The Marowitz
Shakespeare

The Marowitz Shakespeare

Adaptations and collages of *Hamlet, Macbeth, The Taming of the Shrew, Measure for Measure,* and *The Merchant of Venice*

Charles Marowitz

MARION BOYARS . LONDON

First Published in Great Britain in 1978
By Marion Boyars Publishers Ltd.
18 Brewer Street, London W1R 4AS

Australian distribution by Thomas C.·Lothian
4-12 Tattersalls Lane, Melbourne, Victoria 3000

ISBN 0 7145 2650 9 Cased edition
ISBN 0 7145 2651 7 Paperback

Set by Gilbert Composing Services
Leighton Buzzard

Printed in England by Hillman Printers (Frome) Ltd., Somerset

This book is dedicated to the misfit in any given cast who, by swimming against the tide, earns the antagonism of every other member. To the crank and the freak, the maverick and the loner who desolately nurtures his contempt for the safety and tameness of the proven way. To the jackass and the loony who cannot keep a straight face amidst the intense solemnity of serious-minded people. May the special god who protects outcasts watch over him, and long may he thrive.

Contents

Introduction

It is generally accepted that today, Shakespeare can be reinterpreted for modern audiences either in the manner practised by the Royal Shakespeare and National Theatre companies, or in some more flamboyant or 'loose' way as, for instance, in the pop musical *Two Gentlemen of Verona* or *Catch My Soul*, the rock version of *Othello*. Before 1960 it was common practice for directors to put new slants onto Shakespearian narratives, although a gentlemen's agreement existed in regard to the plays' original structures. Today this agreement has been abrogated and many of Shakespeare's plays are used only as a kind of trampoline for modern directors and writers to perform what somersaults they choose. Apart from bouncing off of original Shakespearian works, there is also the practice of bouncing contemporary works off of Shakespeare—as in the cases of Tom Stoppard's *Rosencrantz and Guildenstern are Dead* and Edward Bond's *Lear*.

In all of these convolutions, there is an underlying assumption that the new work, no matter how extrapolated, still owes some kind of debt to its original source and, indeed, in the more successful treatments, the spirit of the original can be discerned coursing through the coagulated matter from which the Frankenstein monster has been assembled.

The Victorians, who took their own liberties with Shakespeare, would probably be horrified at the excesses to which contemporary adaptors have gone to wrench new meanings from these standard sources. They would insist

7

that their own pruning and revisions were, at least, born out of a deep-seated respect for Shakespeare and consisted of relatively minor changes compared to the sweeping overhauls of rock musicals or experimental collages. Technically they would be quite right; but what is significant is the impulse, as rife today as it was in Victorian England, to doctor works which the mainstream public regard as classics. Not heeding Artaud's exhortations to destroy masterpieces, the contemporary tendency is to reassemble them by means of elaborate, sometimes outrageous surgery which may stop short of wholesale decimation but need not necessarily do so.

However, not all classical tinkering is aimed at sweeping overhauls. There is, for instance, the invisible mending which has become the stock-in-trade of John Barton at Stratford. Compressing the York-Lancaster cycle into the epic trilogy *The Wars of the Roses*, (*Henry VI*, *Richard III* and the newly fashioned *Edward IV*), Barton grafts together historically related plays and cunningly removes the joins. A new pattern emerges which provides a fresh perspective on each of the works used to make up the trilogy. Barton's Shakespearian pastiche, when it is concealing amendments is thoroughly successful because the blending process is indiscernible. But when he grows bolder, as he did in the 1974 production of *King John* (versifying the conflicts of the Common Market) or his fanciful rewrite of Marlowe's *Doctor Faustus*, the mixture of modernity and classic brews can sour the palate.

Bertolt Brecht's incursions into the classics are remarkable mainly because he chooses those plays which are already predisposed to his own ideology. It is a moot point which is the more radical play, Farquhar's *The Recruiting Officer* or *Trumpets and Drums*, Brecht's overstated version of it. (There is no question at all as to which is the better play.) The same question can be asked of *Coriolanus* which neon-lights a point about demagogic pride already well-illuminated by Shakespeare—but here, the finished work was done after Brecht's death and so is perhaps not a fair example. Brecht's adaptation of Marlowe's *Edward II*, in collaboration with Leon Feuchtwanger, emphasises the homosexual bond between Edward and Gaveston but is less politically sophisticated than Marlowe's original which underscores the background manoeuvres that actually determine the actions of the Crown. His version of *Antigone* is, again, a reduction-through-oversimplification. The play forfeits its moral balance by loading the dice against Creon. (Anouilh's treatment, due in large part to the time it first appeared in occupied France, actually adds new dimensions to Sophocles.) Brecht is much more effective when he cuts loose from the original source and follows his own bent. A play like *The Resistable Rise of Arturo Ui,* animated by the spirit of *Richard III,* imaginatively converts Shakespeare to Brechtian uses and is at once better Brecht and a more interesting form of classical allusion. And *The Threepenny Opera,* compared to John Gay's *Beggar's Opera* which gave rise to it, is a staggering example of how a 20th century spirit can extend and elaborate an 18th century impulse, with each work enhancing the integrity of the other.

In passing, perhaps one should touch upon those Shakespearian adaptations which cut right across the works being discussed here; adaptations which, far from being experimental, are usually extremely commercial and thoroughly popular. Musicals such as *The Boys from Syracuse* (from *Comedy of Errors),* *Kiss Me Kate* (from *Taming of the Shrew),* *West Side Story* (from *Romeo and Juliet)* and the aforementioned *Two Gentlemen of Verona* and *Catch My Soul* which are basically riffs on their originals using the basic story as a clothes line on which to hang an assortment of fetching new attire. Being expressly 'free' treatments specifically designed to change the medium of expression, they have a different set of priorities from a work which deals with the intellectual structure of the original play and confines itself, more or less, to the given material. Being preoccupied with the additions of song, dance and updated comedy, the musicals made use only of the myth of the originals, the generally accepted gist of the plays rather than their actual units. But the fact remains that in a work like *Kiss Me Kate* for instance, what is compulsive, quite as much as the singing and dancing, is the developing narrative line about a temperamental actress and an actor attempting to subdue her will. Also, there is a cunning aptness about a Kate who is a prima donna and a Petruchio who personifies theatrical egotism. One is clearly, if subterraneously, being nourished by the original play. In *West Side Story,* the sense of warring communities, violent bigotry and victimized lovers is every whit as potent as it is in *Romeo and Juliet*—which is not to draw irrelevant comparisons, but only to point out that when the contemporary parallels have a direct pipeline to the actions on which they are based, the new work rests on a solid foundation and, resting so, can build upwards as far as it likes. *The Boys from Syracuse* takes little more than the idea of confused identities from *Comedy of Errors*, which Shakespeare himself lifted from the *Menaechmi,* but this buoyant Rodgers and Hart musical is thoroughly imbued with the zaniness that Shakespeare extracted from Plautus. *(A Funny Thing Happened on the Way to the Forum* owes a similar debt.)

Catch My Soul is already a different species, being more a rock recital inspired by the alleged funkiness of the Moor than a full-fledged musical comedy treatment depending upon character and developing situation. The original story is, as it were, 'quoted' while singers and dancers project a variety of obliquely related musical numbers which simultaneously oversimplify and overintensify the ingredients of the play; which is to say, they respond to the imperatives of amplified rock music rather than those of the drama.

As a tendency, musicalized Shakespeare is full of potential and to be encouraged. But the underlying principles are exactly the same as those which apply to Brecht or anyone else. In order to derive value from the original, new dimensions with contemporary substance have to be uncovered or imposed. It is leaden and deadly simply to 'set Shakespeare to music' without some organizing drive that justifies and ultimately enriches the media change. *Kiss Me Kate,* by embracing the spirit of *Taming of the Shrew*, leaves Shakespeare in credit. *Catch My Soul,* by musically paraphrasing only the narrative elements in *Othello,* confers no great distinction either to Shakespeare or itself. When Shakespeare appropriated Boccacio or Holinshed, it was always in the name of that rampaging personal egotism that was ultimately responsible for the transformation and improvement of the sources from which he borrowed.

In all of these unrelated activities, each adaptor has his own intentions and priorities, and any attempt to bring them into line, to foist a generalization wide enough to cover, say, Brecht's *Coriolanus* and Jerome Robbins' *West Side Story*, must produce one of those phoney definitions to which academics are so prone: a kind of new nomenclature which, once devised, is employed to bend a multitude of divergent tendencies into something like an orderly system. The result of these stretched critical tendons is to create a sense of uprightness where none exists. And so to avoid this pitfall, I shall say right from the start that I speak for no one but myself, and that no matter how dogmatic my tone may become, I do not presume that my work is the frontrunner of any kind of 'zeitgeist'—nor do I propogate it in order to attract converts.

* * * *

Since about 1956, I have had a curious love-hate relationship with certain old plays—mostly those of Shakespeare—and in the past ten years or so have found myself dealing with them in various ways. What all of this portends I really do not know, but what I *do* know, and what is very often lost sight of, is that my experiments have been conducted in a very small arena (usually a London theatre seating a maximum of 200 persons) and that most of the other classical innovations have likewise been directed to a very small public, so that whatever 'tendency' is being delineated here, it affects only very slightly the ways in which the majority of theatregoers receive the works of Shakespeare.

The first exercise of mine along these lines was the direct result of conversations with Peter Brook in which we discussed the possibilities of conveying theatrical meaning without reliance on narrative. Would it be possible, we conjectured, to convey the multitude of nuances and insights which are to be found in *Hamlet* through a kind of cut-up of the work which thoroughly abandoned its progressive story line? If the story proper would not be conveyed through such a drastic reassembly, what would? The result was a twenty-eight minute collage stitched together from random selections of the play and wedged into an arbitrary structure (viz. the soliloquy 'How all occasions do inform against me')* The intention to fragment the work and then play it

---

* *The Marowitz Hamlet*. London: Penguin, 1968: also contained an adaptation of Marlowe's *Doctor Faustus* (now out of print).

discontinuously forced us to devise a performance technique which would project such a collage form. This was in many ways a more fascinating problem than the assembly of the work itself, for it encouraged the actors to forego all the conventional means by which they usually achieved their effects. Nothing could build, for instance, for longer than two or three minutes; no scene could *develop* to a logical conclusion because no scene ever concluded but was abruptly intersected by another, invariably with a different texture and from another part of the play. The sustenance of character became secondary to the transmutation of character as a result of jumps in time and location. The collage was eventually extended to eighty minutes after which time the pressure of discontinuity became almost unbearable.

It became fashionable to say that if you already knew *Hamlet*, this was a fascinating rescension which would provide a kind of salutary shock. But the fact is the collage was played before hundreds of people who had never read *Hamlet* or seen the film, and their impressions (derived from discussions after the performance) were as valid, and often as knowledgeable, as those of scholars and veteran theatregoers. I had always contended that the ideas contained in the collage were derived from Shakespeare's original and could be transferred back to a straightforward production of the play proper. In Gothenberg and then again in Wiesbaden. I had the opportunity to put that theory to the test. Whatever my misgivings about each production, what became abundantly clear was that every notion which seemed so far-fetched in the context of the collage, was viable in terms of the original work and could be conveyed through conventional interpretation. Which begs the question: why cut it up in the first place?

In my view, radical theatrical experiments need to be justified, if at all, only when they fail. The *Hamlet* collage was, on the whole, successful, and earned a certain credibility of its own. But if one were hard-pressed for justification, I would say that the re-structuring of a work, the characters and situations of which are widely known, is an indirect way of making contact with that work's essence. Just as the human organism is understood differently when its metabolism is scrutinized in isolation, so certain 'classical' works are understood differently when their components are re-formed. This 'different understanding' is not only the result of a new vantage-point (although this advantage should not be under-estimated), but the consequence of changing the play's time-signature. A collage form bequeaths speed, and when you have the advantage of speed in the theatre (without, one must add, the loss of definition), not only do you change the nature of what is being said, you also change the purpose for saying it. Shakespeare's Aristotelian dramatic format obliged him to 'unfold' stories, 'develop' characters and 'illustrate' themes. But a collage version of a known play assumes a pre-knowledge of the original and although it tends to cover familiar ground (refers to characters, alludes to situations, comments on themes), it is more concerned with the application of all these things in order to foster another concept. If the old material was not being redistributed for the sake of this other concept, the collage form would simply be another way of cutting meat; a stylistic mechanism which rearranged material simply for the sake of rearranging it. The change of form inescapably affects the nature of content, but that in itself is not enough. The content must not be accidentally 'affected' in the way that a pedestrian might be 'affected' if he were hit by a bus. It must be refashioned as if, to pursue the metaphor, a pedestrian were hit by a bus driven by a clinical psychiatrist whose aim in knocking him down was to investigate his rate of recovery in response to highly specialized therapies of his own making. Which is a circuitous way of saying that a collage must have a purpose as coherent and proveable as any conventional work of art.

Apart from the stylistic techniques deployed in the *Hamlet* collage, I attempted to delineate a criticism of the type of person Hamlet was and, by inference, to indict the values which he represented; values which (i.e. misdirected moral concern, intellectual analyses as action-substitute, etc.) were, in my view, disreputable in our society and which derived much of their respectability and approval from traditional works such as Shakespeare's *Hamlet*. In short, by assaulting the character of Hamlet, one was deriding the supreme prototype of the conscience-stricken but paralyzed liberal: one of the most lethal and obnoxious characters in modern times.

I now accept that the stylistic innovations in the work were so overwhelming it was difficult to insinuate this idea very lucidly, and I fully accept the fact that most of the public which responded to the collage were more taken with its theatricality than its thesis; but without that thesis none of that theatricality would have had any coherent motive nor, as I have already said, any purpose. I derive some small consolation from the fact that any artefact which is immediately reducible to its theoretical components must be facile and unworthy, but am simultaneously chastened by the knowledge that many artists imagine they are communicating clear-cut intentions when, in fact, they are conveying something entirely ambiguous which, being approved for unexpected reasons, persuades them (hypocritically) to relinquish their original demands in regard to their work.

In *Macbeth**, as with *Hamlet,* the collage treatment had the intention of transmitting experience from the play through the eyes of the central protagonist. The technique was more appropriate in *A Macbeth* because one had decided to forage about in the black magical undergrowth that lay behind the work, and a fragmented structure helped to create the desired nightmarish effect. But again, one was putting an interpretation suggested by the play itself: Macbeth, victim of a witchcraft plot masterminded by Lady Macbeth (the chief witch of a coven which included the three witches), progressively destroyed by forces he could not envisage and therefore not understand, is, for me, a construction direct from Shakespeare's work. The intense paranoia of the man in the final stages of dissolution is remarkably like the hallucination of one possessed. 'Possession' vibrates through every page of the original play from Lady Macbeth's murderous preoccupation with Duncan, to Banquo's obsession with the witches' prophecy, to Macduff's all-consuming dream of revenge—not to mention the overriding spell with which Lady Macbeth confounds her husband and monitors him towards acts which, after her own madness, seem difficult to accept merely as the cunning ploys of an ambitious wife.

One also tried to dramatize the peculiar knot of trinities

---

*First published as *A Macbeth*. London : Calder & Boyars, 1971. (Now out of print.)

that winds its way through the play; three witches, three murderers, three murders; hence in the collage, three personified aspects of Macbeth, the Timorous, the Ambitious, the Nefarious. One tried to restore the play to its pre-Christian, Manichean origins; tried to locate its metaphysical centre and peel away the pseudo-religious and irrelevantly-political gauzes that had woven themselves around the work.

Having said all that I must also add that for me, *A Macbeth* was always something of a bloodless exercise in cut-up techniques. The excitements of the collage-format happened organically in *Hamlet*, aided by the fact that there were so many disparate pieces to put together in new and unexpected ways. The redistribution of its parts was like a multifarious recipe which incorporated many different ingredients. But cutting up *Macbeth* was a little like slicing salami. However one changed its structure (in fact, there was very little change), one was always left with that dark-textured, relentlessly plot-laden Warner Brothers movie about the man who rubbed out Mr. Big and, perforce, had to continue to rub out all the other members of the mob. Clearly, Shakespeare's *Macbeth* has none of the rambling paths and hidden rivulets of *Hamlet*. In its remorseless journey from crime to retribution, it is more like a motorway. Because its intellectual base is less complex than *Hamlet*, one becomes more aware of the technique *qua* technique. However, in the play's tumultuous coda where Macbeth's downfall is more labyrinthine and more terrible than any other of Shakespeare's tragic heroes, the collage-treatment provides an interior view of dissolution more vividly than one would get from the churn of a sequential narrative. Having lived inside of Macbeth's skin from the very start, the slow crumble of the spirit within that skin is, in some ways, more harrowing because more directly experienced. I say this not to draw snide comparisons with Shakespeare's original play, but to point out that the different vantage-point of a collage (i.e. an inside view of external developments) can alter the entire resonance of a theatrical experience. Of course, an X-ray is not the same thing as a work of art but an X-ray of a work of art may claim to fall into a different category.

The Shrew had a premature delivery. The idea of converting Shakespeare's comedy into a Gothic tragedy had been knocking around in my head for many months and I always promised myself that one day I would sit down and think it all out. But in the winter of 1974, having promised the Hot Theatre in The Hague a production of Brecht's *The Messingkauf Dialogues,* one of those unexpected human-relations disasters struck The Open Space and after one promising rehearsal it was impossible to follow through on the Brecht project. Having already signed contracts for a date only three weeks away, I was exhorted by my partner Thelma Holt to 'pull something out of the bag'. I protested that mine was a very meagre, ordinary bag, not a magical rucksack, and one could not simply 'pull something out' without having first spent many months storing something up. As so often happens at The Open Space, the promise of a large sum of money and the theatre's desperately wobbly circumstances dislodged whatever block it was that made me insist we must cancel, and I hauled out my loosely-conceived Gothic *Shrew*. I outlined it to Thelma Holt and Nikolas Simmonds (both casting casualties from the abandoned Brecht work) and I was urged, more out of desperation than enthusiasm, to get on with it. The play, not yet written and only barely conceived, was cast within twenty-four hours and, in forty-eight hours, rehearsals began on a batch of hastily-assembled, photocopied sheets scrounged out of Shakespeare's play the night before.

The plan called for a young man and woman who would improvise a series of contemporary scenes roughly parallel to the Shakespearian ones derived from *The Taming of the Shrew.* Jeremy Nicholas and Kay Barlow, two very game actors who were as much in the dark as the director and adaptor, worked up a series of improvisations based on the courtship of a young working-class youth and upper middle-class girl. I siphoned off from these scenes enough juice to concoct some viable material and in the ensuing weeks, something was hashed together.

The thematic problems of *The Shrew* became clearer each time we played it. The parallel scenes were too baldly parallel to the Petruchio and Kate scenes, and the message that seemed to screech out of the modern scenes in which She (cum-Bianca) domineered and manipulated He (cum-Hortensio) was that nothing very much had changed since the 17th century; that cruelty and power-play were still the active components of relationships and that whereas, in the good old days, the man could brutalise the woman using physical means, today the woman could tyrannise the man using the more subtle weapons of psychology and social exploitation. Clearly, this was a statement not worth making — and certainly not worth cutting up a Shakespearian play in order to make. But the novelty of seeing *The Shrew* played as Grand Guignol was so enthralling to London audiences that the play had a hefty run at The Open Space, was revived, toured throughout England and ultimately wound up in Italy and Yugoslavia. Throughout all of these productions (there were three), I came to loathe the work I had done. It was no justification to explain that it had been done hastily and under great pressure. The result was intellectually contemptible and no amount of superb playing by Thelma Holt and Nikolas Simmonds could alter my own jaundiced view of it.

My desire was to flush the play down the drain, to discard it as a hashed exercise in theatrical expediency; but the script continued to be requested on the continent, in America, in Australia and in Germany where I was invited to direct it at the Staatstheater in Stuttgart. It was then that I decided to 'do the right thing' by the work and tacitly resolved that the play performed in Stuttgart would be a revised, rethought and rewritten work. In short, I would do in Germany, with six full weeks of rehearsal, what I had neither time nor money to do in England. I would make the adaptation I had dimly conceived before the Dutch pressure brought the play prematurely into being.

This involved a careful reassessment of the play's ideology, or, rather, the ideology of the contemporary scenes—for this was where the trouble lay. I did not intend to say that things never change, that cruelty between human beings is a constant factor which only alters its methods but not its intentions. What I wanted to say was, in fact, much more dismal and depressing, namely, that no human relationship has the stamina to withstand long periods of intimate exposure; that familiarity not only breeds contempt but dissipation and stasis; that deep within the very fabric of human relationships, relationships founded on love and togetherness, there was an insidious canker which slowly but surely gnawed away at the euphoria that infused every love affair; that there was something at the core of human nature which was irrevocably abusing and self-consuming; and that the irony of this cancer was that it lurked quietly but potently in a context of love, watching love slowly corrode and growing gradually bolder and bolder until, ultimately, it conquered all. And, irony of ironies, it was at this very juncture that the diseased lovers often sought in the institution of marriage a kind of miracle drug which would transform everything. One wanted to show that for many people, despite the raging permissiveness of our times, Marriage, the hoked-up endlessly-spoofed Magic Ritual, still held out a promise of salvation; a hope that an ancient ceremony could transform a grubby reality; that a solemn rite could, by virtue of its intrinsic ceremonial magic, right the wrongs of years.

To tell such a story Shakespeare's combative couple had to leave the realms of farce and transmute themselves into a kind of Grimm Fairy Tale world, a world of sinister archetypes and hopeless victims. Petruchio, transformed into a kind of Mafiosa-monster who still covets Baptista's fortune and is fully prepared to instigate a bloodless courtship to obtain it is now motivated even more strongly by the detestable independence of spirit that throbs inside of Katherine. The classic encounter of elegance and vulgarity rather than female high-spiritedness and the urge for male sexual conquest. The tragedy of Kate, in this new dispensation, is that she underestimates the magnitude of Petruchio's bestiality. How could she not? The rich daughter of a rich father; the recipient of, if not love, then certainly luxury, education and breeding? Compare such a woman to a strolling fortune-hunter who goes sniffing for rich game and makes no distinction between material gain and amoristic conquest; for whom, indeed, the latter is only a means of acquiring the former. A wastrel, a bogus cavalier; a man who never read Castiglione but who knows the only way to get on in the world is to emulate his type. A man whose peculiar psychosis insists on total subservience as the emblem of love; who counterfeits with the grim, convincing deportment of the crypto-psychopath; who embodies and glories in all the characteristics Wilhelm Reich attributes to the Phallic-Narcissist.

The modern technique for brainwashing is, almost to the letter, what Petruchio makes Katherine undergo. Deprivation of food, deprivation of sleep, disorientation of faculties; cruelty camouflaged as kindness; a reversal of moral values which turns the tormentor into a holy man and the tormented into a hopeless sinner. Petruchio's evil genie punishes Katherine for the greatest crime of all—social rebellion. A woman she can be, she must be; but not *her* kind of woman—rather, the social cipher that Baptista prefers, that Bianca unquestionably is, that Hortensio would have all women be, that Petruchio labours to create. If Katherine can be made to represent breeding and elegance, and one is able to discard the tirades of the traditional termagent, her downfall becomes truly pathetic, for it then represents the abandonment of personal style in the face of a brutalising conformity. If she is shrilly vituperative and conventionally shrewish (Elizabeth Taylor swinging frying-pans), then all she receives is come-uppance and the conventional charade of subterranean longings for Petruchio clear the way for her wholesale conversion to domesticity; a conversion which, in my view, is never alleviated by a tang of irony in the final speech. Katherine accepts nothing and struggles against her cruel punishment to the very end. The only victory available to the Petruchio-Baptista-Bianca axis is the artificially induced spectacle of a mesmerized or drugged victim droning the words her tormentors could not make her speak voluntarily. A victory of these dimensions is hollow indeed.

What rots Katherine is the quicklime of Petruchio's spirit. What rots the contemporary Boy and Girl is the indeterminate moral pollution which many would blame on the social context but whose toxin is discharged through the pores of the human beings which constitute that society. There is no villain or villainess in the contemporary scenes. Whatever personal failings the Boy and Girl may have, they are typical not unique. What happens to them happens to many people. Their 'tragedy', if you like, is built into their human metabolism. They can never escape, and their danger is never, like Katherine's, apparent and challengeable. Katherine is felled by the will of a destructive force she can feel and see. She knows where to do battle and she does so valiantly— right up until the end. The Boy and Girl go through the motions of living and loving, of jealousy and possessiveness, of separations and reunions—like experimental mice that caper and cavort, feed and defecate, but whose destiny is sealed the moment they enter their laboratory cages. I am not alluding here to anything as simple as predestination. Perhaps there *is* another way out for the Boy and Girl; perhaps marriage will replenish their love-cells; but as we see them, they haven't the power to do anything more than feed off each other, try to elude boredom, hope for transformations in their inner lives, and ultimately, settle for less—the inescapable 20th century compromise. The Boy and Girl dwindle into social statistics; Katherine's defeat defines the grandeur of a spirit that has been brought down by overwhelming odds. There is something noble in that defeat because in its resistance, an alternative way of life, a higher degree of individuality, has been implied. The Boy and Girl gradually disappear into the feckless, wholly expedient, mutually exploitative morass of modern life. It is hard to say, viewed that way, which represents the greater tragedy.

Whereas *The Shrew* quite deliberately mixed modern and classical ingredients and made no bones about the mixture, in *Measure for Measure* one tried, by the use of narrative guile, to persuade the audience they were seeing Shakespeare's play—more or less—as he wrote it. That is, the story began, as Shakespeare's did, and appeared to go in the same direction. It was only at that point where most people felt reassured that this was *Measure* as they knew it that one began to switch rails. Isabella, offered Claudio's life in return for her body, resists with all the purity that befits her calling, but there are no arbitrary stratagems from the Duke to divert her from her course to Angelo's bed; nothing standing between his authority and the satisfaction of his desires. Isabella makes the (in Shakespeare's terms) uncharacteristic sacrifice and discovers that Angelo, unlike the contrite deputy of the original, deliberately breaks his bargain. Claudio, the object of a terrible sacrifice, is himself sacrificed. Angelo's wrong is unmitigated and cries out for punishment, and the betrayed Isabella is there clamouring for justice, but to a Duke too wily not to realise that high office must occasionally have its lecherous perks and that political expediency dictates that an efficient civil servant should not be toppled by an hysterical ex-virgin silly enough to believe that justice for the powerful is the same as justice for the lowly.

One concedes immediately that this is a betrayal, not only of Isabella's character, but of the author's intentions. This is patently not what Shakespeare intended—despite the fact that his original source, George Whetsone's *History of*

Promos and Cassandra actually provides the seduction that Shakespeare's bed-trick avoids. Shakespeare's intentions are different from Whetstone's, and mine are different from Shakespeare's. What concerns me is the traditional morality of *Measure for Measure* tested in a contemporary society where Watergate-styled corruptions are often the rule and not the exception. I wanted the audience to be angry with the Duke, Escalus and Angelo in a way that Shakespeare's narrative would never permit. That anger was chemically related to the fury I hoped women would feel against Petruchio after his debasement of Katherine. It is an anger that *I* feel when I see the workings of society—particularly that branch which pompously calls itself The Law but shows no need to reconcile notions of 'legal' and 'illegal' with like-concepts of good and bad. The Law is more than an ass, it is the deadly mechanism by which favour and prejudice are allowed to trample innocence and dissent. Its course is smoothed, certainly in England, with eye-catching ceremonial trappings and theatrical assumptions of pomp—all of which blurs, but does not conceal, the wickedness of its workings. The ceremony of judicial process is an important part of this treatment. Whenever Angelo, the Duke or Escalus are on stage, the panoply of justice glitters and intimidates. When the cruel injustice has been perpetrated against Isabella and Angelo has got away scot-free, these officials remove their robes of state and underneath we should see the kind of attire we associate with frivolous and irresponsible persons who, in their social guises, give a very different impression. The facade of the law, its elaborate stage-management, its imposing rituals, divert us from its manifest evil. As *Measure for Measure* is a play about 'false seeming' so is the practice of justice in most Western countries; those very countries which pride themselves on their democratic institutions and see themselves as the antithesis of totalitarian regimes.

For *Measure* to achieve its effects, it had to stick as closely as possible to Shakespeare's original storyline, veering away at precisely those points where the moral impact would be greatest. The same approach was employed in *Variations on the Merchant of Venice* although here there were certain inherent problems which required different tactics.

It is difficult, almost impossible, to come to a play like *The Merchant of Venice,* whose central character is an orthodox Jew, without bringing to the experience all one has learned and read about the Jews in the past 2000 years; difficult to obliterate from the mind the last seventy-five years of Jewish history which includes European pogroms, the Hitler 'death camps', the rise of Jewish Nationalism and the Arab-Israeli conflicts. Of course, Shakespeare had no knowledge of any of these things and it is undeniable that none of these factors enter into *The Merchant of Venice*—and yet, can they be excluded from the consciousness of the spectator who attends the play? They can, I suppose, if one is prepared to put the contemporary sensibility to sleep and concentrate only on the fairy-tale elements of Shakespeare's play; if one is prepared to say of Shakespeare's Jew, as of Shakespeare's Moor, that he has no actual contemporary parallel; that a red-wigged, joke-Jew has no real affinities with an Israeli business-man or a modern Hebraic scholar—just as an Elizabethan 'Moor' has no discernible connection to a ghetto black. But it is a difficult thesis to sustain because there is a cultural tendon that links all Jews with their history (even their history in Shakespearian plays) and all blacks with *their* antecedents—even the 'noble Moor' who, though he knows nothing of Sharpeville or American race-riots, is still subjected to Venetian racial prejudice and considered an 'outsider' in *his* society.

Rather than indulge in those strenuous mental calisthenics which enable us to separate our contemporary consciousness from that of Shakespeare's, I prefer to join them up; to yoke them together despite the differences and seeming incompatibilities. What had always angered me about *Merchant* was that contemptible trial scene in which Shylock is progressively humiliated, stripped of all property and dignity and sent packing from the courtroom a forced convert, a disreputable father, an unmasked villain. It was to try to redress this balance that I decided to reorder *Merchant* and 'vary' its moral implications.

So long as Antonio remained 'a good man', Shylock must be a villain and so I set about putting Antonio's character into question. By setting the action in Palestine during the period of the British mandate, one had a ready-made villain. The anti-semitism engendered during this period was mainly the result of the policies of Clement Atlee's Middle East policy which severely restricted immigration to Jerusalem, thereby forcing hundreds of thousands of escaping Jews to return to Europe and the concentration-camps that awaited them. These policies were (quite unfairly) personified by Ernest Bevin, the Foreign Secretary of the time. By identifying Antonio with Bevin and the lethal policies of the Atlee government and lining up Shylock with the nationalist forces, particularly the more extreme groups like the Irgun, one created a completely different balance between the social forces in the play. The Venetian capitalists and adventurers were transformed into British colonialists and the Jews (I materialized Shus, briefly mentioned by Shakespeare as an outright terrorist, and turned Tubal into a kind of Zionist front-man) depicted as committed nationalists. Shylock himself retained a certain ambiguity—vigorously playing the caricature Jew in the midst of Antonio, Bassanio and their Jew-baiting British cohorts, but tucking into a cold, Talmudic stoic when amongst his own people; a man with means who knows he is most effective to his own cause by not showing his true mettle, except when he holds the upper hand. As a result of this reorganization of character, and sections lifted from Christopher Marlowe's *Jew of Malta*, it becomes possible to arrive at that detestable trial scene and make it turn out differently.

My own misgivings about *Variations* are twofold. It is not easy to integrate styles as different as Marlowe's and Shakespeare's—particularly in a play as well known as *Merchant of Venice* and so, every time Shakespeare's fluent tone-of-voice is interrupted by Marlowe's artifice, the tone tends to droop accordingly. Also, the ending, unless it is *played against*, tends to be melodramatic in a way that diminishes the political significance of what is being depicted. The spectre of Eric Ambler hovers rather too closely to an adaptation concerned with inflammatory events such as the demolition of the King David Hotel, the treacheries of the Stern Gang and the oppressions of the occupying British forces. This may never be remediable in production—although it is worth taking precautions.

In a sense, both *Measure* and *Merchant* are 'variations' in that they depend on establishing the original events of Shakespeare's play before creating arbitrary diversions. This is not often appreciated by critics who, after *Hamlet* and *Macbeth,* expected every 'treatment' of Shakespeare to be a shattering of a play's original parts for the sake of some radical new rescension. It is pointless to consider which approach is 'better'. Undertaken for different purposes, an adaptation is obliged to resort to different methods.

What eventually emerges from a survey of my own work and work similar to it, is that there are three basic requisites in regard to adaptations of this kind. Firstly, the director-adaptor has got to have something specific to say: that is, he has to shape his material in such a way that the new pattern, despite the existence of familiar source material, delivers a quite specific and original message; a message which does not merely duplicate the statements of the ur-text. Secondly, the material, weighted as it is with the author's original intentions and the accumulation of four or more hundred years of fixed associations, has to have the elasticity to bend in the desired direction. It is when the nature of the contemporary comment goes against the grain of the given material that one usually winds up with those fractured, aberrant, wilfully 'avant-garde' productions where minds, patently inferior to Shakespeare's, are trying to foist ideas which wilt in comparison. The third requirement is to recognise that when the ideas generated by the given material are not reconcilable with the work as it stands, it is politic to change the original rather than, out of respect or timidity, produce a set of clanging incompatibles. One should not back away from an idea which could not possibly have existed in Shakespeare's time if that idea has been inspired by Shakespeare's material. The resolution of what appear to be antithetical elements is often the first step towards the creation of a viable new form.

Ultimately, this kind of re-interpretation has little to do with 'new slants' on traditional material; it eschews the stunning nuances of unexpected verse delivery or the clever innuendoes of costume and set-design. It sets no premium on new approaches to characterisation or novel forms of staging. It is nothing more nor less than a head-on confrontation with the intellectual substructure of the plays, an attempt to test or challenge, revoke or destroy the intellectual foundation which makes a classic the formidable thing it has become. Paradoxically, one can view this as a very traditional exercise. It does not annihilate the content of the original play for the sake of establishing some wholly new aesthetic. It combats the assumptions of the classic with a series of new assumptions and forces it to bend under the power of a new polemic. And, of course, it doesn't always win. Sometimes the play's original ethic is so overpowering that an assault from an opposed viewpoint only confirms its original authority. In the course of these tussles, a certain number of theatrical effects will be produced, and an audience may be diverted by these effects—for their own sake—without realising that, despite dazzling superficies, the play's original premise remains entirely intact. (In my view, this was the case with Peter Brook's *Midsummer Night's Dream* which decked out the play in an entirely new and unexpected wardrobe, but in no way altered its essential biology.) This is a traditional and entirely acceptable mode of Shakespearian interpretation: the Quick Flash method which disorients our visual expectations of what should be happening in a work of art but ultimately comforts us because we are shown that these 'differences' are still at the service of the original, and no matter how unorthodox the play's deportment, it remains inherently 'loyal' to Shakespeare. The experiments to which I would contrast this approach are brazen acts of treason and heinous acts of infidelity which shake to their very foundations the pillars of the original work. Such works, when they succeed, are creations in their own right: ideological extensions of the work from which they sprang.

The question is not, as it is so often put, what is wrong with Shakespeare that we have to meddle with his works, but what is wrong with us that we are content to endure the diminishing returns of conventional dramatic reiteration; that we are prepared to go to the theatre and pretend that what dulls our minds and comforts our world-view is, by dint of such reassurances, culturally uplifting; not to realise that there is nothing so insidious as art that perpetuates the illusion that some kind of eternal truth is enshrined in a time-space continuum called 'a classic'; not to challenge the notion that its theatrical performance is *automatically* an experience because our presumption of a play's established worth guarantees us that experience. We all dupe ourselves in the theatre because we have been sold a bill of goods for a good quarter of a century before we enter. We get what we expect and we expect what we have been led to expect, and it is only when we don't get what we have been led to expect that we are on the threshold of having an experience. It is this cultural anticipation which swirls in our brains before the curtains rise on *Hamlet* or *Macbeth* or *Caesar* or *Lear* which is the catalytic agent which makes it possible for theatregoers to 'have an experience'; to have it precisely because it is not the one they have been anticipating. We lose sight of the fact that, aesthetics notwithstanding, the theatre is primarily a social and psychological habit, and a great deal of what theatre artists prepare is based on the need to accommodate and feed that habit. Paradoxically, this is often done by persons asking themselves: how can we surprise our audiences, keep them from guessing what comes next; how can we give them 'something new'? The answers to these questions produce the pap of the boulevard theatre; the murder-mysteries, suspense-dramas, comedies and farces that suspend our disbeliefs only to fortify the age-old beliefs in whose name they have been only temporarily suspended. The same thinking also conditions the production of classics and so-called 'serious plays'. Even the 'Serious Artist' is primarily concerned with how to distribute stale goods in dazzling new wrappers. It is only when the assumptions of art drastically change that a theatrical experience is possible. *Ubu Roi*, in a sense, did that because it proceeded from a radical reconsideration of what a play could be and, fortunately, the audience's rejection of that idea fanned the flames of the new experience. In our time, *Waiting for Godot*, using an entirely negative aesthetic, did something like the same thing. It put a premium on what had always been taken to be an unquestioned liability: the absence of events, the non-happening. By so doing, it forced us to alter the readings on our cultural thermostat; to receive drama in a very different frame of mind and at a very different tempo. No new theatrical experience proceeds from the same assumptions as the last one. That is why there is nothing so lethal as 'trends' in art for, in standardizing what began life as an original impulse, it insults the integrity of the new experience by parodying it with reasonable facsimiles, thereby putting us further and further away from the possibility of yet another new experience. And, of course, our inability to distinguish artistic experiences from generally approved reasonable facsimiles is only a symptom of our lack of perception in life. How often is the myth of a party or a date or a romance escalated from the insensate reality on which it is based? If we could not idealize life, we could not bear it. And in the theatre our idealizations are supported by art myths, education myths, media myths, innate desires for self-delusion and the insatiable craving for magic. The theatre artist has all this to contend with. An audience is like the implacable face of a stopped clock that will resist all efforts to be wound to the correct time out of an obsessive desire to maintain the integrity of its broken mechanism. It is no wonder that art must occasionally give it a good shake to get it ticking again.

Charles Marowitz
1978

Hamlet

CAST

HAMLET   CLOWN-POLONIUS*
FORTINBRAS   OPHELIA
GHOST   LAERTES
QUEEN   ROSENCRANTZ
KING   GUILDENSTERN
              COURTIER (female)

*Polonius is played by the same actor who plays the
clown, either by making a swift change in vocal
characterization or, for example, by putting a grey-
gloved hand to his chin to suggest a beard.

HAMLET *and* FORTINBRAS *stand facing each other. After a moment,* FORTINBRAS *moves down to meet the* CAPTAIN. HAMLET *falls in behind the* CAPTAIN *like a soldier in the ranks.*

FORTINBRAS.   Go, Captain, from me greet the Danish King.
    Tell him that by this licence Fortinbras
    Craves the conveyance of a promis'd march
    Over his kingdom.

HAMLET. *(Aside to* CAPTAIN)
    Good sir, whose powers are these?

CAPTAIN. *(Aside to* HAMLET) They are of Norway, sir.

FORTINBRAS.   You know the rendezvous.

HAMLET. *(Aside)* How purpos'd, sir, I pray you?

CAPTAIN. *(Aside)* Against some part of Poland.

FORTINBRAS.   If that his Majesty would aught with us,
    We shall express our duty in his eye,
    And let him know so.

CAPTAIN. *(Marching off)* I will do't, my Lord.

HAMLET.   Who commands them, sir?

CAPTAIN. *(Almost off-stage)*
    The nephew to old Norway, Fortinbras.

*(*HAMLET *moves downstage into a spot of his own.*

FORTINBRAS, *standing strongly behind him. slowly fades out.)*

HAMLET. How all occasions do inform against me,
    And spur my dull revenge. What is a man
    If his chief good and market of his time
    Be but to sleep and feed? A beast, no more:
    Sure that he made us with such large discourse
    Looking before and after, gave us not
    That capability and god-like reason . . . .

FORTINBRAS. *(Accusingly)* To rust in us unus'd.

GHOST. If thou hast Nature in thee bear it not.

    (Cut into new scene)

HAMLET. Murder?

GHOST. Murder most foul, as in the best it is;
    But this most foul and unnatural.

HAMLET. Haste, haste me to know it,
    That I with wings as swift
    As meditation or the thoughts of love
    May sweep to my revenge.

QUEEN. *(Entering placating)*
    Come let me wipe thy face.

HAMLET. *(To* GHOST) Speak, I am bound to hear.

OPHELIA. *(Entering)* You are keen, my Lord, you are keen.

QUEEN. I prithee stay with us, go not to Wittenberg.

GHOST. The serpent that did sting thy father's life . . .

QUEEN. Do not forever with thy vailed lids
    Seek for thy noble father in the dust.

GHOST. Now wears his crown.

KING. How is it the clouds still hang on you?

QUEEN. Thou know'st 'tis common, all that lives must die . . .

GHOST. By a brother's hand
    Of life, of crown and Queen at once dispatch'd.

QUEEN. Passing through Nature, to Eternity.

HAMLET. *(To* GHOST) Mine uncle?

GHOST.   Ay, that incestuous, that adulterate beast,
  With witchcraft of his wits, with traitorous gifts won
   to his shameful lust
  The will of my most seeming-virtuous Queen.

QUEEN.   Why seems it so particular with thee?

HAMLET.   *(To* QUEEN*)*
  Seems, Madam? nay, it is: I know not it seems!

(The next two speeches are counterpointed with the
KING's in prominence, and the GHOST's *as a dulled*
accompaniment.)

KING.	GHOST.
'Tis sweet and commendable in your nature, Hamlet,	With juice of a cursed hebenon in a vial
To give these mourning duties to your father.	. . . swift as quicksilver it courses through
But you must know, your father lost a father,	The natural gates and alleys of the body;
That father lost, lost his, and the survivor bound	And with a sudden vigour it doth posset
In filial obligation for some term	And curd, like eager droppings into milk,
To do obsequious sorrow.	The thin and wholesome blood . . .

HAMLET.   *(To himself)* Hold my heart:
  And you my sinews grow not instant old:
  But bear me stiffly up.

KING.   Fie, 'tis a fault to Heaven,
  A fault against the dead, a fault to Nature,
  To reason most absurd whose common theme
  Is death of fathers.

HAMLET.   If he but blench I know my course.

CLOWN.   *(Suddenly appearing)* What is he that builds stronger
  than either the mason, the shipwright or the carpenter?

HAMLET.   *(Soberly to the* KING) The gallows-maker, for
  that frame outlives a thousand tenants.

CLOWN.   I like thy wit well, in good faith, the gallows does well; but
  how does it well? It does well to those that do ill. To't again.
  Who builds stronger than a mason, a shipwright or a carpenter?

KING. We pray you throw to earth
This unprevailing woe, and think of us
As of a father.

FORTINBRAS.
Think of us as of a father.

CLOWN.
Think of *us* as of a father.

QUEEN.
Thou has thy father much offended.

LAERTES.
And so have I a noble father lost.

(Sound-Montage: all lines are chant-ed and overlap.)

(Coming out of Sound-Montage.)

GHOST.
If thou didst ever thy dear father love . . .

KING. Remain
Here in the cheer and comfort of our eye,
Our chiefest courtier, cousin, and our son.

HAMLET. O villain, villain, smiling damned villain!

KING. Why 'tis a loving and a fair reply.

CLOWN. *(Coming in for tag-line)* Cudgel thy brains no
more about it; say a grave-maker, the houses that
he makes last . . .

GHOST.
Till the foul crimes done in my days of Nature
Are burnt and purged away.

CLOWN. *(Seeing Ghost—backing away)*
How long will a man lie in the earth ere he rot?

GHOST. *(To* HAMLET*)* By a brother's hand
Of life, of crown, and Queen at once dispatch'd.

HAMLET. Mine uncle.

GHOST. Cut off even in the blossoms of my sin,
Unhousel'd . . .

HAMLET. A murderer and a villain . . .

GHOST. Disappointed . . .

HAMLET. A slave . . .

GHOST. Unaneled . . .

HAMLET. A cutpurse of the empire and the rule . . .

GHOST.
>No reckoning made, but sent to my account
>With all my imperfections on my head.

HAMLET. A king of shreds and patches!

>*(Cut into new scene. KING and LAERTES play oblivious of HAMLET.)*

LAERTES. *(Suddenly)* Where is my father?

KING. Dead.

LAERTES. I'll not be juggled with.
>To hell allegiance; vows to the blackest devil.

HAMLET. *(Weakly trying to match LAERTES' passion)*
>Yea, from the table of my memory
>I'll wipe away all trivial fond records . . .

LAERTES. Conscience and grace to the profoundest pit.

HAMLET. All saws of books, all forms, all pressures past.

LAERTES. I dare damnation.

HAMLET. I have sworn it.

LAERTES. . . . to this point I stand,
>That both the worlds I give to negligence,
>Let come what comes: only I'll be revenged
>Most throughly for my father.

HAMLET. O thou vile King,
>Give me my father.

KING. *(Calming LAERTES)*
>Make choice of whom your wisest friends you will,
>And they shall hear and judge 'twixt you and me:
>If by direct or collateral hand
>They find us touch'd, we will our Kingdom give,
>Our Crown, our life, and all that we call ours
>To you in satisfaction.

HAMLET.
>So excellent a King that was to this Hyperion a satyr.

KING. *(Turning on Hamlet, tauntingly)*
Was your father dear to you?
Or are you like a painting of a sorrow,
A face without a heart?

GHOST. *(Off-stage)* Remember me!

HAMLET. O all you host of heaven. O earth what else?
And shall I couple hell—Remember thee!

(Now swinging on rope which has suddenly appeared from above.)

Ay thou poor ghost; while memory holds a seat in this
distracted globe.

(Cut into Closet Scene.)

QUEEN. *(At right of HAMLET)*
This is the very coinage of your brain
This bodiless creation ecstasy
Is very cunning in.

HAMLET. *(Still on rope)* Ecstasy?
My pulse as yours doth temperately keep time
And makes as healthful music. Mother, for love of Grace,
Lay not a flattering unction to your soul
That not your trespass but my madness speaks.
Confess yourself to Heaven,
Repent what's past, avoid what is to come,
And do not spread the compost on the weeds
To make them ranker.

(Coming off rope.)

I did love you once.

OPHELIA. *(At left of HAMLET)*
Indeed my Lord, you made me believe so.

HAMLET. You should not have believed me. For virtue
cannot so inoculate our old stock but we shall relish
of it.

OPHELIA. I have remembrances of yours,
That I have longed long to redeliver.
I pray you now, receive them.

HAMLET. No, I never gave you aught.

OPHELIA.   My honour'd Lord, you did,
    And with them words of so sweet breath compos'd
    As made the things more rich.

HAMLET.   *(To* OPHELIA*)* Are you honest?

QUEEN.   O Hamlet, speak no more;
    Thou turn'st mine eyes into my very soul,
    And there I see such black and grained spots
    As will not leave their tinct.

HAMLET.   *(To* OPHELIA*)* Are you fair?

QUEEN.   These words like daggers enter in mine ears.

HAMLET.   Get thee to a nunnery. Why wouldst thou be a
    breeder of sinners?

CLOWN.   Cannot you tell that? Every fool can tell that.

OPHELIA.   Thou hast cleft my heart in twain.

POLONIUS.   My Lord, the Queen would speak with you,
    and presently.

HAMLET.   Do you see that cloud that's almost in shape
    like a camel?

POLONIUS.   *(Studying it)*
    By the mass, and it's like a camel indeed.

HAMLET.   Methinks it is like a weasel.

OPHELIA.   I was the more deceived.

HAMLET.   If thou dost marry, I'll give thee this plague for thy
    dowry. Be thou as chaste as ice, as pure as snow . . .

    (To QUEEN*)*

    Go not to my uncle's bed,
    Assume a virtue if you have it not!

    (To OPHELIA*)*

    Thou shalt not escape calumny.
    Get thee to a nunnery. Or if thou wilt needs marry, marry
    a fool: for wise men know what monsters you make of
    them.

POLONIUS.   *(Still studying the cloud)*
    It *is* back'd like a weasel.

HAMLET. Or like a whale?

POLONIUS. Very like a whale.

HAMLET. *(Facetiously, of* POLONIUS*)*
O what a noble mind is here o'erthrown.

*(*ROSENCRANTZ *and* GUILDENSTERN, *as vaudeville team, dance on. They are linked by a long rope that connects one to the other.)*

BOTH. They bore him barefac'd on the bier,
Hey nonny, nonny, hey nonny, no.
And on his grave rain'd many a tear,
Hey nonny, nonny, no.

CLOWN. *(Pained by their performance)*
The *time* is out of joint.

HAMLET. Good lads, how do you both?

BOTH. As the indifferent children of the earth.

ROSENCRANTZ. Happy, in that

GUILDENSTERN. We are not overhappy;

ROSENCRANTZ. On Fortune's cap

GUILDENSTERN. We are not the very button.

HAMLET. Nor the soles of her shoe?

BOTH. Neither, my Lord.

HAMLET. Then you live about her waist, or in the middle of her favour?

BOTH. *(Clutching balls)* Her privates we. *(All yoke it up.)*

HAMLET. In the secret parts of Fortune: Oh, most true; she is a strumpet.

(From opposite side a separate scene between KING *and* ROSENCRANTZ *and* GUILDENSTERN.*)*

KING. I entreat you both
That you vouchsafe your rest here in our Court
Some little time: so by your companies
To draw him on to pleasures, and to gather
So much as from occasions you may glean
That open'd lies within our remedy.

HAMLET. *(In former scene)*
What have you, my good friend deserv'd at the hands of Fortune that she sends you to prison hither?

ROSENCRANTZ. Prison, my Lord?

HAMLET. Denmark's a prison.

QUEEN. Your visitation shall receive such thanks As fits a King's remembrance.

(They are paid; KING and QUEEN exit.)

ROSENCRANTZ. We think not so, my Lord.

HAMLET. Why then 'tis none to you, for there is nothing either good or bad but thinking makes it so.

(All laugh)

CLOWN. *(As referee.)* A hit, a hit, a palpable hit!

ROSENCRANTZ. Why then, your ambition makes it one; 'tis too narrow for your mind.

HAMLET. O God, I could be bounded in a nutshell and count myself a King of infinite space, were it not that I have bad dreams.

(All turn to CLOWN for judgement.)

CLOWN. Nothing, neither way.

(Cut into new scene.)

GUILDENSTERN. *(Secretively)* Good my Lord.

HAMLET. *(Taken off to one side)* What's the news?

GUILDENSTERN. Vouchsafe me a word with you.

HAMLET. *(Facetiously)* Sir, a whole history.

GUILDENSTERN. The King, sir . . .

HAMLET. *(Pleasantly)* I know the King and Queen have sent for you.

GUILDENSTERN. *(Ignoring him)* . . . is in his retirement marvellously distempered.

HAMLET. With drink, sir.

(MUGS does a little dance-step.)

GUILDENSTERN.   Good my Lord, put your discourse into
some frame, and start not so wildly from my affair.

HAMLET.   *(Still clowning)* I am tame, sir, pronounce.

GUILDENSTERN.   My Lord, you once did love me.

HAMLET.   Were you not sent for? Come, deal justly with me;
nay, speak.

ROSENCRANTZ.   Good my Lord, what is your cause of
distemper? You do surely bar the door of your own liberty,
if you deny your griefs to your friend.

HAMLET.   But to the purpose, what make you at Elsinore?

GUILDENSTERN.   To visit you, my Lord. No other occasion.

(HAMLET *grabs them both by the neck.*)

HAMLET.   Be even and direct with me, whether you were
sent for or no.

GUILDENSTERN.   What should we say, my Lord?

HAMLET.   If you love me hold not off. *(Applies pressure)*

ROSENCRANTZ   *(gurgling)* My Lord, we were sent for.

(HAMLET *shoves them both away, towards the* KING,
*but still keeps a tight rein on them—literally, holds the rope
to which both are attached.*)

KING.   And can you by no drift of circumstance
Get from him why he puts on this confusion,
Grating so harshly all his days of quiet
With turbulent and dangerous lunacy?

ROSENCRANTZ.   He does confess he feels himself distracted.
But from what cause he will by no means speak.

KING.   Did he receive you well?

ROSENCRANTZ.   *(With a look back to* HAMLET *who holds
his rein)* Most like a gentleman.

(HAMLET *yanks* ROSENCRANTZ's *rope,* ROSENCRANTZ
is pulled back to HAMLET.)

GUILDENSTERN.   But with much forcing of his disposition.

(HAMLET *yanks* GUILDENSTERN's *rope, and he is pulled
back to* HAMLET. HAMLET *unties them, pushes*

ROSENCRANTZ *forward and out, and boots*
GUILDENSTERN *solidly on the rump.)*

GUILDENSTERN. *(Rubbing backside)*
Now cracks a noble heart.

(Exits)

(Cut into new scene)

QUEEN. *(Suddenly discovered)* Why, how now Hamlet?

HAMLET. *(Of the booted-off* ROSENCRANTZ *and*
GUILDENSTERN)
My excellent good friends,
Whom I will trust as I will adders fang'd!

QUEEN. This is mere madness.

HAMLET. I must to England; you know that?

QUEEN. Nay then, I'll set those to you that can speak.

HAMLET. Do not come your tardy son to chide.

(Cut into school flashback.)

QUEEN. *(As teacher)* Come, come and sit you down,
And these few precepts in thy memory
See thou character.

(LAERTES, OPHELIA, *and the* CLOWN *sit down in a
line in front of* HAMLET. *Teacher and class start
beating out the iambic rhythm with their fingers against
their palms, and the next is chanted out in a strictly
scanned sing-song.)*

Give thy thoughts . . . *(points to* OPHELIA.*)*

OPHELIA. No tongue.

QUEEN. Nor any unproportion'd thought his . . . *(to*
HAMLET.*)*

HAMLET. Act.

QUEEN. Be thou familiar but . . .

CLOWN. *(Brightly, teacher's pet)* By no means vulgar.

QUEEN. *(To class)*
The friends thou hast, and their adoption tried,
Grapple them to thy soul with hoops of steel.

But do not dull thy palm with entertainment
Of each unhatch'd, unfledg'd comrade.

(Scanning ends here.)

Beware of entrance into a quarrel but being in
Bear it that the opposed may beware of thee.
Give every man thine ear, but . . . *(to* LAERTES)

LAERTES. *(After being coached by all)* . . . few thy voice.

QUEEN. Take each man's censure but . . . *(to* OPHELIA)

OPHELIA. Reserve thy judgement. *(Slaps him without reason)*

QUEEN. Costly thy habit as thy purse can buy
But not express'd in fancy; rich not g—

CLOWN. *(Impetuously)* Not gaudy!

QUEEN. *(Who had intended that one for herself)*
For the apparel oft proclaims the man.
Neither a . . . *(Cues each pupil accordingly)*

HAMLET. Borrower.

OPHELIA. Nor a

LAERTES. Lender . . .

CLOWN. Be.

ALL. *(Skipping in a circle)*
For loan oft loses both itself and friend;
And borrowing dulls the edge of husbandry.

QUEEN. This above all . . .

(All stand formally in a line and recite in a childish sing-song.)

ALL. To thine own self be true,
And it must follow as the night the day
Thou canst not then be false to any man.

QUEEN. *(After a teasing pause)* Farewell.

(All dash out as if at the end of a school session, but FORTINBRAS *catches* HAMLET *before he has a chance to go)*

FORTINBRAS. Come, come and sit you down;

You shall not budge
till I set you up a glass
Where you may see the inmost part of you.

(On rostrum, KING *and* GHOST *stand back to back as if discovered in a picture frame.)*

Look here upon this picture and on this—
The counterfeit presentment of two brothers.
See what a grace was seated on this brow:

GHOST. *(Of himself)*
Hyperion's curls, the front of Jove himself,
An eye like Mars to threaten or command;
A station like the herald Mercury,
New-lighted on a heaven-kissing hill;

FORTINBRAS. *(Summing-up)*
A combination and a form indeed
Where every god did seem to set his seal
To give the world assurance of a man.

QUEEN. *(From the side, as a starstruck teenager)*
He was a man, take him for all in all
I shall not look upon his like again.

FORTINBRAS. Look you now what follows:
A murderer and a villain;
A slave that is not twentieth part the tithe
Of your precedent Lord.

KING. *(Of himself)* A vice of kings,
A vice of kings,
A cutpurse of the empire and the rule
That from a shelf the precious diadem stole
And put it in his pocket.

(The QUEEN *is scooped up into the* KING's *arms, and he proceeds to kiss and undress her. The* GHOST *steps down from the picture frame and directs the next to the embracing couple.)*

GHOST. O Hamlet, what a falling-off was there,
From me, whose love was of that dignity
That it went hand in hand, even with the vow
I made to her in marriage: and to decline
Upon a wretch whose natural gifts were poor

To those of mine.
                              O horrible, horrible, most horrible.
If thou hast nature in thee bear it not.

HAMLET. *(Trying not to see the* KING *and* QUEEN *making love before his eyes)* I have of late, but wherefore I know not, lost all my mirth, foregone all custom of exercise; and indeed it goes so heavily with my disposition, that this goodly frame the earth seems to me a sterile promontory; this most excellent canopy the air, look you, this brave o'erhanging firmament, this majestical roof fretted with golden fire:

(GHOST *and* FORTINBRAS, *disgusted with* HAMLET, *exit consulting together.)*

Why, it appears no other thing to me than a foul and pestilent congregation of vapours.
Man delights not me . . .

OPHELIA. *(Trying to seduce* HAMLET. *Singing)*
By Gis, and by Saint Charity,
Alack and fie for shame:
Young men will do't, if they come to't.
    By Cock they are to blame.
Quoth she, before you tumbled me,
    You promis'd me to wed.
So would I ha' done, by yonder sun,
    And thou hadst not come to my bed.

HAMLET. *(Unmoved by all advances)*
. . . no nor woman neither.

(GHOST *suddenly enters with his arm around* FORTINBRAS, *as if he were his son and confiding in him.)*

GHOST. *(Colloquially)* If thou didst ever thy dear father love
Revenge his foul and most unnatural murder.

FORTINBRAS. *(Imitating* HAMLET)
Haste, haste me to know it
That I with wings as swift . . .

HAMLET. *(Seeing his place usurped by* FORTINBRAS)
As meditation or the thoughts of love
May sweep to my revenge.

*(Repeating speech, both play child's game—fist over fist—
to win toy sword. HAMLET wins then leaps forward
gallantly.)*

HAMLET. *(Centre stage; consciously performing)*
Rightly to be great
Is not to stir without great argument.

CLOWN. *(With script, like exasperated director)*
Speak the speech, I pray you, as I pronounced it to you,
trippingly on the tongue.

HAMLET. But greatly to find quarrel in a straw . . .

CLOWN. Nor do not saw the air too much with your hand
thus, but use all gently.

HAMLET. . . . greatly to find quarrel in a straw,
When honour's at the stake.

CLOWN. Be not too tame neither.

HAMLET. *(Fiercely)* How stand I then
That have a father kill'd, a mother stain'd . . .

CLOWN. Suit the action to the word, the word to the
action.

HAMLET. *(Gesturing)*
That have a father kill'd a mother stain'd,
Excitement of my reason and my blood
And let all sleep.

CLOWN. *(Now as POLONIUS)* Fore God, my Lord, well
spoken with good accent and good discretion.

(HAMLET, *exhausted and humiliated, has sunk to the
ground. CLOWN has gone. Enter OPHELIA.)*

OPHELIA. *(Mock concern)*
The glass of fashion and the mould of form,
The observed of all observers, quite, quite down
(Sighs)

*(The following scene is played out against flicker-wheel
effect—like an old-time silent film. HAMLET sits on
floor, entranced by all he sees. Shortly the CLOWN
joins him, and both watch the film.)*

KING. *(Suddenly embracing OPHELIA)*

There's matter in these sighs.
These profound heaves
You must translate: 'tis fit we understand them.
What is't, Ophelia?

OPHELIA. *(Modestly)*
So please you, something touching the Lord Hamlet.

KING. *(Suddenly releasing her, jealously)*
What is between you, give me up the truth.

OPHELIA. He hath, my Lord, of late made many tenders
Of his affection for me.

KING. You speak like a green girl
Unsifted in such perilous circumstance.
Do you believe his tenders, as you call them?

OPHELIA. I do not know, my Lord, what I should think.

KING. Think yourself a baby
That you have ta'en his tenders for true pay
Which are not sterling. Tender yourself more dearly.

OPHELIA. My Lord, he hath importun'd me with love
In honourable fashion.

KING. Ay, fashion you may call it; go to, go to.

OPHELIA.
And hath given countenance to his speech, my Lord,
With all the vows of Heaven.

KING.
Love, his affections do not that way tend.
Do not believe his vows; for they are brokers,
Not of that dye which their investments show,
But mere implorators of unholy suits,
Breathing like sanctified and pious bawds,
The better to beguile.
I would not, in plain terms, from this time forth,
Have you so slander any moment leisure
As to give words or talk with the Lord Hamlet;
Look to't, I charge you.

OPHELIA. I shall obey, my Lord.

(The KING, regretting his harshness, embraces her.)

KING. Pretty Ophelia.

(They kiss—and the scene dissolves.)

CLOWN. *(As prompter)*
A father kill'd . . . a mother stain'd . . .

(HAMLET, *still transfixed by the scene, does not stir.*
As the movie lights come on again, the QUEEN *is*
discovered in KING's *arms;* OPHELIA *has vanished.)*

QUEEN. *(After kiss)*
Since my dear soul was mistress of my choice
And could of men distinguish, her election
Hath seal'd thee for herself. For thou has been
As one in suffering all, that suffers nothing.
A man that Fortune's buffets and rewards
Hath ta'en with equal thanks. And blest are those
Whose blood and judgement are so well commingled
That they are not a pipe for Fortune's finger
To sound what stop she please. Give me that man
That is not passion's slave, and I will wear him
In my heart's core, ay, in my heart of heart
As I do thee.

(The QUEEN *kisses* CLAUDIUS, *and the scene*
dissolves. When lights fade up, it is the GHOST
discovered in the QUEEN's *arms. He sits wearily.*
HAMLET *and* CLOWN, *still engrossed by film,*
continue to gape.)

GHOST. Faith I must leave thee, and shortly too.

QUEEN. *(Soothingly)* You are so sick of late,
So far from cheer, and from your former state
That I distrust you: yet though I distrust,
Discomfort you, my Lord, it nothing must.
For women's fear and love holds quantity
In neither aught or in extremity.
Now what my love is, proof hath made you know
And as my love is siz'd, my fear is so.

GHOST. *(Wearily)*
My operant powers their functions leave to do:
And thou shalt live in this fair world behind,
Honour'd belov'd and haply, one as kind
For husband shalt thou . . .

QUEEN. O confound the rest:

Such love must needs be treason in my breast.
In second husband let me accurst,
None wed the second, but who kill'd the first.

GHOST. I do believe you think what now you speak,
But what we do determine, oft we break.

QUEEN. The instances that second marriage move
Are base respects of thrift, but none of love.
A second time, I kill my husband dead
When second husband kisses me in bed.

GHOST. The world is not for aye, nor 'tis not strange
That even our loves should with our fortunes change.
The great man down, you mark his favourite flies,
The poor advanc'd makes friends of enemies.
But orderly to end where I begun,
Our wills and fates do so contrary run,
That our devices still are overthrown,
Our thoughts are ours, their ends none of our own.
So think thou wilt no second husband wed:
But die thy thoughts, when thy first Lord is dead.

QUEEN. *(Pledging)* Nor earth to me give food, nor Heaven light,
Sport and repose lock from me day and night.
Each opposite that blanks the face of joy,
Meet what I would have well, and it destroy.
Both here, and hence, pursue me lasting strife,
If once a widow, ever I be wife.

CLOWN. *(From floor)*
Well spoken with good accent and good discretion.

(HAMLET, *still transfixed, shushes the* CLOWN.)

GHOST. *(Lying down)* Sleep rock thy brain,
And never come mischance between us twain.

(When GHOST *is asleep, the* KING, *as Murderer,
suddenly appears beside the* QUEEN. *The* QUEEN, *no
longer the loving wife, appears as Accomplice. They both
stare down at the sleeping man, and then abruptly turn
on* HAMLET. *The silent-screen convention is abruptly
broken.* KING *and* QUEEN *bearing down on* HAMLET.)

QUEEN.   Thoughts black,

KING.   hands apt

46

HAMLET

QUEEN.   drugs fit,

KING.   and time agreeing

QUEEN.   Confederate season,

KING.   else no creature seeing.

QUEEN. *(With vial)* With Hecat's ban thrice blasted, thrice
> infected.
> Thy natural magic and dire property

> *(The vial is forced into* HAMLET's *hands.)*

KING. On wholesome life, usurp immediately.

> (KING *and* QUEEN *force a helpless* HAMLET *to pour
> poison into the ears of his sleeping father.)*

GHOST. *(Shrieking, rising up and speaking straight into*
> HAMLET's *face)* If thou has Nature in thee bear it not!

> *(The shriek has suddenly dissolved the entire scene, and
> HAMLET, with all the apparitions fled, is left entirely
> alone. The* CLOWN *stealthily sneaks back.)*

CLOWN. *(As prompter)* A father kill'd . . . a mother stain'd . .

HAMLET. *(Dully)* A father kill'd . . . a mother stain'd . . .

CLOWN. *(Decides to prompt from other part of speech)*
> Bestial oblivion . . .

HAMLET. *(Revved up again)* Now whether it be
> Bestial oblivion or some craven scruple
> Of thinking too precisely on the event,

> (CLOWN *breathes sigh of relief and departs, thankful
> he's got the show on the road again.)*

HAMLET. *(Continues)*
> A thought which quarter'd hath but one part wisdom
> And ever three parts coward, I do not know
> Why yet I live to say, 'This thing's to do'
> Sith I have cause . . .

FORTINBRAS. *(Urging)*
> . . . and will and strength and means . . .

HAMLET. *(Limply)* To do it.

FORTINBRAS. 'This thing's to do.' *(Hands him toy sword)*

HAMLET. Now might I do it pat.

(The Court suddenly appears in an eighteenth-century elaborately ornamented theatre box. Applause. The GHOST as Player-King downstage giving his performance.)

This play is the image of a murder done in Vienna: Gonzago is the Duke's name, his wife, Baptista: you shall see anon: 'tis a knavish piece of work, but what o' that? Your Majesty and we that have free souls, it touches us not: let the gall'd jade winch, our withers are unwrung.

KING. *(In box)* What do you call the play?

HAMLET. The Mouse-Trap.

(The GHOST, playing as old-time tragedian (Player-King), begins.)

GHOST. *(Histrionically)*
But soft, methinks I scent the morning's air:
Brief let me be: sleeping within my orchard,
My custom always in the afternoon,
Upon my secure hour . . . *(Kneels down)*

HAMLET. Now he is praying,
And now I'll do it.
And so he goes to Heaven,
And so I am revenged. That would be scanned:
A villain kills my father, and for that
I his sole son do this same villain send
To heaven . . .
Oh, this is hire and salary not revenge.

(CLAUDIUS is suddenly discovered kneeling in GHOST's position.)

KING. *(Hamming)* What if this cursed hand
Were thicker than itself with brother's blood,
Is there not rain enough in the sweet heavens
To wash it white as snow?

HAMLET. He took my father grossly full of bread
With all his crimes broad blown, as flush as May,
And how his audit stands who knows, save Heaven?
And am I then revenged,
To take him in the purging of his soul,
When he is fit and seasoned for his passage?

KING. Whereto serves mercy
But to confront the visage of offence?
And what's in prayer but this twofold force,
To be forestalled ere we come to fall,
Or pardoned being down? Then I'll look up . . .
My fault is past. But oh, what form of prayer
Can serve my turn?

(The Court applauds the KING's histrionics and rushes out of box to congratulate him.)

HAMLET. *(Appealing to audience)*
Am I a coward?
Who calls me villain; breaks my pate across?
Plucks off my beard and blows it in my face?
Tweaks me by the nose; gives me the lie in the throat
As deep as to the lungs? Who does me this?
Ha why, I should take it; for it cannot be
But I am pigeon-liver'd and lack gall
To make oppression bitter or ere this
I should have fatted all the region kites
With this slave's offal, *(to KING)* bloody, bawdy,
villain.

KING. *(as Player-King, apologizing for performance)*
Forgive me my foul murder.

HAMLET. *(Faltering)*
Remorseless, treacherous, lecherous, kindless villain.

KING. *(As himself, kneels)*
Oh my offence is rank, it smells to Heaven,
It hath the primal eldest curse upon it.
A brother's murder. Pray can I not,
Though inclination be as sharp as will,
My stronger guilt defeats my strong intent,

HAMLET. And like a man to double business bound
I stand in pause where I shall first begin
And both neglect.

GHOST. If thou . . . hast . . . nature . . . in thee . . .
bear . . . it not.

FORTINBRAS. I with wings as swift
As meditation or the thoughts of love . . .

HAMLET. *(as if having been coached)* may sweep to my . . .

49

QUEEN. *(Seeing* HAMLET *with sword)* Help, help, hoa.

HAMLET. O vengeance!

(Stabs the KING *who is kneeling before him. Blackout as his sword enters. Lights up. The* KING *still praying, unhurt. Repeated twice. On third stab,* POLONIUS *falls forward.)*

POLONIUS. Oh, I am slain! *(Falls forward, dead.)*

(All, crying like banshees, dash out leaving HAMLET, *the dead* POLONIUS, *and the* QUEEN, *grief-stricken at the corpse.)*

HAMLET. Dead for a ducat, dead.

(Cut sharply into new scene.)

OPHELIA. You are merry, my Lord?

HAMLET. Who I?

OPHELIA. Ay, my Lord.

HAMLET. O God, your only jig-maker; what should a man do but be merry? For look you how cheerfully my mother looks, and my father died within's two hours.

QUEEN. *(With* POLONIUS's *corpse)*
Oh me, what hast thou done?

HAMLET. *(To* QUEEN)
Such an act
That blurs the grace and blush of modesty
Calls virtue hypocrite, takes off the rose
From the fair forehead of an innocent love
And sets a blister there.
Lady, shall I lie in your lap?

OPHELIA. No, my Lord.

HAMLET. I mean, my head upon your lap.

OPHELIA. Aye, my Lord.

HAMLET. Do you think I meant country matters?

OPHELIA. I think nothing, my Lord.

HAMLET. That's a fair thought to lie between maids' legs.

OPHELIA. What is, my Lord?

HAMLET. Nothing.

(HAMLET kisses her roughly and lays her down, then leaves; OPHELIA, now distracted, slowly recovers.)

OPHELIA. *(Sings)*
How should I your true love know
   From another one?
By his cockle hat and staff
   And his sandal shoon.
He is dead and gone, Lady,
   He is dead and gone,
At his head a grass-green turf.
At his heels a stone.
And will he not come again?
And will he not come again?
   No, no, he is dead,
   Go to thy death-bed,
He will never come again.

(Before OPHELIA's plaintive song is finished the Gravedigger's merry one has already begun.)

CLOWN. *(As Gravedigger)*
In youth when I did love, did love,
   Methought it was very sweet,
To contract O the time for my behove,
   O methought there was nothing meet.
But Age with his stealing steps
   Hath claw'd me in his clutch:
And hath shipped me until the land
   As if I had never been such.

(As OPHELIA wanders off aimlessly and the dead POLONIUS sings his song from the prone position, HAMLET and LAERTES suddenly appear from opposite sides, each brandishing a wooden toy sword. They clank swords together and then begin elaborate warming-up exercises, while the KING, QUEEN, and Court troop on and group themselves formally, awaiting the commencement of the duel.)

HAMLET. Come on, sir.

LAERTES. Come, my Lord.

KING. If Hamlet give the first or second hit,

Or quit in answer of the third exchange,
Let all the battlements their ordnance fire.
The King shall drink to Hamlet's better health,
And in the cup a union shall he throw
Richer than that, which four successive Kings
In Denmark's Crown have worn.

                              Come begin.
And you the judges bear a wary eye.

(They duel mechanically, then stop.)

LAERTES.   Too much of water has thou, poor Ophelia,
And therefore I forbid my tears.

*(The Court applaud enthusiastically. LAERTES
acknowledges with a bow. They duel again, then stop.)*

HAMLET.   *(Trying his style)*
Doubt thou, the stars are fire,
Doubt that the Sun doth move,
Doubt truth to be a liar
But never doubt, I love.

(The Court boo and hiss his paltry effort.)

LAERTES.   *(Still dueling. Stops)*
Both the worlds I give to negligence,
Let come what comes: only I'll be revenged
Most throughly for my father.

(The Court cheer LAERTES' poetry. The duel continues.)

HAMLET.   *(Limply competing)*
The play's the thing
Wherein I'll catch the conscience of the King.

(All boo and hiss HAMLET's lame reply.)

LAERTES.   *(Flamboyantly)*
I have a speech of fire that fain would blaze.

(All cheer wildly.)

HAMLET.   *(Desperately rattling them off)*
O what a rogue and peasant slave am I
O that this too too solid flesh would melt
There's a divinity that shapes our ends,
Frailty thy name is woman—the rest is silence.
Judgement.

CLOWN. *(Grudgingly)* A hit, a very palpable hit.

> (FORTINBRAS, *all by himself, very slowly and deliberately applauds* HAMLET *as the Court stonily looks on.* HAMLET *draws more encouragement from this than, objectively, he should.* ROSENCRANTZ *and* GUILDENSTERN *come forward while* HAMLET *duels coolly with* LAERTES, *who, unlike* HAMLET, *is fencing laboriously.)*

ROSENCRANTZ. What have you done, my Lord, with the dead body?

HAMLET. Alas, poor Yorick.

GUILDENSTERN. Where's Polonius?

HAMLET. At supper.

GUILDENSTERN. At supper? Where?

HAMLET. Not where he eats, but where he is eaten, a certain convocation of politic worms are e'en at him.

ROSENCRANTZ. My Lord, you must tell us where the body is, and go with us to the King.

HAMLET. The body is with the King, but the King is not with the body. The King is a thing—

GUILDENSTERN. A thing, my Lord?

HAMLET. . . . of shreds and patches. Did you think I meant country matters? Another hit, what say you? *(Running* LAERTES *through.)*

LAERTES. *(Dropping his sword)*
A touch, a touch, I do confess.

ROSENCRANTZ and GUILDENSTERN. Where is Polonius?

HAMLET. In heaven; send thither to see. If your messenger find him not there seek him in the other place yourself.

ROSENCRANTZ. O my Lord, if my duty be too bold, my love is too unmannerly.

HAMLET. *(Proffering sword as if it were a recorder)*
Will you play upon this pipe?

GUILDENSTERN. My Lord, I cannot.

HAMLET. *(to* ROSENCRANTZ) I pray you.

ROSENCRANTZ. Believe me, I cannot.

HAMLET. I do beseech you.

GUILDENSTERN. *(Humouring him)* I know no touch of it, my Lord.

HAMLET. 'Tis as easy as lying; govern these ventages with your finger and thumb, give it breath with your mouth, and it will discourse most eloquent music. Look you, these are the stops.

(Waggles the point near ROSENCRANTZ *and* GUILDENSTERN; *they look on frightened. He mimes playing the sword as if it were a pipe, then offers it to* ROSENCRANTZ *and* GUILDENSTERN *to play upon. They hesitate out of fear and confusion; then, to humour him, come forward to pick up the sword—at that moment he grabs them both and threatens them with the toy, which has now become lethal.)*

GUILDENSTERN. *(Struggling free)* Nay, good my Lord, this courtesy is not of the right breed.

HAMLET. Why look you now, how unworthy a thing you make of me: you would pluck out the heart of my mystery; you would sound me from my lowest note to the top of my compass. Why do you think I am easier to be played on than a pipe? Call me what instrument you will, though you can fret me, you cannot play upon me.

*(*HAMLET *does a wild step around* ROSENCRANTZ *and* GUILDENSTERN *and ends by stabbing them both with the toy sword. After being stabbed, they consult each other, and decide to die, which they do, quite falsely.)*

CLOWN. A hit, a very palpable hit!

HAMLET. *(Now mad with power)*
Come for the third, Laertes; you but dally.
I pray you, pass with your best violence,
I am afeared you make a wanton of me.

(Exits brandishing sword, with CLOWN.
Cut to Burial Scene.
All gathered around OPHELIA's *tomb,* LAERTES
with the CLERGYMAN.)*

LAERTES. *(Soberly)*
What ceremony else?

DOCTOR. Her obsequies have been as far enlarged
As we have warranty. Her death was doubtful,
And but that great command o'ersways the order,
She should in ground unsanctified have lodged
Till the last trumpet.

LAERTES. Must there no more be done?

DOCTOR. No more be done!
We should profane the service of the dead
To sing sage requiem and such rest to her
As to peace-parted souls.

LAERTES. Lay her in the earth
And from her fair and unpolluted flesh
May violets spring.

(LAERTES *leaps past grave and mourners into flashback with* OPHELIA *who sits miming sewing.*)

LAERTES.
My necessaries are embarked; farewell,
And sister, as the winds give benefit
And convoy is assistant, do not sleep
But let me hear from you.

OPHELIA. *(At loom)*
Do you doubt that?

LAERTES. For Hamlet, and the trifling of his favours,
Hold it a fashion, and a toy in blood;
A violet in the youth of primy nature:
Forward, not permanent, sweet, not lasting,
The perfume and suppliance of a minute,
No more.

OPHELIA. No more but so.

LAERTES. Perhaps he loves you now,
And now no soil nor cautel does besmirch
The virtue of his will. But you must fear
His greatness weighed, his will is not his own.
Be wary then, best safety lies in fear.

OPHELIA.   I shall the effect of this good lesson keep
As watchman to my heart;
'Tis in my memory lock'd
And you yourself shall keep the key of it.

LAERTES.   *(Back in former scene)*
I tell thee, churlish priest,
A ministering angel shall my sister be
When thou liest howling.
Hold off the earth awhile,
Till I have caught her once more in mine arms:

(Leaps into grave. The funeral group suddenly freeze into a tableau. Reappears with dead OPHELIA in his arms.)

Now pile your dust upon the quick and dead
Till of this flat a mountain you have made
To o'ertop old Pelion or the skyish head
Of blue Olympus.

HAMLET.   *(Reappearing)*
What is he whose grief
Bears such an emphasis? whose phrase of sorrow
Conjures the wandering stars and makes them stand
Like wonder-wounded hearers. This is I,
Hamlet the Dane.

CLOWN.   *(As prompter)* Speak the speech, I pray you, as
I pronounced it to you, trippingly on the tongue.

HAMLET.   *(To LAERTES)* Woo't drink up eisel? eat a
crocodile? I'll do't.

CLOWN.   *(Whispering)* Nor do not saw the air too much with
your hand thus, but use all gently.

HAMLET.   Dost thou come here to whine,
To outface me with leaping in her grave?
Be buried quick with her, and so will I.

CLOWN.   Be not too tame neither.

HAMLET.   And if thou prate of mountains let them throw
Millions of acres on us.

CLOWN.   Suit the action to the word, the word to the
action.

HAMLET.   Throw Millions of acres on us, till our ground

Singeing his pate against the burning zone
Make Ossa like a wart. Nay, and thou'lt mouth.
I'll rant as well as thou.

QUEEN.   Alas, how is't with you?
That you bend your eye on vacancy,
And with the incorporal air do hold discourse.
Whereon do you look?

(Funeral ceremony still frozen in tableau.)

HAMLET.   *(Looking toward funeral scene)*
Do you see nothing there?

QUEEN.   Nothing at all, yet all that is I see.

HAMLET.   Nor did you nothing hear?

QUEEN.   No, nothing but ourselves.

(Pause)

HAMLET.   *(Collapsing into* QUEEN's *lap)*
Your noble son is mad.

(Tableau dissolves.)

QUEEN.   *(The mum, consoling)*
Here Hamlet, take my napkin; rub thy brow.

HAMLET.   *(Nestling in her bosom)*
You must needs have heard how I am punished
With sore distraction. What I have done
That might your nature, honour and exception
Roughly awake, I here proclaim was madness.

QUEEN.   Come, let me wipe thy face.

HAMLET.   *(Still nestling)*
I lov'd Ophelia; forty thousand brothers
Could not with all their quantity of love
Make up my sum.

QUEEN.   *(Rocking* HAMLET *like a babe)*
Hamlet, Hamlet . . .

HAMLET.   *(Suddenly up; facing* QUEEN)
Go not to my uncle's bed.

(Pause)

QUEEN.   No more.

HAMLET. *(Still restrained)*
>You cannot call it love; for at your age
>The hey-day in the blood is tame, it's humble,
>And waits upon the judgement.

QUEEN. Hamlet, speak no more.

HAMLET. *(Losing control)*
>Nay, but to live
>In the rank sweat of an enseamed bed
>Stew'd in corruption; honeying and making love
>Over the nasty sty.

KING. *(Entering)*
>Good Gertrude, set some watch over your son.

HAMLET. *(Pushing her away)*
>O shame! Where is thy blush? Rebellious Hell
>If thou canst mutine in a matron's bones,
>To flaming youth, let virtue be as wax
>And melt in her own fire.

QUEEN. Why, how now Hamlet?

HAMLET. *(As if there had been no outburst)*
>What's the matter now?

QUEEN. Have you forgot me?

HAMLET. *(To the* KING)
>No, by the rood;
>You are the Queen, your husband's brother's wife
>But would you were not so.
>You are my mother.

KING. Thy loving father, Hamlet.

HAMLET. Father and mother is man and wife; man and wife
is one flesh, and so my mother.

KING. *(Moving off)*
>He is far gone; far gone.

QUEEN. O heavenly powers, restore him.

KING. Mad as the seas and wind when both contend
>Which is the mightier.

(KING and QUEEN, *shaking heads, move away.)*

HAMLET. *(To audience)* I am mad but north-north-west;

when the wind is southerly, I know a hawk from a handsaw.

ALL. Judgement! Judgement! Judgement!

(A trial is swiftly arranged: HAMLET placed in the dock by FORTINBRAS, who acts as counsel. The KING acts as Judge.
All are seated behind a long tribunal table.)

QUEEN. Hamlet, thou hast thy father much offended.

HAMLET. Mother, you have my father much offended.

KING. *(As Judge)* Come, come, you answer with an idle tongue.

HAMLET. Go, go, you question with an idle tongue.

KING. Ophelia, prithee speak.

OPHELIA. *(Soberly giving testimony)*
My Lord, as I was sewing in my chamber,
Lord Hamlet with his doublet all unbrac'd,
No hat upon his head, his stockings foul'd
Ungarter'd and down-gyved to his ankle,
Pale as his shirt, his knees knocking each other,
And with a look so piteous in purport,
As if he had been loosed out of hell,
To speak of horrors, he comes before me.

FORTINBRAS. *(Explaining)* Mad for thy love.

OPHELIA. My Lord, I do not know.

KING. What said he?

OPHELIA. He took me by the wrist and held me hard;
Then goes he to the length of all his arm,
And with his other hand thus o'er his brow,
He falls to such perusal of my face
As he would draw it. Long stay'd he so.
At last, a little shaking of mine arm;
And thrice his head thus waving up and down,
He rais'd a sigh so piteous and profound
As it did seem to shatter all his bulk
And end his being. That done, he lets me go,
And with his head over his shoulder turn'd,
He seemed to find his way without his eyes

For out a doors he went without their help,
And to the last bended their light on me.

FORTINBRAS. *(to Court)*
This is the very ecstasy of love
Whose violent property fordoes itself,
And leads the will to desperate undertakings
As oft as any passion under Heaven
That does afflict our natures.

OPHELIA. *(Slowly turning mad)* I hope all will be well.
We must be patient, but I cannot choose but weep to think
they should lay him in the cold ground: my brother shall
know of it, and so I thank you for your good counsel.
Come, my coach: good night Ladies, good night sweet
Ladies, good night, good night.

(Exits as if in the seat of a coach and six.)

LAERTES. *(Of OPHELIA)*
O treble woe,
Fall ten times treble on that cursed head
Whose wicked deed thy most ingenious sense
Depriv'd thee of.

(Makes for HAMLET.)

HAMLET. Away thy hand!

KING. Pluck them asunder.

FORTINBRAS. *(Aside, to HAMLET)*
Good my Lord, be quiet.

(To Court)

Was't Hamlet wrong'd Laertes? Never Hamlet.
If Hamlet from himself be ta'en away
And when he's not himself does wrong Laertes,
Then Hamlet does it not. Hamlet denies it.
Who does it then?

CLOWN. *(Impulsively)* His madness.

FORTINBRAS. If't be so, Hamlet is of the faction that is
wrong'd. His madness is poor Hamlet's enemy.

CLOWN. *(To others behind table)*
That he is mad, 'tis true;
'tis true, 'tis pity, and pity 'tis, 'tis true.

60

GUILDENSTERN. My Lord, the Queen would speak.

QUEEN. *(Rising)* Hamlet in madness hath Polonius slain.

ALL. *(Suddenly thumping table)* Vengeance!

QUEEN. In his lawless fit,
Behind the arras, hearing something stir,
He whips out his rapier and cries, A rat, a rat,
And in this brainish apprehension kills
The unseen good old man.

(The CLOWN, *as* POLONIUS, *rises and bows his head.
All at the table bow their heads in condolence.)*

KING. It had been so with us had we been there.

FORTINBRAS. Of that I shall have also cause to speak,
Wherein . . .

QUEEN. His liberty is full of threats to all; To you yourself,
to us, to everyone.

(All thump table vengefully, as before.)

HAMLET. *(Rising to defend himself;* FORTINBRAS
struggles to keep him seated.) Indeed my lord,
I am very proud, revengeful, ambitious, with more
offences at my beck than I have thoughts to put them
in, imagination to give them shape, or time to act them
in. What should such fellows as I do, crawling between
heaven and earth. We are arrant knaves all, believe none
of us.

*(The Court bristles with contempt and all agitatedly
consult the* KING. FORTINBRAS *talks urgently to*
HAMLET *and forces a paper into hands.)*

FORTINBRAS. *(Trying to undo* HAMLET'*s harm)*
My lord, will the King hear this.

HAMLET. *(Rises, under sufferance, and reads prepared
statement)* "This presence knows,
And you must needs have heard how I am punish'd
With sore distraction. What I have done
That might your nature, honour and exception
Roughly awake, I here proclaim was madness."

LAERTES. Madness!
And so have I a noble father lost,

A sister driven into desperate terms.
Whose worth (if praises may go back again)
Stood challenger on the mount of all the age
For her perfections. But my revenge will come.

HAMLET.   Hear you, sir:
What is the reason that you use me thus?
I lov'd you ever.

LAERTES.   *(Bristling with anger)*
You mock me, sir.

HAMLET.   Not by this hand.

LAERTES.   *(Springing on* HAMLET)
The devil take your soul.

(Others part LAERTES *and* HAMLET. *General
scuffle stopped suddenly by the* GHOST*'s entrance.)*

GHOST.   Mark me.

HAMLET.   Alas, poor ghost.

KING.   Speak.

HAMLET.   Do not come your tardy son to chide
That laps'd in time and passion lets go by
Th' important acting of your dread command.

KING.   I charge thee, speak.

GHOST.   *(Directly to King)*
In the corrupted currents of this world,
Offence's golden hand may shove by justice,
And oft 'tis seen the wicked prize itself
Buys out the Law; but 'tis not so above,
There is no shuffling, there the action lies
In his true nature, and we ourselves compell'd
Even to the teeth and forehead of our faults,
To give in evidence.

(Suddenly turns to HAMLET, *who averts his gaze.)*

HAMLET.   *(To himself)* How all occasions do inform . . .

GHOST.   Eyes without feeling, feeling without sight,
Ears without hands, or eyes, smelling, sans all
Or but a sickly part of one true sense
Could not so mope.

62

HAMLET. *(Swearing to himself)*
    Thy commandment all alone shall live . . .

GHOST. Let . . . not . . . the royal bed . . . of Denmark . . .
    be . . . a Couch . . . for luxury and damned . . . incest.

HAMLET. *(Kneeling before Father)*
    Thy commandment all alone shall live,
    Within the book and volume of my brain,
    Unmix'd with baser matter; yes, yes, by Heaven.
    I have sworn't.

QUEEN. *(Rising)*
    And thus awhile the fit will work on him:
    Anon as patient as the female dove,
    When that her golden couplets are disclosed,
    His silence will sit drooping.

(All rise for verdict.)

KING. Confine him.
    Madness in great ones must not unwatch'd go.

(As Court moves off in all directions, HAMLET *tries to stop them with the next speech.)*

HAMLET. Let me speak to th' yet unknowing world,
    How these things came about. So shall you hear
    Of carnal, bloody and unnatural acts,
    Of accidental judgements, casual slaughters,
    Of deaths put on by cunning, and forc'd cause,
    And in the upshot, purposes mistook,
    Fall'n on the inventors' heads. All this can I
    Truly deliver.

(By the time HAMLET *has finished his speech, he is ranting to the empty air as the Court have all disappeared.* FORTINBRAS, *sitting alone, looks up at him.* HAMLET *sinks down exhausted at his side.)*

FORTINBRAS. So oft it chances in particular men
    That for some vicious mole of nature in them
    As in their birth—wherein they are not guilty,
    Since nature cannot choose his origin,—
    By the o'ergrowth of some complexion,
    Oft breaking down the pales and forts of reason;
    Or by some habit that too much o'er-leavens
    The form of plausive manners; that these men,

Carrying, I say, the stamp of one defect,
Being nature's livery or Fortune's star,
Their virtues else, be they as pure as grace,
As infinite as man may undergo,
Shall in the general censure take corruption
From that particular fault.

HAMLET. *(As if not understanding the implication)*
Does it not, think'st thee, stand me now upon?
He that hath kill'd my King, and whor'd my mother,
Popped in between the'election and my hopes,
Thrown out his angle for my proper life,
And with such cozenage: is't not perfect conscience,
To quit him with this arm? and is't not to be damn'd
To let this canker of our nature come
In further evil?

FORTINBRAS. *(Patronizing)* Ay, marry is't.

HAMLET. *(Acting)* Now could I drink hot blood,
And do such bitter business as the day
Would quake to look on.

FORTINBRAS *(trying another tack)* Rightly to be great
Is not to stir without great argument
But greatly to find quarrel in a straw
When honour's at the stake.

HAMLET. *(Hearing it for the first time)* How stand I then,
That have a father kill'd, a mother stain'd,
Excitements of my reason and my blood,
And let all sleep.

FORTINBRAS. *(Urging direct action)*
Then trip him that his heels may kick at Heaven
And that his soul may be as damn'd and black
As Hell, whereto it goes.

(Pause.)

HAMLET. No.
When he is drunk asleep, or in his rage,
Or in the incestuous pleasure of his bed . . .

FORTINBRAS *(He's heard it all before)*
Ay sure, this is most brave.

HAMLET. *(On the defensive)* The spirit that I have seen

May be the devil . . . the devil hath power
To assume a pleasing shape.

(FORTINBRAS, *unmoved by this ruse, regards*
HAMLET *knowingly.*)

Do not look upon me,
Lest with this piteous action you convert
My stern effects; then what I have to do
Will want true colour.

FORTINBRAS.   That we would do
We should do when we would; for this 'would' changes,
And hath abatements and delays, as many
As there are tongues, are hands, are accidents,
And this 'should' is like a spendthrift sigh
That hurts by easing.

HAMLET.   *(Seeking escape hatch)*
How all occasions . . .

FORTINBRAS.   *(Taking him by the shoulders)*
What would you undertake
To show yourself your father's son in deed
More than in words?

HAMLET.   *(Squirming)*
I'll . . . observe his looks; I'll . . . tempt him to the quick,
I'll have grounds more relative than this.

FORTINBRAS.   *(Washing his hands of him completely)*
Thus conscience does make cowards of us all,
And thus the native hue of resolution
Is sicklied o'er with the pale cast of thought
And enterprises of great pith and moment
With this regard their currents turn awry
And lose the name of action. *(Exits)*

(Long pause.)

HAMLET.   *(Bid to audience)*
Had *he* the motive and the cue for passion
That I have, he would drown the stage with tears
And cleave the general ear with horrid speech,
Make mad the guilty and appal the free,
Confound the ignorant and amaze indeed
The very faculty of eyes and ears.
                              Yet I

A dull and muddy-mettled rascal . . .
Peak like . . .
John a' Dreams . . . and
                              can do nothing.

(Before the end of this speech, the GHOST *and all the other characters have walked on very slowly. They form a semi-circle around the bent figure of* HAMLET. *Eventually, the* GHOST *comes forward. He is holding* HAMLET's *toy sword.)*

GHOST. *(Mock frightened)*
Angels and ministers of grace defend us:
Be thou a spirit of health, or a goblin damn'd,
Bring with thee airs from Heaven or blasts from Hell?
Be thy intents wicked or charitable,
Thou comest in such a questionable shape
That I will speak to thee. I'll call thee Hamlet.

(Puts toy sword under HAMLET's *arm, like a crutch. The Cast, now fully assembled, expresses its delight over the* GHOST's *send-up.)*

CLOWN. *(Acknowledging its wit)*
A hit, a very palpable hit.

GHOST. *(Still playing it up like mad)*
Speak, I am bound to hear.

(A long pause, during which everyone's sarcastic laughter gradually mounts.)

HAMLET. *(Weakly)*
To be or not to be that is the question.

(All laugh.)

(Weakly) The play's the thing wherein I'll catch the conscience of the King.

(All laugh again.)

(Vainly trying to find the right words) There is something rotten in the state of Denmark.

(The laughter sharply cuts out. A powerful, stark silence issues from everyone. No one moves. Slowly HAMLET's *frame begins to bend, gradually his knees sag and his back arches until he slumps down on to his knees.*

Then his head slowly rolls forward on to his chest and he sinks even further, on to his haunches. He leans on his toy sword for support. This descent takes a good deal of time, and occurs in total silence.)

FORTINBRAS. *(Coming out of semi-circle, sarcastically)*
What a piece of work is man.

(Chants)

How noble in reason.

ALL. *(Chanting)* Noble in reason.

FORTINBRAS. *(Chants)* How infinite in faculty.

ALL. *(Chanting)* Infinite in faculty.

FORTINBRAS. *(Chanting)*
In form and moving, how express and admirable.

ALL. *(Chanting)* Express and admirable.

FORTINBRAS. *(Chanting)* In action, how like an angel.

ALL. *(Chanting)* How like an angel.

FORTINBRAS. *(Chanting)* In apprehension, how like a god.

ALL. *(Chanting)* How like a god.

(After this choral send-up led by FORTINBRAS, *all look again to* HAMLET, *who has not stirred.)*

OPHELIA. *(Like old-time tragedienne, dashing forward)*
O what a noble mind is here o'erthrown.

ALL. *(Make a cry of being aghast.)*

OPHELIA. The courtier's, soldier's, scholar's eye, tongue, sword.

ALL. *(Make a sound of great mock anguish)*

OPHELIA. The expectancy and rose of the fair State.

ALL. *(Make a sound of mock pity)*

OPHELIA. And I of ladies most deject and wretched
That suck'd the honey of his music vows.

ALL. *(Make a sound commiserating with the girl's wretchedness)*

OPHELIA. Now see that noble, and most sovereign reason,

Like sweet bells jangled out of tune, and harsh,
That unmatch'd form and feature of blown youth,
Blasted with ecstasy. O woe is me . . .

ALL. *(Wailing)* Woe is meeeeee . . .

OPHELIA. T' have seen what I have seen,

(Looks disgustedly at the slouched HAMLET)

See what I see.

(There is another stony silence, during which all watch the motionless HAMLET.)

GHOST. *(Coming forward; the father of old)*
If . . . thou . . . hast . . . Nature . . . in . . . thee . . .
bear . . . it . . . not!

HAMLET. *(Still slumped, making a vow)*
Thy commandment all alone shall live
Within the book and volume of my brain.

GHOST. Swear.

HAMLET. All saws of books . . .

GHOST. Swear . . .

HAMLET. All forms . . .

GHOST. Swear . . .

HAMLET. All pressures past . . .

GHOST. Swear!

HAMLET. *(rising)*
Thy commandment all alone shall live.

(As he has struggled to his feet, ROSENCRANTZ *and* GUILDENSTERN *come up to him—and at that moment, he collapses into their arms and is borne—like a dead soldier—to the pedestal.)*

FORTINBRAS. Bear Hamlet like a soldier to the stage
For he was likely (had he been put on)
To have prov'd most royally.

(HAMLET, *slumped on circular pedestal, summons up one last burst of energy.)*

HAMLET. O Vengeance!

(Thrusts his toy sword into host of imaginary victims. After each thrust, a character falls to the ground, truly slain, until the corpses of all the characters lie strewn around HAMLET *like a set of downed ninepins.)*

From . . . this . . . time . . . forth

(The corpses, still stretched out, begin derisive laughter.)

My thoughts be bloody or be nothing worth.

(Corpses, laughing hysterically, mock HAMLET *with jeers, whistles, stamping and catcalls, till final fade out.)*

CURTAIN

EXERCISES TO A MACBETH

The more one goes through the motions of play-production,
the more one realizes the inappropriateness of the conventional rehearsal process. What is the premise behind most
rehearsals? Mainly, that in a limited period of time, actors are
expected to learn a certain number of words and a certain
number of moves in order to achieve a half-decent state-of-
readiness before an audience. Even in Continental companies
where the rehearsal-period is sometimes eight and twelve weeks,
the additional time is spent polishing results usually achieved in
three or four weeks' time. The essential requirement, and one
would have thought the most obvious, has either been ignored
or heedlessly taken for granted; namely, that actors have to
undergo a certain number of pressures and impacts to make
them ready to deliver the experience contained in their play.
This may sound like walloping the obvious, but the one factor
missing from most rehearsal-periods is precisely that of
experience, i.e. the living-through of those tensions and
revelations which charge characters with emotions and endow
them with insights. The 'experience' of most rehearsal-periods
is what actors usually refer to as "getting the technical things
straight"; the memorization of words, the mapping-out of
moves, the assimilation of props and costume. One does not
underestimate these 'technical' needs by pointing out that in
preparing to convey something of the shape and feel of life,
one needs more than the mechanistic fluency of its surface.
Nor am I proposing an endless period of depth-analysis a la
Stanislavsky—although time could be worse spent—what I am
saying is that the richness of the experience delivered in
performance is in direct ratio to the *experience* undergone
in preparation. It is too easily forgotten that the surest factor

70

in any production is the *text* which has been furnished from the outset. The most difficult requisite is the sub-textual physiology that qualifies actors to speak the text; that brings them to that state of artistic maturity which makes certain manifestations inevitable. Which is why, for instance, in rehearsing *The Hostage,* Joan Littlewood was right to deny her actors any knowledge of what Brendan Behan had written and instead, had them march around the barred roof of her theatre inculcating the experience of regimentation. And why Grotowsky, to cite an even more convincing example, spends most of his preparation-period in exploring the archetypal underbelly of his play leaving sound (words or musical expressions of same) to the very last.

The first stage of any rehearsal-period should introduce actors to the forms and images they will subsequently discover working on the play. By exposing them to naked physical syntax, they are given the means with which they will eventually construct the action-language of the production.

To the best of my knowledge, these are original exercises, devided by myself for use with The Open Space Company, but like all scientific inventions, I would not be surprised to learn that variations are being used in Prague, Paris, Zagreb, and Canarsie.

Warm-Up

Actors in pairs using subtle hand-and-finger signals try to match up each other's movements. The face is kept expressionless. All emotional attitudes are conveyed by means of the hand-and-finger movements. The acting-partner, face expressionless, also using only hands and fingers, reacts.

Adjustments

One actor is seated at a table. He is utterly neutral–without character, situation or intention. A second actor enters the scene and, by playing his chosen character, situation and intention, automatically transforms the first actor into a relevant partner. The first actor, as quickly as possible, adapts to the situation imposed on him by the second actor. Before the scene is allowed to finish, a third actor enters (this being the cue for the first actor's exit) and, playing an entirely different situation forces the second actor to adjust to a completely new set of circumstances. Etc. etc. etc. The most delicate point of contact—apart from the obvious adjustment of first actor to second, is the moment the third actor intrudes on the scene already in progress between actors 1 and 2. If the rhythm of the exercise is right, there is a split-second cut (without pause) between the entrance of actor 3 and the exit of actor 1. So that scenes never actually finish but unexpectedly dissolve into new ones.

The acting-exercise is the greatest challenge an actor has; greater even than the demands of a role. Using a flexible form which accommodates improvisation and physical invention, he is asked to conjure up something telling and creative. Very often, the exercise is devoid of any substance except that which he brings to it. A role, no matter how large or small, gives the actor some kind of framework and textual base. No matter how feeble his own personal contribution, there is always some given content to fall back on. The exercise is an invitation to unveil himself completely; to dazzle and overwhelm using his own personal stock of imagery, his own innate style, his own peculiar brand of genius. It lays bare his talent—which is why it is such a terrifying act.

The Clothesline

A well-known line from Shakespeare is chosen, i.e. 'If it were done when 'tis done t'were well it were done quickly' or 'Is this a dagger I see before me, the handle toward my hand' etc. etc.

The Company is placed in a circle. Each actor is given one word of the line.

1 The first actor begins a definite 'reading' of the line—using only the first word of the line. The second actor (on his right) attempts to pick up the colour of that line-reading and continue it on his word. The other actors, in their turn, do likewise. If successful, once the line has rippled through the entire company, it has been given a definite and comprehensible group-rendering. When unsuccessful, each actor will have simply mimicked the attitude of the first, and the result is a slightly-modified repetition of one emotional colour. A good test is to re-play the line to see if it would pass muster in any sort of interpretation of the

speech. If the line has been successfully rendered, it should then be reversed—with the actor holding the last word playing out the final colour (as he ended) and everyone else obliged to recreate their original word-reading.

2 The same line is played out without emotional consistency. Each actor is obliged to choose an emotional colour as far removed as possible from the one preceding him.

3 The same line is played out with an extravagant, non-naturalistic physical action. A gesture or movement is selected—in a split second—which has no relation whatsoever to the one preceding. There should be no seconds allowed for preparation, the choice being made almost involuntarily.

4 The same line is played out with an attempt at consistent physical action. The first actor makes the first motion of a gesture. Each actor in turn is obliged to fulfil the natural tendency of that gesture. Here too, there is the danger of mimicry; that each actor will only perform a slightly varied version of the first gesture instead of allowing it to graduate naturally.

5 The Shakespearian line is put to a familiar tune. In this variation, the first actor is allowed three or four words so that the gist of the melodic line can be recognized; the object then being for the melody to be continued—without break—from one to the other. (The bugaboo of this exercise is the unequal musical knowledge of any given company; what is an 'old standard' for one actor is totally unknown to another. It is best to stick to songs with a popular national character or indisputable standard such as 'Happy Birthday To You' and 'Silent Night'.

6 The line is played out in a stock accent: Irish, Scots, Brooklynese, Yiddish, etc. The first actor has only one word with which to establish the accent. Again, one should try for some kind of dramatic variety in the line so as to avoid the tendency for each actor merely displaying their version of Scots, Irish, Yiddish, etc.

7 The line is then played out only in physical movements. The aim of the group-movement should be to unify the emotional colouring of the line—(as with 1). The same pitfalls of mimicry and imitation should be avoided. The physical action of each actor should be as precise and fragmented as the words were in Exercise 1.

In all of these variations, the prime requisite is the unbroken continuity of the exercise. If there are preparational gaps between words, or if the line loses the fluency of a natural speech rhythm, it is a failure. It is easy for these exercises to dwindle into isolated party-pieces which, of course, destroys the collective purpose for which they have been devised.

Death Circle

The actors form a circle and begin intoning any prayer of their own choice. The circle moves around the perimeter of the room. At some point on that perimeter, a white mark has been painted. On a signal, the praying and circling stops abruptly. Whoever has reached the white mark is obliged to die in some way of his own choosing. The rhythm, style and manner of his death is entirely up to the actor—hence it can be straight, comic, abrupt, elongated or whatever. No two actors may perform the same death. The dead actor remains on the floor until the entire group dies.

Howdown

The company forms a circle. A leader is selected, and he or she begins to clap out a rhythm which the others quickly duplicate, syncopate and embellish. An actor steps into the centre of the circle and begins performing a speech from the play—adjusting the rhythm of his delivery to the tempo of the group's clapping. As the clapping tempo changes (and the changes should not simply go from fast to slow, but contain differences of volume, texture, and dramatic character), the actor changes his speech accordingly. As soon as he feels he has had enough, without interruption, he resumes his place in the circle cueing another actor into his place in the centre. Throughout the exercise, the object is for the actor to perform the group will. His interpretation is entirely regulated by the changes occurring in the tempi of the group. Eventually, the leader can be forsaken altogether, and the group should be able to ring its changes by itself. When this can be brought about smoothly, it indicates a highly-developed sense of group-contact.

Macbeth Stew

Different scenes from the play are divided between five couples. The scenes should be short, compact and, wherever possible, self-sufficient, i.e. the Malcolm-Macduff Scene (IV.3), the Conspiracy Scene between Macbeth and Lady Macbeth (I.7), Banquo and Macbeth (III.1) etc. Since several scenes may include Macbeth, he should be played by as many different actors as is feasible.

1 The scenes are played out straight.
2 The scenes are conditioned by unrelated physical actions (i.e.Macbeth and Lady Macbeth playing tennis, taking ballet instructions, doing the dishes, etc. with the scene's original intentions observed as faithfully as possible.
3 The scenes, with unrelated physical business, are played so that intentions are radically changed; changed, that is, in accordance with the dictates of the new business (i.e. Macbeth petulant at having to wash while Lady M. dries; Lady Macbeth irritated by Macbeth's ineptitude at ballet instructions, etc. etc.)
4 On a signal, the couples playing their scenes simultaneously, split up and begin playing their scenes with other characters. Now a Lady Macbeth may be playing her Conspiracy Scene with a Macduff who is playing his Testing Scene. The more dominant physical action dominates the scene, and the words become nothing more than a sound-cover for sub-textual meanings wholly unrelated to the text, (i.e. Macduff, still using the words of his original scene, may be playing the henpecked husband of a domineering wife; Macduff, using his original text, may be urged to murder by a shrewish Lady Macbeth, etc.)
5 Signals are then given in quick succession with only one or two minutes pause between. On each signal, characters break away from their original partners, and quickly match up with another; any other. As they do so, their scene automatically changes its action, attitude and intention. In every case, the more dominant idea should be allowed to prevail; the playing-partner adapting as quickly as possible.

The reason for fracturing a Shakespearian scene—altering the original meaning of its text but keeping the words intact, complicating its situation with incongruous business and unrelated acting-partners, is to compel actors to control both disparate and multiple elements. One part of the actor's technique is dealing with words, another with feelings, a third with actions, a fourth with contact, and all the while, all these elements are shifting, changing, reversing, returning. The overall effect, from the audience's standpoint, is simultaneity, but within this jumble of words and actions, the actor is the regulator of a highly sophisticated piece of equipment: himself. Therefore, jumbled as it certainly is, it is never unaccountable chaos; unless of course, the actor sinks beneath the multiple pressures. When successful, it is a rich fusion of several elements which, like the components of a printing-press, create an impression of impossible complexity, and yet, when the printing-press slows down, are individually recognizable.

These kinds of exercises deal with the actor as mechanism because the human being which animates the actor *is* a mechanism; just as theatre is the synthesis of many mechanisms. The danger is that the performance of these mechanisms produces a purely *mechanistic* effect—which of course has nothing to do with the intentions of art. In such a case, it would be as if the complicated machinery of the printing-press was functioning only to demonstrate the facility of its equipment, without actually printing anything. It is important that the end for which these mechanisms are being lubricated is always kept in mind; so that exercises never *lose* themselves in displays of technique, but *utilise* technique to express more than could be expressed if technique were not that highly sophisticated.

The actor who complains he is being treated like a robot is often bawling for the self-indulgence of the mono-celled performer. Give me my lines and moves, cries his sub-text, and I will give you a thundering exhibition of my immovable cliches. If there were no other benefit to these exercises, it would be sufficient that they rob the actor of the complacency which type-casting and artistic sloth engender in his being. The actor is always asking for a 'challenge' until he actually gets one; then you realize what he meant was a big, showy part for himself.

Male-Female

A male actor chooses a typical female situation (i.e. instruction on childbirth, trying on lingerie, receiving

beauty-parlour treatment) and plays it out in his own character
but with all the appropriate female choices. There should be no
attempt at phoney-female voices or female-parody. The object
of the exercise is for the male to assimilate the female situation
as faithfully as possible in his own character.

Multiples

Best performed with a group of twelve. All standing in a circle.

1ST ACTOR.   Lays down a basic rhythmic beat (not a melody)
which serves as a bass-accompaniment to the exercise.

2ND ACTOR.   Augments this beat with a rhythm of his own
which, in range and texture, is as dissimilar as possible but
still fits into the given rhythm.

3RD ACTOR.   Does likewise.

4TH ACTOR.   Does likewise.

5TH ACTOR.   Chooses the name of a disease and performs
that rhythmically, i.e. 'laryngitis'—broken down into sound-
components: *lah*-ryn-gi-tis, lah-*ryn*-gi-tis, lag-ryn-*gi*-tis, etc.
etc.

6TH ACTOR.   Continually repeats four bars of a popular
song.

7TH ACTOR.   Plays out an advertising slogan augmenting the
group-rhythm: 'Daz Washes Whiter', 'Guinness is Good For
You', 'Keep Britain Tidy' etc. etc.

8TH ACTOR.   Punctuates group-rhythm with a cry. No
matter how searing the cry, it must—in some way—fit into
the collective rhythm and must never be rhythmically
arbitrary.

9TH ACTOR.   Using only plosives, non-vocalized sounds,
adds to the collective rhythm.

10TH ACTOR.   Using his body as an instrument, claps out a
beat which fits into the collective rhythm.

11TH ACTOR.   Using sharp, rhythmic gestures, adds movements that fit into the collective rhythm.

12TH ACTOR.   Begins to tell the story of his life in a dry,
matter-of-fact, conventional style.

N.B.   The group-rhythm must never be imitative but always
complimentary; that is, everyone's contribution, by being
tonally or texturally different from what has gone before,
must enrich the overall texture of the whole.

Once the group-rhythm is under way, the director uses the
Biographist (12th Actor) as a soloist, relegating everyone else
to the level of accompaniment. He conducts the Biographist to
the centre and signals for the background-actors to subside in
volume. In this way, the soloist's biography becomes the main-
line of the exercise; the others providing a dulled, but
discernable, repeated accompaniment. Ideally, they are
listening to the soloist while performing their own repeated
contributions. Then the conductor (director) signals to another
actor to become the Biographist-soloist. The new Biographist
abandons his own rhythmic contribution and begins telling
the story of his life while the previous Biographist (12th
Actor) retires to the background still speaking his biography,
but now as part of the dulled accompaniment. This process
continues until all have become Biographists. (During the
soloist's performance, the director-conductor regulates the
group's performance as he wishes—changing tempi and
dynamics).

Towards the end of the exercise, soloists, instead of being
waved into the background, remain in the centre telling their
stories while other soloists are signalled in. Eventually, there
are four or five biographies being spoken simultaneously;
then eight, nine, ten, etc. Eventually, everyone is speaking
their biography at the same time. Again, the din is a concentration factor, and the object is to retain the line of one's own
story in the midst of the jumble-of-speech on every side.

Help Play

The room is littered with numerous obstacles; overturned
chairs, banana-peels, balls, heavy equipment, trays of water,
etc. One set of actors (the Movers) are blindfolded; alongside
them a second set of actors (the Helpers). The Helpers' job
is to guide the Movers from one end of the room to the other
without colliding against any of the obstacles. This is done
by the Helpers whispering instructions into the ears of the
Movers. If there are six or seven people performing the
exercise at the same time, the din of everyone talking at once

is a useful complicating factor encouraging greater concentration. Once the Movers have successfully traversed the room, they become the Helpers and vice versa.

In preparing this version of *Macbeth,* there are three acting priorities.

1 The company has to mesh together so perfectly that sub-textual meaning registers as strongly as text and, (another way of putting the same idea), that familiar text—which is what *Macbeth* is—does not override the new emphases and nuances projected through it.
2 That resources are opened for the actor with which he can transcend the conventional means of performing Shakespearian language—so that, for instance, when the spirit moves him, he can create a sound, a movement, a gesture or a cry which is dramatically appropriate and still connected to the literary framework from which it springs.
3 That personal conceptions of the play's meaning are able to find original modes of expression which reinforce the production's meaning, and do not tumble into that ever-open pit of 'stylistic jazziness' which tempts the actor into flashy novelties which are subsequently rationalized as 'originality'.

Postscript Any scene from this version of the play which could occur just as easily in a conventional production of Shakespeare's *Macbeth* must be stylistically incorrect.

A Macbeth

CAST

MACBETH	2ND WITCH
2ND MACBETH	3RD WITCH
3RD MACBETH	DUNCAN
LADY MACBETH	BANQUO
1ST WITCH	MACDUFF

MALCOLM

Lights come up on effigy of MACBETH. *In front of it, back to audience, stands* LADY MACBETH. *On a signal, the three* WITCHES *enter and surround the effigy. Each adds bits to it until it clearly resembles* MACBETH. *After a pause,* LADY MACBETH *begins to intone an incantation.*

LADY MACBETH.   I'll drain him dry
    as hay
  Sleep shall neither night nor day
  Hang upon his penthouse lid.
  He shall live a man forbid.
  Weary seven-nights nine-times-nine
  Shall he dwindle, peak and pine.

  (One of the WITCHES *hands* LADY MACBETH *a smoking poker. With it, she slowly obliterates the wax eyes of the effigy. The lights fade.)*

  (Lights up. Enter DUNCAN, BANQUO, MALCOLM and MACDUFF. *The stage is filled with a pleasant, summery glow. Birds are chirping in the background.)*

KING.   This castle hath a pleasant seat; the air
  Nimbly and sweetly recommmends itself
  Unto our gentle senses.

BANQUO.   This guest of summer,
  The temple-haunting martlet, does approve
  By his loved mansionry that the heaven's breath
  Smells wooingly here; no jutty, frieze,
  Buttress, nor coign of vantage, but this bird
  Hath made his pendent bed and procreant cradle;
  Where they most breed and haunt I have observed
  The air is delicate.

(Enter LADY MACBETH)

KING.   See, see, our honoured hostess—
      The love that follows us sometimes is our trouble,
      Which still we thank as love. Herein I teach you
      How you shall bid 'God 'ield us' for your pains,
      And thank us for your trouble.

LADY MACBETH.   All our service
      In every point twice done and then done double
      Were poor and single business to contend
      Against those honours deep and broad wherewith
      Your majesty loads our house. For those of old,
      And the late dignities heaped up to them,
      We rest your hermits.

KING.   Where is the Thane of Cawdor?
      We coursed him at the heels and had a purpose
      To be his purveyor; but he rides well,
      And his great love, sharp as his spur, hath holp him
      To his home before us.
      Fair and noble hostess,
      We are your guest tonight.

LADY MACBETH.   Your servants ever
      Have theirs, themselves, and what is theirs, in compt,
      To make their audit at your highness' pleasure,
      Still to return your own.

KING.   Give me your hand;
      Conduct me to mine host. We love him highly,
      And shall continue our graces towards him.

      (Others pass through door, but as DUNCAN *and*
      BANQUO *are about to enter,* MACBETH *suddenly*
      appears. He stabs DUNCAN. LADY MACBETH *stabs*
      BANQUO. WITCHES *quickly spirit away* DUNCAN,
      BANQUO *and* LADY MACBETH. *Blackout.)*

      (Lights up. MACBETH *surrounded by* MACBETHS 1
      & 2 dash downstage together and begin the next speech
      MACBETHS 1 & 2 *whisper the words* MACBETH
      speaks.)

MACBETH.   *(Breathlessly)*
      If it were done when 'tis done, then 'twere well

It were done quickly. If the assassination

Could trammel up the consequence, and catch
With his surcease success—that but this blow
Might be the be-all and the end-all!—here,
But here, upon this bank and shoal of time,
We'd jump the life to come. But in these cases
We still have judgement here—that we but teach
Bloody instructions, which, being taught, return
To plague the inventor. This even-handed justice
Commends the ingredience of our poisoned chalice
To our own lips
(Turning quickly—to LADY MACBETH)
He's here in double trust.

LADY MACBETH. Was the hope drunk
Wherein you dress'd yourself. Hath it slept since?
And wakes it now to look so green and pale?

MACBETH. I am his kinsman and his subject
Strong both against the deed.

LADY MACBETH. Wouldst thou be afear'd
To be the same in thine own act and valour
As thou art in desire?

MACBETH. His virtues
Will plead like angels, trumpet-tongued against
The deep damnation of his taking-off.

LADY MACBETH. Wouldst thou have that
Which thou esteem'st the ornament of life,
And live a coward in thine own esteem?
Letting 'I dare not' wait upon 'I would'
Like the poor cat in the adage.

(Cut to:)

DUNCAN. I have begun to plant thee and will labour
To make thee full of growing.

MACBETH. *(Kneeling)*
The service and the loyalty I owe
In doing it, pays itself.

LADY MACBETH. From this time
Such I account thy love.

DUNCAN.   More is thy due than more than all can pay.

MACBETH.   *(Back with* LADY MACBETH)
    He hath honour'd me of late, and I have bought
    Golden opinions from all sorts of people . . .

DUNCAN.   *(To* BANQUO)
    No more that Thane of Cawdor shall deceive
    Our bosom interest. Go pronounce his present death.

MACBETH.   I should against his murderer shut the door
    Not bear the knife myself.

LADY MACBETH.   The sleeping and the dead
    Are but as pictures: tis the eye of childhood
    That fears a painted devil.

MACBETH.   We will proceed no further in this business.

LADY MACBETH.   Thou shalt be what thou art promis'd.

    (Cut to:)

BANQUO.   You shall be king.

1ST WITCH.   And Thane of Cawdor too.

MACBETH.   *(To* WITCH)
    The Thane of Cawdor lives; a prosperous gentleman.

1ST WITCH.   Go pronounce his present death.

2ND WITCH.   And with his former title greet Macbeth.

MACBETH.   Why do you dress me in borrowed robes?

WITCHES.   Hail to thee, Thane of Glamis
                    Thane of Cawdor,
    All hail Macbeth.

LADY MACBETH.   That shalt be king hereafter.

MACBETH.   To be king
    Stands not within prospect of belief
    More than . . .

DUNCAN.   Is execution done on Cawdor?

MACBETH.   *(Limply)* To be Cawdor.

DUNCAN.   *(To* BANQUO*)* There's no art
    To find the mind's construction in the face.

He was a gentleman on whom I built
An absolute trust.

MACBETH. *(To* LADY MACBETH*)* Prithee peace:
I dare do all that may become a man
Who dares do more is none.

2ND MACBETH. What beast was't then
That made you break this enterprise to me?
When you durst do it, then you were a man,
And to be more than what you were, you should
Be so much more the man.

(Pause)

DUNCAN. Look how our partner's rapt?

LADY MACBETH. Are you a man?

MACBETH. *(Fiercely)* Ay, and a bold one.

LADY MACBETH. Ay, in the catalogue ye go for men
As hounds and greyhounds, mongrels, spaniels, curs,
Shoughs, water-rugs and demi-wolves are clept
All by the name of dogs.

BANQUO. I dreamt last night of the three weird sisters.
To you they have showed some truth.

MACBETH. *(To* BANQUO) I think not of them.

(To LADY MACBETH)

We will proceed no further in this business.

LADY MACBETH. I have given suck and know
How tender 'tis to love the babe that milks me.
I would, while it was smiling in my face,
Have pluck'd my nipple from his boneless gums
And dash'd the brains out had I so sworn.

MACBETH. Prithee peace.

BANQUO. Good sir, why do you start and seem to fear
Things that do sound so fair?

WITCHES. *(Overlapping* BANQUO's *last word)*
Is foul and foul is fair
Glamis—Cawdor—King—All.

MACBETH. *(To himself)* This supernatural soliciting
    Cannot be ill, cannot be good.
    If ill,
    Why hath it given me earnest of success
    Commencing in a truth? I am Thane of Cawdor.

WITCHES. And shalt be King hereafter!

2ND MACBETH. Oftentimes, to win us to our harm
    The instruments of darkness tell us truths;

3RD MACBETH. Win us with honest trifles, to betray's
    In deepest consequence.

    (MACBETH, *considering this, turns suspiciously to*
    LADY MACBETH.)

LADY MACBETH. *(Nonchalantly)*
    So foul and fair a day I have not seen.

MACBETH. *(Hotly, to* WITCHES)
    Say from whence
    You owe this strange intelligence;
    Speak, I charge you!

LADY MACBETH. *(Calming him; taking him round)*
    Hie thee hither
    That I may pour my spirits in thine ear
    And chastize with the valour of my tongue
    All that impedes thee from the golden round
    Which fate and metaphysical aid doth seem
    To have thee crowned withal.

    (Led by LADY MACBETH *and* WITCHES *into a circle.)*

3RD WITCH. Look what I have.

2ND WITCH. Show me, show me.

3RD WITCH. *(Grabbing* MACBETH's *thumb)*
    Here I have a pilot's thumb
    Wracked as homeward he did come.

    (Places MACBETH's *hand onto his sword)*

WITCHES. A drum! A drum!
    Macbeth doth come.

    (While this is chanted, the WITCHES *beat a tattoo on*

their sides. It is repeated until MACBETH *is crowned in a mock-coronation ceremony)*

1ST WITCH.   Hail to thee Thane of Glamis.

2ND WITCH.   Hail to thee, Thane of Cawdor.

3RD WITCH.   All Hail Macbeth.

LADY MACBETH.   *(Kneeling before him)*
That shalt be king hereafter.

MACBETH.   *(Breaking ceremony, to* LADY MACBETH*)*
If we should fail.

LADY MACBETH.   We fail.

2ND MACBETH.   *(Rallying him)*
But screw your courage to the sticking place

3RD MACBETH.   And we'll not fail.

DUNCAN.   *(Insistently)* Is execution done on Cawdor?

MACBETH.   *(Defensively)* The Thane of Cawdor lives.

WITCH.   And shalt be king hereafter.

BANQUO.   If you can look into the seeds of time
And say which grain will grow
And which will not.
Speak to me then who neither beg nor fear
Your favours nor your hate.

WITCHES.   *(By-passing* MACBETH *perform crowning
ceremony on* BANQUO*)*
Hail, hail, hail.
Lesser than Macbeth, yet much happier.

1ST WITCH.   Thou shalt get kings, though thou be none.

MACBETH.   No son of mine succeeding?

WITCHES.   All hail, Banquo.

MACBETH.   The seeds of Banquo, kings?

2ND WITCH. Lesser than Macbeth . . .

MACBETH.   A fruitless crown . . .

3RD WITCH.   Yet much happier . . .

MACBETH. A barren sceptre?

DUNCAN. *(With* BANQUO)
Noble Banquo
That hast no less deserv'd, nor must be known
No less to have done so, let me enfold thee
And hold thee to my heart.

MACBETH. For Banquo's issue have I filed my mind.

DUNCAN. *(To* MACBETH, *agreeing)*
True, worthy Banquo.

MACBETH. For them the gracious Duncan have I murdered?

BANQUO. *(Holding out hand)* It will be rain tonight.

2ND MACBETH. ⎱
3RD MACBETH. ⎰ Then let it come down

(MACBETH *issues signal;* BANQUO *dies.* MACBETHS
2 *and* 3 *remove the static figure of* BANQUO *as if it
were a store-dummy.)*

MACBETH. *(To* WITCHES)
Shall Banquo's issue ever
Reign in this kingdom?

1ST WITCH. Be bloody,

2ND WITCH. bold,

3RD WITCH. and resolute;

1ST WITCH. Laugh to scorn the power of man
For none of woman born
Shall harm Macbeth.

MACBETH. Shall Banquo's issue ever reign . . .

WITCH. ⎱
WITCH. ⎰
Macbeth shall never vanquished be until
Great Birnam Wood to High Dunsinane Hill
Shall come against him.

MACBETH. That will never be.

LADY MACBETH. Then come,
Bend up each corporal agent to this terrible feat

Spurn fate . . .

MALCOLM. *(Building in volume)*
  Bloody, luxurious, avaricious . . .

LADY MACBETH. Scorn death.

MALCOLM. False, deceitful, sudden, malicious . . .

LADY MACBETH. Bear your hopes 'bove wisdom, grace and fear.

MALCOLM. Smacking of every sin that hath a name.
  (Turns to MACBETH)
  If such a one be fit to govern, speak.

MACBETH. *(Lamely to MALCOLM)*
  The spirits that know all mortal consequences
  Have pronounced me thus:
  Fear not Macbeth; for none of woman born

WITCHES. *(Whispering with MACBETH)*
  Shall ere have power upon thee.

MALCOLM. God above deal between thee and me
  When I shall tread upon this tyrant's head
  Or wear it in my sword.

LADY MACBETH. *(Brazenly goading MACBETH)*
  What's the boy Malcolm?

MALCOLM. *(To LADY MACBETH imperiously)*
  The son of Duncan
  From whom this tyrant holds the due of birth
  Which we now claim as ours.

MACBETH. Were I from Dunsinane away and clear
  Profit again should hardly draw me here.

LADY MACBETH. O proper stuff!
  Wouldst thou live a coward . . .
  To kiss the ground before Malcolm's feet
  And to be baited with the rabble's curse?

MACBETH. *(Surveying all)*
  I dare do all that may become a man.

MACDUFF. *(To other MACBETHS)*
  Wife?

2ND MACBETH. Aye.

MACDUFF. Children?

3RD MACBETH. Aye.

MACDUFF. Servants, all?

2ND MACBETH. Aye.

MACDUFF. *(To* MACBETH)
Turn hellhound, turn!
Thou bloodier villain
Than terms can give thee out.

BANQUO. *(Turning on him)*
O Horror, horror, horror!
Tongue nor heart cannot conceive or name thee.

MALCOLM. Not in the legions of horrid hell can come
A devil more damned in evil.

DUNCAN. *(Turning on him)* Speak if you can. What are you?

(MACBETH, *hemmed in by* DUNCAN, BANQUO *and*
MACDUFF, *backs away towards* WITCHES.)

WITCHES. By the pricking of my thumbs
Something wicked this way comes.

MACBETH. I bear a charmed life which must not yield
To one of woman born.

WITCHES. *(With tattoo, as before)*
A drum! A drum!
Macbeth doth come.

MACBETH. Macbeth shall never vanquished be until
Great Birnam Wood to high Dunsinane Hill
Shall come against him.

(All circle MACBETH, LADY MACBETH, *with effigy,
spell-casting in Background.)*

WITCHES. A drum. A drum.
Macbeth doth come.

MACBETH. I bear a charmed life . . .

WITCHES. A drum. A drum.
Macbeth doth come.

(MACBETH *is subdued. Cry. Blackout.*)

BANQUO. *(As in the scene after the* WITCHES' *disappearance)*
  The earth hath bubbles as the water has,
  And these are of them. Whither are they vanished?

MACBETH. Into the air; and what seemed corporal
  Melted, as breath into the wind.

BANQUO. Were such things here as we do speak about?
  Or have we eaten on the insane root
  That takes the reason prisoner?

MACBETH. Your children shall be kings.

BANQUO. You shall be king.

MACBETH. And Thane of Cawdor too, went it not so?

BANQUO. To the self same tune and words
  Hail King of Scotland, for so thou art.

MACBETH. Hail root and father of many kings, for so
  thou art.

BANQUO. Who's here?

2ND MACBETH. *(Entering)*
  The King hath happily received, Macbeth,
  The news of thy success; and when he reads
  Thy personal venture in the rebels' fight
  His wonders and his praises do contend
  Which should be thine, or his,
  And, for an earnest of a greater honour,
  He bade me from him call thee Thane of Cawdor
  In which addition, hail, most worthy thane,
  For it is thine.
  (Kneels)

WITCHES. *(Off)* All hail Thane of Cawdor.

BANQUO. What! Can the devil speak true?

MACBETH. The Thane of Cawdor lives, a prosperous
    gentleman.
  Why do you dress me in borrowed robes?

2ND MACBETH. Who was the Thane lives yet, but under
    heavy judgement

91

Bears that life which he deserves to lose.
But treasons capital, confessed and proved
Have overthrown him.

MACBETH.   Do you not hope that your children shall be
          kings
        When those that gave the Thane of Cawdor to me
        Promised no less to them?

BANQUO.   That trusted home
        Might yet enkindle you unto the crown
        Besides the Thane of Cawdor. But tis strange.

(MACBETH *gives* BANQUO *one last look and strides
out.* MACBETHS 1 *and* 2 *superciliously confront a
startled* BANQUO. *The group stands motionless until*
LADY MACBETH *strides between them commencing
the next scene, and then they vanish.*)

LADY MACBETH.   Glamis thou art, and Cawdor, and shalt be
        What thou art promised.

1ST WITCH.   The King comes here tonight.

LADY MACBETH.   Thou'rt mad to say it!

1ST WITCH.   So please you, it is true. Our Thane is coming;

LADY MACBETH.   The raven himself is hoarse
        That croaks the fatal entrance of Duncan
        Under my battlements.

(During this speech, WITCHES *come forward and take
hold of* LADY MACBETH. *They whisper the words she
speaks.*)

(Formally, as invocation)

Come, you spirits
That tend on mortal thoughts, unsex me here
And fill me from the crown to the toe top-full
Of direst cruelty. Make thick my blood;
Stop up the access and passage to remorse,
That no compunctious visitings of nature
Shake my fell purpose, nor keep peace between
The effect and it. Come to my woman's breasts
And take my milk for gall, you murdering ministers,
Wherever, in your sightless substances,

92

You wait on nature's mischief. Come, thick night,
And pall thee in the dunnest smoke of hell,
That my keen knife see not the wound it makes,
Nor heaven peep through the blanket of the dark
To cry, 'Hold, hold!'

(WITCHES *take up position behind* LADY MACBETH
facing upstage. Enter MACBETH.)

Great Glamis, worthy Cawdor!
Greater than both by the all-hail hereafter!
Thy letters have transported me beyond
This ignorant present and I feel now
The future in the instant.

MACBETH. My dearest love. *(They kiss)*
Duncan comes here tonight.

LADY MACBETH. And when goes hence?

MACBETH. Tomorrow, as he purposes.

LADY MACBETH. O never
Shall sun that morrow see!

(Cut to:)

DUNCAN. O worthiest cousin!
The sin of my ingratitude even now
Was heavy on me. Thou art so far before,
That swiftest wing of recompense is slow
To overtake thee. Would thou hadst less deserved,
That the proportion both of thanks and payment
Might have been mine. Only I have left to say,
'More is thy due than more than all can pay.'

MACBETH. The service and the loyalty I owe,
In doing it, pays itself. Your highness' part
Is to receive our duties; and our duties
Are to your throne and state, children and servants,
Which do but what they should by doing everything
Safe toward your love and honour.

KING. I have begun to plant thee, and will labour
To make thee full of growing.

LADY MACBETH. Your face, my thane, is as a book where
men

> May read strange matters. To beguile the time
> Look like the time, bear welcome in your eye,
> Your hand, your tongue: He that's coming
> Must be provided for.

BANQUO. I dreamt last night of the three weird sisters.
> To you they have showed some truth.

MACBETH. I think not of them.

LADY MACBETH. I will acquaint you with the perfect spy
> o' the time
> The moment on't; for it must be done tonight.

MACBETH. We will speak further.

BANQUO. Yet, when we can entreat an hour to serve,
> We would spend it in some words upon that business
> If you grant the time.

LADY MACBETH. Put this night's great business into my
> dispatch.
> It shall make honour for you.

MACBETH. *(To* LADY MACBETH *harshly)*
> So I lose none
> In seeking to augment it, but still keep
> My bosom franchis'd and allegiance clear.

BANQUO. Good repose the while.

MACBETH. Thanks sir, the like to you.

LADY MACBETH. Leave all the rest to me.

MACBETH. We—will—speak—further.

> (LADY MACBETH *and* BANQUO, *speaking simultaneously,
> repeat the words of their scene. Pouring them, like liquid,
> into* MACBETH's *ears.)*

BANQUO.	LADY MACBETH.
I dreamt last night of the three weird sisters. To you they have showed some truth Yet when we can entreat an hour	I will acquaint you with the perfect spy o' the time The moment on't for it must be done tonight. Put this night's great business into my dispatch

We would spend it in
some words upon that
business
If you grant the time.
Good repose the while.

It shall make honour for
you.
Leave all the rest to me.

(As MACBETH *cuts downstage, he is confronted by*
MACBETHS 2 *and* 3. BANQUO *and* LADY MACBETH
exit.)

MACBETH. *(Reasoning)* He's here in double trust:
First, as I am his kinsman and his subject,
Strong both against the deed; then, as his host,
Who should against his murderer shut the door,
Not bear the knife myself.

2ND MACBETH. *(Facetious)* Besides, this Duncan
Hath borne his faculties so meek, hath been
So clear in his great office, that his virtues
Will plead like angels, trumpet-tongued against
The deep damnation of his taking-off;

3RD MACBETH. And Pity, like a naked new-borne babe
Striding the blast, or heaven's cherubim, horsed
Upon the sightless couriers of the air,
Shall blow the horrid deed in every eye,
That tears shall drown the wind.

(Pause. MACBETHS 2 *and* 3 *regard the petrified*
MACBETH.)

2ND MACBETH. *(To* MACBETH 3)
Were I king,
I should cut off the Nobles for their lands,
Desire his jewels, and this other's house,
And my more-having would be as a sauce
To make me hunger more.

3RD MACBETH. *(To* 2ND MACBETH)
Were I king,
Your wives, your daughters
Your matrons and your maids could not fill up
The cistern of my lust.

2ND MACBETH. I should forge
Quarrels unjust against the good and loyal,
Destroying them for their wealth.

3RD MACBETH.   I should
       Pour the sweet milk of concord into Hell
       Uproar the universal peace, confound
       All unity on earth.

MACBETH.   *(Trying to blot out the thoughts of* MACBETHS
       2 *and* 3)
       Stars, hide your fires,
       Let not light see my black and deep desires,
       The eye wink at the hand; yet let that be
       Which the eye fears, when it is done, to see.

3RD MACBETH.   Thou wouldst be great,
       Art not without ambition, but without
       The illness should attend it.
       Wouldst not play false,

2ND MACBETH.   And yet would wrongly win.
       Thou'dst have great Glamis
       That which cries 'Thus thou must do' if thou have it,
       And that which rather thou dost fear to do
       Than wishest should be undone.

MACBETH.   I have no spur
       To prick the sides of my intent but only . . .

2ND MACBETH.   *(Snide)*
       Vaulting ambition which o'erleaps itself
       And falls on the other.

3RD MACBETH.   *(Exhorting)*
       Was the hope drunk
       Wherein you dressed yourself?

2ND MACBETH.   Art thou afear'd to be the same in thine
           act and valour as thou art in desire?
       When you durst do it, then you were a man.

MACBETH.   *(Lamely rationalizing)*
       My thought, whose murder yet is but fantastical,
       Shakes so my single state of man
       That function is smothered in surmise.

2ND MACBETH.   *(Washing hands of him)*
       Go prick thy face and over-red thy fear,
       Thou lily-livered boy!

3RD MACBETH. *(Reasoning)*
Present fears are less than horrible imaginings.

2ND MACBETH. *(Still ill-tempered)*
Blood hath been shed ere now.

(MACBETH *hesitates.* MACBETHS 2 *and* 3 *close in.*)

3RD MACBETH. Laugh to scorn
The power of man.

2ND MACBETH. For none of woman-born
Shall harm Macbeth.

(Daggers are placed into his grip.)

MACBETH. *(Quietly)*
Thou marshall'st me the way I was going
And such an instrument I was to use . . .

3RD MACBETH. Come what come may,
Time and the hour runs through the roughest day.

(MACBETHS 1 *and* 2 *arrange his stance so that it
suggests a murderer about to strike. Then step back.*)

MACBETH. *(With daggers)* I am settled; and bend up
Each corporal agent to this terrible feat.
From this moment,
The very firstlings of my heart shall be
The firstlings of my hand.

2ND MACBETH. *(Gaily)* Away

3RD MACBETH. And mock the time

2ND MACBETH. with fairest show,

3RD MACBETH. False face

2ND MACBETH. must hide

3RD MACBETH. what the false heart

2ND MACBETH. doth know.

*(A sepulchral bell begins to toll in the distance.
LADY MACBETH and WITCHES congregate around
around MACBETH who stands transfixed with
daggers.)*

MACBETH.   Now o'er the one half-world
    Nature seems dead, and wicked dreams abuse
    The curtained sleep. Witchcraft celebrates
    Pale Hecate's offerings; and withered murder,
    Alarumed by his sentinel the wolf,
    Whose howl's his watch, thus with his stealthy pace,
    With Tarquin's ravishing strides, towards his design
    Moves like a ghost. Thou sure and firm-set earth,
    Hear not my steps, which way they walk, for fear
    The very stones prate of my whereabout
    And take the present horror from the time
    Which now suits it. Whilst I threat, he lives:
    Words to the heat of deeds too cold breath gives.

(Tolling continues)

I go, and it is done; the bell invites me.
Hear it not, Duncan, for it is a knell
That summons thee to heaven or to hell.

(Exit)

(Lights fade up dimly on	VOICE OF LADY MACBETH
DUNCAN's chamber.	When Duncan is asleep,
MACBETHS 1 and 2	Whereto the rather shall
play DUNCAN's grooms)	his hard day's journey
(GROOMS are discovered	Soundly invite him—his
dicing at foot of	two chamberlains
DUNCAN's bed. WITCHES	Will I with wine and
arrive, lure the GROOMS	wassail so convince
to drink. When GROOMS	That memory, the
topple over drunk,	warder of the brain,
WITCHES circle	Shall be a'fume, and the
DUNCAN's bed and take	receipt of reason
up formal positions.	a Limbeck only. When
During this opening	in swinish sleep
action, the VOICE of	Their drenched natures
LADY MACBETH has	lie as in a death,
been heard (on tape)	What cannot you and I
speaking the accom-	perform upon
panying speech.)	The unguarded Duncan?
	What not put upon
	His spongy officers, who
	shall bear the guilt
	Of our great quell.

(When the WITCHES *are in position around the bed, they begin chanting a prayer for the dead, the text of which is alongside. The speech is on tape as well as whispered during the scene.)*

(MACBETH, *with bloody hands, slowly enters the chamber. He stands hesitating for a moment, then proceeds towards the bed. The drunk* GROOMS *stir. He stops. Waits. Then moves forward again. One of the* GROOMS, *having a nightmare, suddenly shakes himself awake with a cry which rouses the other. Both now awake, confront* MACBETH *and stare at his hands. Then, strangely calm, in no way surprised by* MACBETH'*s presence in the chamber, they kneel and begin to pray.* MACBETH *watches them for a moment, and then blesses them. With each blessing a* GROOM *topples over dead until both are lying motionless on the floor. The* WITCHES *place two daggers into* MACBETH'*s hands, and, still praying, usher him over to the*

Witches' Prayer
One cried 'God bless us'
  and 'Amen' the other
As they had seen me with
  these hangman's hands.
Listening their fear I
  could not say 'Amen'
When they did say 'God
  bless us'.
But wherefore could not
  I pronounce 'Amen'?
I had most need of
  blessing, and 'Amen'
Stuck in my throat.
Methought I heard a voice
  cry 'Sleep no more'
Macbeth does murder
  sleep—the innocent
  sleep
Sleep that knits up the
  ravelled sleeve of care,
The death of each day's
  life, sore labour's
  bath,
Balm of hurt minds,
  great nature's second
  course,
Chief nourisher in life's
  feast.
Still it cried 'Sleep no
  more' to all the house;
'Glamis hath murder'd
  sleep and therefore
  Cawdor
Shall sleep no more,
  Macbeth shall sleep
  no more'.

sleeping DUNCAN. *The*
WITCHES *then hoist up the*
sleeping KING *and present*
him to MACBETH. DUN-
CAN, *now roused from*
sleep, confronts MACBETH,
his eyes wild and frightened.
MACBETH *raises the*
daggers and then lowers them.
Continues staring into
DUNCAN's *terrified eyes.*
Raises his daggers again.
At that moment, LADY
MACBETH *appears, takes*
hold of MACBETH's *hands*
and drives the daggers into
DUNCAN's *heart.*
There is an ear-splitting cry
from DUNCAN *which is*
picked up by the WITCHES.
All vanish immediately on
the Blackout.

(Lights up. MACDUFF *enters.)*

MACDUFF.   O horror, horror, horror!
Tongue nor heart cannot conceive nor name thee!
Confusion now hath made his masterpiece;
Most sacrilegious murder hath broke ope
The Lord's annointed temple and stole thence
The life o' the building.
Awake, awake!
Ring the alarum bell! Murder and treason!
Banquo and Donalbain, Malcolm, awake!
Shake off this downy sleep, death's counterfeit,
And look on death itself! Up, up, and see
The Great Doom's image! Malcolm, Banquo,
As from your graves rise up and walk like sprites
To countenance this horror. Ring the bell!

(Bell rings. Real bell now sounds. Enter LADY
MACBETH. *During scene,* WITCHES *stand motionless*
in background.)

LADY MACBETH.   What's the business,

That such a hideous trumpet calls to parley
The sleepers of the house? Speak, speak!

MACDUFF. O gentle lady,
Tis not for you to hear what I can speak.
The repetition in a woman's ear
Would murder as it fell.

(Enter BANQUO*)*

O Banquo, Banquo!
Our royal master's murdered.

LADY MACBETH. Woe, alas!
What, in our house!

BANQUO. Too cruel, anywhere.
Dear Duff, I prithee contradict thyself
And say it is not so.

(Enter MACBETHS*)*

2nd MACBETH.
Had I but died an hour before this chance
I had lived a blessed time.

(Enter MALCOLM*)*

MALCOLM. What is amiss?

3RD MACBETH. You are, and do not know't.
The spring, the head, the fountain of your blood
Is stopped, the very source of it is stopped.

MACDUFF. Your royal father's murdered.

MALCOLM. By whom?

2ND MACBETH.
Those of his chamber, as it seemed, had done't:
Their hands and faces were all badged with blood,
So were their daggers, which, unwiped, we found
Upon their pillows: they stared and were distracted;
No man's life was to be trusted with them.

MACBETH.
O yet I do repent me of my fury,
That I did kill them.

MACDUFF. Wherefore did you so?

MACBETH.
>Who can be wise, amazed, temperate and furious,
>Loyal and neutral, in a moment? No man. *(Knocking)*
>The expedition of my violent love
>Outruns the pauser reason. *(Knocking)* Here lay Duncan,
>His silver skin laced with his golden blood,
>And his gashed stabs looked like a breach in nature
>For ruin's wasteful entrance, *(Knocking)* there the
>>murderers
>Steeped in colours of their trade, their daggers
>>*(Knocking)*
>unmannerly breeched with gore. Who could refrain,
>That had a heart to love, and in that heart
>Courage to make's love known?

(For a moment no-one speaks. All regard MACBETH's hands. He then looks down at them as well.)

LADY MACBETH. *(Swooning.)* Help me hence, ho!

MACDUFF. Look to the lady!

BANQUO. *(to MACDUFF.)*
>Why do we hold our tongues,
>That most may claim this argument for ours?

MALCOLM.
>What should be spoken here where our fate,
>Hid in an auger-hole, may rush and seize us?
>Let's away. Our tears are not yet brewed.

MACDUFF. Nor our strong sorrow upon the foot of motion.

BANQUO. And when we have our naked frailties hid
>That suffer in exposure, let us meet
>And question this most bloody piece of work.
>Fears and scruples shake us.
>In the great hand of God I stand, and thence,
>Against the undivulg'd pretence, I fight
>Of treasonous malice.

MACDUFF. And so do I.

MALCOLM. And so do I.

BANQUO. And so do all. *(They pledge and exit.)*

(Sepulchral knocking is heard by MACBETH*)*

MACBETH.   Whence is that knocking?
How is't with me when every noise appalls me?
What hands are here! Ha—they pluck out mine eyes!

*(*WITCHES *with* MACBETH *effigy during speech.)*

Will all great Neptune's ocean wash this blood
Clean from my hand? No, this my hand will rather
The multitudinous seas incarnadine,
Making the green one red.

(Enter LADY MACBETH. *Sepulchral knocking
becomes real.)*

2ND MACBETH.   I hear a knocking at the south entry.

3RD MACBETH.   Retire we to our chamber.
A little water clears us of this deed.

2ND MACBETH.   Your constancy hath left you unattended.

3RD MACBETH.   Hark! More knocking!

2ND MACBETH.   Get on your nightgown, lest occasion
          call us
And show us to be watchers.
Be not lost so poorly in your thoughts.

(They exit.)

MACBETH.
To know my deed 'twere best not know myself.

(Knocking persists. MACBETH *approaches door, opens
it, a bloody* DUNCAN—*in shroud*—appears on
threshold. Blackout. On DUNCAN's appearance, the*
WITCHES *emit a fearful but exaggerated cry of
fright and, on Blackout, come downstage—sans
stocking masks.)*

2ND WITCH.   *(of* DUNCAN*)*
What bloody man is that?

(All laugh.)

3RD WITCH.
Who would have thought the old man had so much
blood in him.

(All laugh.)

3RD WITCH. *(Parodying* MACBETH*)*
I have done the deed.

*(*2ND WITCH *blows raspberry.)*

3RD WITCH. Didst thou not hear a noise?

1ST WITCH. I hear the owl scream and the cricket cry.
Did not you speak?

2ND WITCH. When?

1ST WITCH. Now.

2ND WITCH. As I descended?

1ST WITCH. Ay. *(Giggles.)*

(All laugh together)

2ND WITCH. Who lies in the second chamber?

3RD WITCH. Donalbain.

2ND WITCH. *(Peering into* 3RD WITCH*'s face)*
This is a sorry sight.

1ST WITCH. *(Irritated.)*
A foolish thought to say a sorry sight.
(Peers into 3RD WITCH*'s face)*
This *is* a sorry sight.
Why did you bring these daggers from the place?
They must lie there. Go, carry them and smear
The sleepy grooms with blood.

2ND WITCH. *(Banging the ground mock-tragically.)*
I'll go no more.
I am afraid to think what I have done;
Look on't again I dare not.

1ST WITCH.
Infirm of purpose! Give me the bloody daggers.
*(She takes them melodramatically, then focuses as if
seeing them for the first time.)*
Is this a dagger which I see before me.
The handle toward my hand?
Come let me clutch thee.
I have thee not. Yet I see thee still.

Art thou not, fatal vision, sensible to feeling as to
    sight?
Or art thou but a dagger of the mind; a false creation
Proceeding from the heat-oppres'd brain.

(WITCHES *applaud* 1ST WITCH's *performance.* 1ST
WITCH *takes a bow. Then suddenly takes up purpose-
ful stance.)*

I go and it is done; the bell invites me.

WITCHES. *(piping high)* Ting-a-ling-a-ling.

1ST WITCH. Hear it not Duncan, for it is a knell.

WITCHES. *(High)* Ting-a-ling-a-ling.

1ST WITCH. That summons thee to heaven.

WITCHES. *(High)* Ting-a-ling-a-ling.

1ST WITCH. Or to hell.

WITCHES. *(In bass register)* Ting-a-ling-a-ling.

(WITCHES *begin to stalk out, all moving forward with
the same foot.* 1ST WITCH *suddenly notices* MACBETH,
*shushes them, they regain their composure, pull on
their masks and quickly depart.* MACBETH *is rolled
downstage in an oversize throne pushed by* MACBETHS
1 *and* 2. *His feet dangle without touching the floor.
He looks like a baby in a high-chair.)*

MACBETH. To be thus . . .

2ND MACBETH. is nothing!

3RD MACBETH. But to be safely thus!

2ND MACBETH. Our fears in Banquo
Stick deep; and in his royalty of nature
Reigns that which would be feared.

3RD MACBETH. Tis much he dares,
And to that dauntless temper of his mind
He hath a wisdom that doth guide his valour
To act in safety.

2ND MACBETH. He chid the sisters
When they first put the name of king upon thee
And bade them speak to him.

And bade them speak to him.

3RD MACBETH.   Then prophet-like,
They hailed him father to a line of kings.

2ND MACBETH.   Upon thy head they placed a
fruitless crown
And put a barren sceptre in thy grip
Thence to be wrenched with an unlineal hand
No son of thine succeeding.

MACBETH.   If it be so
For Banquo's issue have I filed my mind,
For them the gracious Duncan have I murdered,
Put rancours in the vessel of my peace,
Only for them; and mine eternal jewel
Given to the common enemy of man.

2ND MACBETH.   To make them kings.

3RD MACBETH.   The seed of Banquo, kings.

MACBETH.
Rather than so, come fate into the list
And champion me to the utterance.

(BANQUO *enters*)

Here's our chief guest.
If he had been forgot
It had been as a gap in our great feast
And all-thing unbecoming.

(All freeze during BANQUO's *next speech.)*

BANQUO.
Thou hast it now: King, Cawdor, Glamis, all
As the weird woman promised; and I fear
Thou playd'st most foully for't. Yet it was said
It should not stand in thy posterity
But that myself should be the root and father
Of many kings. If there come truth from them
As upon thee, Macbeth, their speeches shine,
Why by the verities on thee made good
May they not be my oracles as well
And set me up in hope?

(Motion.)

MACBETH. Tonight we hold a solemn supper, sir
    And I'll request your presence.

BANQUO.
    Let your highness
    Command upon me, to the which my duties
    Are with a most indissoluble tie
    Forever knit.

MACBETH. Ride you this afternoon?

BANQUO. Ay, my good lord.

    (Static.)

2ND MACBETH. I am one, my liege,
    Whom the vile blows and buffets of the world,
    Hath so incens'd that I am reckless what I do
    To spite the world.

MACBETH. Is it far you ride?

3RD MACBETH. And I another,
    So weary with disasters, tugged with fortune,
    That I would set my life on any chance
    To mend it or be rid on't.

    (Motion.)

BANQUO.
    As far my lord, as will fill up the time
    Twixt this and supper. Go not my horse the better,
    I must become a borrower of the night
    For a dark hour or twain.

MACBETH. Fail not our feast.

BANQUO. My lord, I will not.

    (Static)

MACBETH.
    Every minute of his being thrusts against
    My near'st of life. It must be done tonight.

2ND MACBETH. It is concluded!

3RD MACBETH. Banquo, thy soul's flight,
    If it find heaven, must find it   out tonight.

    (Motion.)

MACBETH.   Hie you to horse. Adieu.
Till you return tonight. Goes Fleance with you?

BANQUO.   Ay my good lord; *(Pause)* our time does call upon's.

MACBETH.
I wish your horses swift and sure of foot
And so I do commend you to their backs.
Farewell.
Let every man be master of his time
Till seven at night. Farewell.

*(BANQUO exits, Murderers—MACBETHS 1 and 2—
follow on each side. Simultaneously, double-bed is
rolled down. LADY MACBETH under sheet; WITCHES
beside her.)*

LADY MACBETH.   Is Banquo gone from court?

WITCH.   Ay madam, but returns again tonight.

LADY MACBETH.   *(Secretly content)*
Say to the King I would attend his leisure
For a few words . . .

*(Settles back in bed. The WITCHES have not moved;
each is silently communing with the other. Eventually,
LADY MACBETH becomes aware of the hesitation;
turns to 1ST WITCH.)*

WITCH.   *(Caught)* Madam, I will.

*(WITCHES in background, stand awaiting LADY
MACBETH's instructions.)*

LADY MACBETH.   *(as MACBETH enters)*
How now, my Lord? Why do you keep alone,
Of sorriest fancies your companions making,
Using those thoughts which should indeed have died
With them they think on? Things without all remedy
Should be without regard; what's done is done.

MACBETH.   What is the night?

LADY MACBETH.
Almost at odds with morning which is which.
Come, we'll to sleep.

(WITCHES begin whispering into MACBETH's ears.)

MACBETH.
>We have scorched the snake, not killed it;
>She'll close and be herself, whilst our poor malice
>Remains in danger of her former tooth,
>But let the frame of things disjoint, both the worlds
>>suffer
>Ere we will eat our meal in fear, and sleep
>In the affliction of these terrible dreams
>That shake us nightly; better be with the dead
>Whom we, to gain our peace, have sent to peace,
>Than on the torture of the mind to lie
>In restless ecstasy. Duncan is in his grave;
>After life's fitful fever he sleeps well;
>Treason has done his worst. Nor steel, nor poison,
>Malice domestic, foreign levy, nothing
>Can touch him further.

LADY MACBETH. Come on,
>Gentle my lord, sleek o'er your rugged looks,
>Be bright and jovial among your guests tonight.

MACBETH.
>O, full of scorpions is my mind, dear wife.

>(WITCHES *abruptly stop whispering.* LADY
>MACBETH *consolingly embraces* MACBETH.)

>There's comfort yet!
>Ere the bat hath flown
>His cloistered flight, ere to black Hecate's summons
>The shard-borne beetle, with his drowsy hums,
>Hath run night's yawning peal, there shall be done
>A deed of dreadful note.

LADY MACBETH. What's to be done?

MACBETH.
>Be innocent of the knowledge, dearest chuck,
>Till thou applaud the deed.

>*(*MACBETH *exits.* WITCHES *congregate around*
>LADY MACBETH *and take up formal positions.*
>*During following invocation,* WITCHES *whisper*
>LADY MACBETH'*s words.)*

LADY MACBETH. Come, seeling night
>Scarf up the tender eye of pitiful day,

And with thy bloody and invisible hand
Cancel and tear to pieces that great bond
Which keeps me pale. Light thickens
And the crow makes wing to the rooky wood;
Good things of day begin to droop and drowse,
While night's black agents to their preys do rouse.

(The two MACBETHS *suddenly appear illuminated.
They beckon to* MACBETH *who joins them.)*

2ND MACBETH.   Come stand with us;
The west yet glimmers with some streaks of day.
Now spurs the lated traveller apace
To gain the timely inn; and near approaches
The subject of our watch.

3RD MACBETH.   Hark, I hear horses!

BANQUO.   *(Within)* Give us a light there, ho!

2ND MACBETH.   Then 'tis he.
The rest that are within the note of expectation,
Already are i' the court.

3RD MACBETH.   His horses go about.

2ND MACBETH.   Almost a mile; but he does usually.
So all men do, from hence to the palace gate
Make it their walk.

(Enter BANQUO *and* FLEANCE, *with a torch.)*

3RD MACBETH.   A light, a light!

2ND MACBETH.   'Tis he.

3RD MACBETH.   Stand to 't!

BANQUO.   It will be rain tonight.

1ST MACBETH.   Let it come down!

BANQUO.   Fly good Fleance. Fly. Fly. Fly.

(They attack BANQUO. *A net is dropped onto*
BANQUO *who is suddenly hoisted up and swung in
space. While* MACBETHS *stab their prey in the trap,*
WITCHES, *at side, tear strips off* BANQUO's *effigy
revealing bright red colouring underneath.
Simultaneously, banquet table is brought out and guests,*

led by MACBETH, *enter in and dance around table. All assemble for banquet, chatting and laughing. But when seated, only* WITCHES *and* MACBETH *are at table. The dance ends drunkenly and breathless.)*

MACBETH.
You know your own degrees, sit down. At first
And last, the hearty welcome.
Ourself will mingle with society
And play the humble host.
Our hostess keeps her state; but in best time
We will require her welcome.

LADY MACBETH.
Pronounce it for me, sir, to all our friends,
For my heart speaks they are welcome.

MACBETH.
See, they encounter thee with their hearts' thanks;
Both sides are even.
Be large in mirth. Anon we'll drink a measure
The table round.

LADY MACBETH. *(Aside)* There's blood upon thy face.

MACBETH. *(Aside)*
'Tis Banquo's then,
Safe in a ditch he bides
With twenty trenched gashes in his head
The least a death to nature.

LADY MACBETH. My royal lord,
You do not give the cheer. The feast is sold
That is not often vouched, while 'tis a-making,
'Tis given with welcome. To feed were best at home;
From thence, the sauce to meat is ceremony,
Meeting were bare without it.

MACBETH. Sweet remembrancer!
Now good digestion wait on appetite,
And health on both!

ALL. Health on both!

(Enter the GHOST OF BANQUO *and sits in* MACBETH's *place. All at table become strangely still, smiling knowingly at each other.)*

MACBETH.
>Here had we now our country's honour roofed,
>Were the graced person of our Banquo present;
>Who may I rather challenge for unkindness
>Than pity for mischance.

3RD MACBETH. *(With knowing smile)* His absence, sir,
>Lays blame upon his promise. Pleas't your highness
>To grace us with your royal company?

MACBETH. The table's full.

2ND MACBETH. *(Sharing the joke)* Here is a place reserved,
>sir.

MACBETH. Where?

2ND MACBETH. Here, my good lord. What is't that moved
>your highness?

MACBETH. Which of you have done this?

ALL. What, my good lord?

MACBETH.
>Thou canst not say I did it; never shake
>Thy gory locks at me.

3RD MACBETH. *(Smiling, unperturbed, remaining seated)*
>Gentlemen, rise. His highness is not well.

LADY MACBETH.
>Sit, worthy friends. My Lord is often thus;
>The fit is momentary; upon a thought
>He will again be well.

MACBETH. Behold! *(All at table become animate again;
talking, laughing, etc.)*

LADY MACBETH. O proper stuff!
>This is the very painting of your fear.
>This is the air-drawn dagger which you said
>Led you to Duncan. O, these flaws and starts,
>Imposters to true fear, would well become
>A woman's story at a winter's fire,
>Authorized by her grandam. Shame itself!
>Why do you make such faces? When all's done
>You look but on a stool.

MACBETH.
>Look! Lo!—How say you? *(All freeze as before)*
>Why, what care I if thou canst nod! Speak, too!
>If charnel-houses and our graves must send
>Those that we bury back, our monuments
>Shall be the maws of kites.

3RD MACBETH.   Quite unmanned in folly?

LADY MACBETH.   Fie, for shame!

MACBETH.   The times has been
>That, when the brains were out, the man would die,
>And there an end. But now they rise again
>With twenty mortal murders on their crowns,
>And push us from our stools.

LADY MACBETH.   My worthy Lord,
>Your noble friends do lack you.

(The table becomes animate again.)

MACBETH.   *(Attempts to ignore the* GHOST*)*
>I do forget.
>Do not muse at me, my most worthy friends:
>I have a strange infirmity, which is nothing
>To those that know me. Come, love and health to all!
>Then I'll sit down. Give me some wine; fill full!

(BANQUO *empties his blood into goblet and proffers it to* MACBETH. *All freeze into tableau.)*

>Avaunt, and quit my sight! Let the earth hide thee!
>Thy bones are marrowless, thy blood is cold.
>Thou hast no speculation in those eyes
>Which thou dost glare with.
>What man dare, I dare.
>Approach thou like the rugged Russian bear,
>The armed rhinoceros, or the Hyrcan tiger,
>Take any shape but that, and my firm nerves
>Shall never tremble. Or be alive again,
>And dare me to the desert with thy sword:
>If trembling I inhabit then, protest me
>The baby of a girl. Hence, horrible shadow!
>Unreal mockery, hence!

(Upsets table. Pandemonium. All exit.)

(Cut into new scene.)

MACBETH.
>I conjure you, by that which you profess,
>Howe'er you come to know it, answer me—
>Though you untie the winds and let them fight
>Against the churches; though the yesty waves
>Confound and swallow navigation up;
>Though bladed corn be lodged and trees blown down;
>Though castles topple on their warders' heads;
>Though palaces and pyramids do slope
>Their heads to their foundations: though the treasure
>Of nature's germens tumble all together
>Even till destruction sicken—answer me
>To what I ask you.

1ST WITCH.   Speak.

2ND WITCH.   Demand.

3RD WITCH.   We'll answer.

1ST WITCH.
>Say if thou'dst rather hear it from our mouths
>Or from our masters.

MACBETH.   Call 'em. Let me see 'em.

ALL.   Come high or low,
>Thyself and office deftly show.

>*(Thunder.* 1ST APPARITION. *Dead DUNCAN is raised up. Eyes cavernous-black.* WITCHES *hold him up to speak through him.* MACBETH *starts but* 3RD WITCH *calms him.)*

MACBETH.   Tell me, thou unknown power—

1ST WITCH.   He knows thy thought
>Hear his speech, say thou naught.

1ST APPARITION.   *(Spoken by* 1ST WITCH)
>Macbeth, Macbeth, Macbeth, beware Macduff!
>Beware the Thane of Fife! Dismiss me. Enough.

>*(He descends into trap.)*

MACBETH.   Whate'er thou art, for thy good caution, thanks;
>Thou hast harped my fear aright. But one word more—

114

1ST WITCH.
>He will not be commanded. Here's another
>More potent than the first.

>*(Thunder. 2ND APPARITION. Dead BANQUO raised up.)*

2ND APPARITION.   Macbeth, Macbeth, Macbeth!

MACBETH.   Had I three ears, I'd hear thee.

2ND APPARITION.   *(Spoken by 2ND WITCH)*
>Be bloody, bold, and resolute; laugh to scorn
>The power of man; for none of woman born
>Shall harm Macbeth.

>*(He descends.)*

MACBETH.
>Then live Macduff; what need I fear of thee?
>But yet I'll make assurance double sure,
>And take a bond of fate. Thou shalt not live;
>That I may tell pale-hearted fear it lies,
>And sleep in spite of thunder.

>*(Thunder. 3RD APPARITION. 2ND MACBETH wearing mask of MACBETH.)*

1ST WITCH.   Listen, but speak not to 't.

3RD APPARITION.   *(Spoken by 3RD WITCH)*
>Be lion-mettled, proud, and take no care
>Who chafes, who frets, or where conspirers are;
>Macbeth shall never vanquished be, until
>Great Birnam Wood to high Dunsinane Hill
>Shall come against him.

MACBETH.   That will never be.
>Who can impress the forest, bid the tree
>Unfix his earth-bound root? Sweet bodements! Good!
>Rebellious dead rise never till the wood
>Of Birnam rise, and our high-placed Macbeth
>Shall live the lease of nature, pay his breath
>To time and mortal custom, Yet my heart
>Throbs to know one thing: tell me, if your art
>Can tell so much, shall Banquo's issue ever
>Reign in this kingdom?

ALL.   Seek to know no more.

(2ND MACBETH *descends.*)

MACBETH.   I will be satisfied! Deny me this
And an eternal curse fall on you!

(WITCH-*chord.*)

And what noise is this?

1ST WITCH.   Show!

2ND WITCH.   Show!

3RD WITCH.   Show!

ALL.   Show his eyes and grieve his heart;
Come like shadows, so depart.

(WITCHES *in a queue behind* MACBETH *take turns putting hands over his eyes.*)

MACBETH.
Thou art too like the spirit of Banquo. Down!
Thy crown does sear mine eye-balls.

NEXT WITCH.
Thou other gold-bound brow, is like the first.

NEXT WITCH.
A third is like the former. —Filthy hags,
Why do you show me this?

NEXT WITCH.   A fourth? Start, eyes!
What, will the line stretch out to the crack of doom?

NEXT WITCH.   Another yet?

NEXT WITCH.   A seventh? I'll see no more!

NEXT WITCH.
And yet the eighth appears, who bears a glass
Which shows me many more. And some I see
That two-fold balls and treble sceptres carry.

(Dead BANQUO *with crown is now thrust before* MACBETH.)

Horrible sight! Now I see 'tis true,
For the blood-boltered Banquo smiles upon me,
And points at them for his. What! Is this so?

1ST WITCH.   Ay, sir, all this is so.

2ND WITCH.   *(Tracing a vision)*
Hark, I did hear the galloping of horses.

3RD WITCH.   *(Divining the vision from* 2ND WITCH*)*
Macduff is fled to England.

(All turn to MACBETH, *as if to say: 'What will you do now?')*

MACBETH.   From this moment
The very firstlings of my heart shall be
The firstlings of my hand.
The castle of Macduff I will surprise,
Seize upon Fife, give to the end o' the sword
His wife, his babes, and all unfortunate souls
That trace him in his line, and even now,
To crown my thoughts with acts, be it thought and
        done.
Come you secret black and midnight hags,
Bring me where they are.

*(*WITCHES, *taking masks, assume characters of*
LADY MACDUFF *and* CHILD.   LADY MACDUFF
*takes babe in her arms. Scene is played out like an old-
fashioned Morality play—in a crude, artificial style.)*

WIFE.   Sirrah, your father's dead.
And what will you do now? How will you live?

SON.   As birds do, mother.

WIFE.   What, with worms and flies?

SON.
With what I get, I mean; and so do they.
My father is not dead, for all your saying.

WIFE.
Yes, he is dead. How wilt thou do for a father?

SON.   Nay, how will you do for a husband?

WIFE.   Why, I can buy me twenty at any market.

SON.   Then you'll buy 'em to sell again.

WIFE.   Thou speak'st with all thy wit,
And yet, i'faith, with wit enough for thee.

SON.   Was my father a traitor, mother?

WIFE.   Ay, that he was.

SON.   What is a traitor?

WIFE.   Why, one that swears and lies.

SON.   And be all traitors that do so?

WIFE.   Every one that does so is a traitor,
And must be hanged.

SON.   And must they all be hanged that swear and lie?

WIFE.   Every one.

SON.   Who must hang him?

WIFE.   Why, the honest men.

SON.   Then the liars and swearers are fools; for there are
liars and swearers enow to beat the honest men and
hang up them.

WIFE.   Now God help thee, poor monkey! But how wilt
thou do for a father?

SON.   If he were dead, you'd weep for him; if you would not,
it were a good sign that I should quickly have a new
father.

WIFE.   Poor prattler, how thou talk'st!

*(3RD WITCH as male is cued on by 1ST WITCH—
irritably because cue was missed.)*

Poor prattler, how thou talk'st!

3RD WITCH.
Bless you, fair dame! I am not to you known,
Though in your state of honour I am perfect.
I doubt some danger does approach you nearly.
If you will take a homely man's advice,
Be not found here. Hence with your little ones!
To fright you thus methinks I am too savage;
To do worse to you were fell cruelty,
Which is too nigh your person. Heaven preserve you!
I dare abide no longer.

(Exit.)

WIFE.   Whither should I fly?
   I have done no harm. But I remember now
   I am in this earthly world, where to do harm
   Is often laudable, to do good sometime
   Accounted dangerous folly. Why then, alas,
   Do I put up that womanly defence
   To say I have done no harm?

(Enter murderers—MACBETHS 2 and 3.)

WIFE.   What are these faces?

2ND MACBETH.   Where is your husband?

WIFE.   I hope in no place so unsanctified
   Where such as thou mayst find him.

3RD MACBETH.   He's a traitor.

SON.   Thou liest, thou shag-haired villain!

3RD MACBETH.   What, you egg,
   Young fry of treachery!

  *(LADY MACDUFF and BABE are stalked then cornered.
  Then, daggers are thrust into MACBETH's hands and he is
  forced to stab LADY MACDUFF and SON. As dagger
  enters SON, MACDUFF, in subsequent scene, is
  heard crying out.)*

  (Cut to:)

MACDUFF.   Ahh!
   My children too!

MALCOLM.   Wife, children, servants, all
   That could be found.

MACDUFF.   My wife killed too?

MALCOLM.   I have said.
   Be comforted.
   Let's make us medicines of our great revenge
   To cure this deadly grief.

MACDUFF.   He has no children.
   All my pretty ones? Did you say all?
   O hell-kite! All? What, all my pretty chickens
   And their dam, at one fell swoop?

MALCOLM. Dispute it like a man.

MACDUFF. I shall do so;
   But I must also feel it as a man.
   I cannot but remember such things were
   That were most precious to me. Did Heaven look
   And would not take their part? Sinful Macduff
   They were all struck for thee.
   Naught for their own demerits but for thine
   Fell slaughter on their souls.
   Heaven rest them now.

MALCOLM. Be this the whetstone of your sword
   Let grief convert to anger. Blunt not the heart.
   Enrage it.

MACDUFF. O, I could play the woman with mine eyes
   And braggart with my tongue! But, gentle heavens
   Cut short all intermission. Front to front
   Bring thou this fiend of Scotland and myself.
   Within my sword's length set him; if he scape,
   Heaven forgive him too.

(Blackout. LADY MACBETH *discovers* WITCHES
removing LADY MACDUFF *gear.)*

LADY MACBETH. *(Angrily)*
   Beldams,
   Saucy and over-bold? How did you dare
   To trade and traffick with Macbeth
   In riddles and affairs of death,
   And I, the mistress of your charms,
   The close contriver of all harms,
   Was never called to bear my part,
   Or show the glory of our art?
   Thou shalt make amends: now get you gone.

(Exits.)

1ST WITCH. Come, let's make haste; she'll soon be back again.

*(*1ST WITCH, *using twig, draws a circle on the
ground.* 2ND *and* 3RD WITCHES *place effigy of*
LADY MACBETH *in centre.* WITCHES *then
chant the following, reinforced with tape in
background:*

'Double, double, toil, trouble
Fire burn, cauldron bubble'
This is endlessly repeated as WITCHES, *facing effigy,*
twitch thumbs in a repeated rhythm and slowly kneel
before it. On a signal, they abruptly end their chant.
Each WITCH, *taking her turn, jabs a sharp, silver*
knitting-needle into the effigy's head. Pause. The
perforated effigy sways gently for a moment in its
frame. Then the 1ST WITCH *tears off a piece of the*
effigy's heart revealing blood-red colouring underneath.
2ND WITCH *tears off another strip from the effigy's*
leg. Blood-red colouring revealed again. 3RD WITCH
tears off a strip from effigy's head. Blood-red colouring
revealed again. Pause. WITCHES *stand silently watching*
the torn effigy swaying in its frame. Suddenly, the
effigy is removed by WITCHES 2 *and* 3. 1ST WITCH
cocks her head hearing someone's approach and backs
slowly up-stage as she says)

1ST WITCH.   By the pricking of my thumbs,
Something wicked this way comes.

(2ND WITCH, now playing GENTLEWOMAN, *enters*
with DOCTOR.)

DOCTOR.   When was it she last walked?

GENTLEWOMAN.   Since his majesty went into the field I
have seen her rise from her bed, throw her nightgown
upon her, unlock her closet, take forth paper, fold it,
write upon't, read it, afterwards seal it, and again
return to bed; yet all this while in a most fast sleep.

DOCTOR.   In this slumbery agitation, besides her walking
and other actual performances, what, at any time, have
you heard her say?

GENTLEWOMAN.   That, sir, which I will not report after
her.

DOCTOR.   You may to me; and 'tis most meet you should.

GENTLEWOMAN.   Neither to you nor anyone, having no
witness to confirm my speech.

(Enter LADY MACBETH *with a taper.)*

Look you! Here she comes. This is her very guise;
and, upon my life, fast asleep. Observe her; stand close.

DOCTOR. How came she by that light?

GENTLEWOMAN. Why, it stood by her. She has light by her
continually; 'tis her command.

DOCTOR. You see her eyes are open.

GENTLEWOMAN. Ay, but their sense are shut.

DOCTOR. What is it she does now? Look how she rubs her
hands.

GENTLEWOMAN. It is an accustomed action with her to
seem thus washing her hands. I have known her continue
in this a quarter of an hour.

LADY MACBETH. Yet here's a spot.

*(DOCTOR ushers GENTLEWOMAN off. WITCHES,
at side, deal with LADY MACBETH effigy throughout
scene. LADY MACBETH wears transparent nightdress.
Carries a long taper.)*

LADY MACBETH.	WITCHES.
Out, damned spot! Out I say.	Fillet of a fenny snake In the cauldron boil and bake
One: two: why then, 'tis time to do't. Hell is murky—Fie, my lord, fie. A Soldier and a'feared?— What need we fear who knows it, when none can call our power to account?— Yet who would have thought the old man to have so much blood in him?	Eye of newt and toe of frog,
The Thane of Fife had a wife; where	Wool of bat, and tongue of dog,

is she now?—What,
will these
hands ne'er be clean.

No more o' that my
Lord, no more o'
that. You mar all
with this
starting. Here's the
smell of
blood still. All the
perfumes
of Arabia will not
sweeten this
little hand. Oh! Oh!
Oh!

Wash your hands; put
on your night-
gown; look not so pale.
I tell
you again, Banquo's
buried; he
cannot come out on's
grave.

(Resisting slightly)
There's a
knocking at the gate.

Adder's fork and blind-
worm's sting
Lizard's leg and howlet's
wing,

Ohhhhhhhhhhhhhhhhhhhhhhh
*(Sympathetic cry turns
shrill and cruel.)*

(Taking her round.)
To bed, to bed.

Come, come, come,
come, give
me your hand.

What's done cannot be
undone.

To bed, to bed, to bed.

*(They shroud her over
in their costumes, snuff
out her light, and carry
her away.)*

*(A funeral procession. A coffin carrying the corpse of
LADY MACBETH enters and is set downstage.*

Surrounding the bier are the WITCHES, MACBETH *and
a* PRIEST. *After a moment's mumbled prayer, the*
PRIEST *comes forward and delivers the eulogy.)*

PRIEST.
Tomorrow and tomorrow and tomorrow
Creeps in this petty pace from day to day
To the last syllable of recorded time
And all our yesterdays have lighted fools
The way to dusty death. Out, out, brief candle
Life's but a walking shadow; a poor player
That struts and frets his hour upon the stage
And then is heard no more. It is a tale
Told by an idiot, full of sound and fury
Signifying nothing.

(The PRIEST *crosses himself. There is a moment's silence.*
MACBETH *looks dazed. He crouches down beside the
bier to peer intently into the corpse's eyes. Then,
suddenly angered, he turns and goes. The others also
move off leaving the three* WITCHES *hovering over the
coffin. After a moment, the* 1ST WITCH *bends down
to take up* LADY MACBETH's *crown. The others
struggle with her for a moment. She pushes them away.
Then very slowly she places the crown onto her head
and gazes imperiously out towards the audience. The
other two* WITCHES *keep their eyes riveted on her.
The lights slowly fade out.)*
(Cut to:
MALCOLM *and* MACDUFF *on two platforms above.
In centre,* MACBETH *is seated on throne. He looks
straight out, fear in his eyes. Clustered around the throne
is a fresco of heads—all the characters of the play. They
intone a dull, smouldering sound—barely audible—while
MALCOLM's *and* MACDUFF's *speeches are played out.)*

MACDUFF.
O Scotland, Scotland!
O nation miserable,
With an untitled tyrant, bloody-sceptred,
When shalt thou see thy wholesome days again?

MALCOLM   Our country sinks beneath the yoke.
It weeps, it bleeds, and each new day a gash
Is added to her wounds.

Each new morn
New widows howl, new orphans cry, new sorrows
Strike heaven on the face, that it resounds
As if it felt with Scotland, and yelled out
Like syllable of dolour.

MACDUFF.   Alas poor country!
Almost afraid to know itself! It cannot
Be called our mother, but our grave; where nothing
But who-knows-nothing is once seen to smile;
Where sighs and groans and shrieks that rent the air
Are made not marked; where violent sorrow seems
A modern ecstasy.

What I believe I'll wail;
What know, believe; and what I can redress,
As I shall find the time to friend, I will.

MALCOLM.
This tyrant whose sole name blisters our tongue!
Not in the legions
Of horrid hell can come a devil more damned
In evils to top Macbeth.
Some say he's mad.

MACDUFF.   Others that lesser hate him
Do call it valiant fury; but for certain
He cannot buckle his distempered cause
Within the belt of rule.

MALCOLM.   Now does he feel
His secret murders sticking on his hands;

MACDUFF.
Now, minutely, revolts upbraid his faith-breach.

MALCOLM.   Those he commands move only in command,
Nothing in love.

MACDUFF.   Now does he feel his title
Hang loose about him like a giant's robe
Upon a dwarfish thief.

MALCOLM.   Who then shall blame
His pestered senses to recoil and start,
When all that is within him does condemn
Itself for being there?

MACDUFF. Well, march we now
　　To give obedience where tis truly owed.

MALCOLM. Gracious England hath
　　Lent us good Seyward and ten thousand men—

MACDUFF. Our power is ready;
　　Our lack is nothing but our leave.

MALCOLM. Macbeth
　　Is ripe for shaking, and the powers above
　　Put on their instruments.

MACDUFF. Forward
　　Make we our march towards Birnam!

(During the scene, the drone has steadily increased in volume. On MACDUFF's last speech it bursts into a wild, chaotic clamour. Blackout.)

(On lights up: All are circled around the perimeter of the stage facing outward—like pillars of a human fortress. They all hold witches' brooms as if they were spears. MACBETH, with sword, in centre. During the next dialogue, each actor turns downstage centre to deliver his line. It is shouted out as if it were a message being called out from a great distance.)

2ND MACBETH. The night has been unruly.

BANQUO. Chimneys were blown down.

MALCOLM. Lamentings heard i' the air.

3RD MACBETH. Strange screams of death
　　And prophesying with accents terrible
　　Of fire combustion and confused events.

MACBETH. The mind I sway by and the heart I bear
　　Shall never sag with doubt nor shake with fear.

MALCOLM. Foul whisperings are abroad.

MACDUFF. The English power is near.
　　Led on by Malcolm.

MACBETH. What's the boy Malcolm?
　　Was he not born of woman?

(All beat the floor with broom-handles; three knocks.)

Who's there?

2ND MACBETH. A farmer that hanged himself
on the expectation of plenty.

MACBETH. *(To himself)*
Why should I play the Roman fool and die
On mine own sword? Whiles I see lives, the gashes
Do better upon them.

(Shouting orders.)

Send out more horses; skirr the country round.
Hang those that talk of fear.
Who's there?

(Three knocks.)

DUNCAN. Old Seyward and ten thousand men.

MACBETH.
Hang out our banners on the outward walls.
Our castle's strength
Will laugh a siege to scorn.

LADY MACBETH. *(Off-stage)* What is that noise?

DUNCAN. *(In a comic voice)*
It was the owl that shriek'd, the fatal bellman
Which gives the stern'st good-night.

(Three knocks.)

MACBETH. Who's there?

DUNCAN. Old Seyward and ten thousand men.

2ND MACBETH. *(Kneeling as* MESSENGER*)*
All is confirmed, my lord, which was reported.

*(*MACBETH, *shaken, rises from throne and takes a
few steps forward; is caught up in* LADY MACBETH's
arms.)*

MACBETH. Dearest chuck.

LADY MACBETH. *(As mother)*
Put this night's great business into my dispatch.

MACBETH. *(Holding her desperately)*
I have lived long enough; my way of life

127

Is fallen into the sere, the yellow leaf;
And that which should accompany old age,
As honour, love, obedience, troops of friends,
I must not look to have.

LADY MACBETH.   Poor prattler, how thou talk'st.

MACBETH.   There's nothing serious in mortality.
All is but toys. Renown and grace is dead.
The wine of life is drawn and the mere lees
Is left this vault to brag of.
Naught's had, all's spent . . .

LADY MACBETH.   Consider it not so deeply.

MACBETH.   I am in blood.
Stepped in so far, that should I wade no more
Returning were as tedious as go o'er.

LADY MACBETH.   *(Cuddling him)*
You lack the season of all natures, sleep.

MACBETH.   *(Held tight in* LADY MACBETH's *arms)*
It will have blood, they say; blood will have blood.
Stones have been known to move and trees to speak;
Augurs and understood relations have,
By maggot-pies, and choughs and rooks brought forth
The secret'st man of blood.

LADY MACBETH.   *(Consoling)*
What's done is done.
MACBETH.   *(Suddenly turning)*
Canst thou not minister to a mind diseased,
And with some sweet, oblivious antidote
Cleanse the stuffed bosom of that perilous stuff
Which weighs upon the heart.

LADY MACBETH.   These deeds must not be thought
After these ways, so it will make us mad.
Blood hath been shed ere now, i' the olden time,
Ere human statute purged the gentle weal;
Ay, and since too, murders have been performed
Too terrible for the ear. We are yet but young in
    deed.

But fear not,
Yet shalt thou take upon you what is yours.

MACBETH. *(Bucked)* Bring forth men-children only,
  For thy undaunted mettle should compose
  Nothing but males.
  We will establish our estate upon
  Our eldest; and signs of nobleness,
  Like stars, shall shine
  On all deservers.

(Turns to her.)

My dearest partner of greatness.

(MACBETH goes to kiss LADY MACBETH. Curiously, she resists; he looks at her quizzically wondering why her tenderness has vanished. LADY MACBETH looks him squarely in the eyes. Transforms.)

LADY MACBETH. The queen, my lord, is dead.

(She becomes immobile. The WITCHES suddenly appear and remove her body. A shriek is heard off-stage.)

2ND MACBETH. Gracious my lord,
  I should report that which I say I saw,
  But know not how to do't.

MACBETH. *(Hysterical)* Well, say, sir!

2ND MACBETH.
  As I did stand my watch upon the hill
  I looked toward Birnam and anon me thought
  The wood began to move.

MACBETH. Liar and slave. If thou speakest false
  Upon the next tree shalt thou hang. If thy speech be
      sooth
  I care not if thou durst for me as much.
  Arm, arm and out! I 'gin to be aweary of the sun
  And wish the estate of the world were now undone.
  Ring the alarum bell.
  They have tied me to a stake. I cannot fly
  But bear-like I must fight the course.
  Ring the alarum bell.

(The circle which had been facing up-stage, slowly turns downstage to face MACBETH. Each character

*holds a witch's broom. There is a long, electric
pause as circle confronts* MACBETH. *Then they begin
to tighten around him.* MACBETH *draws one of his
daggers. As each character comes forward, he strikes at
his broomstick; the character drops broom and retires.)*

What's he
That was not born of woman? Such a one
Am I to fear or none.

*(*MACDUFF *suddenly turns to confront* MACBETH. *He,
unlike all the others in the circle, holds a sword.)*

MACDUFF.
    If thou be'st slain and with no stroke of mine,
    My wife and children's ghosts will haunt me still.

MACBETH. Of all men else I have avoided thee.
    But get thee back; my soul is too much charged
    With blood of thine already.

MACDUFF. I have no words;
    My voice is in my sword, thou bloodier villain
    Than terms can give thee out.

(They duel. MACDUFF *weakens.)*

MACBETH. Thou losest labour.
    Let fall thy blade on vulnerable crests,
    I bear a charmed life which must not yield
    To one of woman born.

MACDUFF. Despair thy charm
    And let the angel whom thou still hast served
    Tell thee Macduff was from his mother's womb
    Untimely ripped.

MACBETH. Accursed be that tongue that tells me so
    For it hath cow'd my better part of man:
    And be these juggling fiends no more believed
    That palter with us in a double sense
    That keep the word of promise to our ear
    And break it to our hope. I'll not fight with thee.

MACDUFF. Then yield thee coward,
    And live to be the show and gaze of the time.
    We'll have thee, as our rarer monsters are,

Painted upon a pole, and underwrit:
"Here may you see the tyrant!"

*(All characters now rise up with their brooms and
stalk MACBETH. MACBETH stands frozen and
helpless. When he is completely surrounded, all begin
to beat him to death with broomsticks. This done,
MACDUFF approaches the heap. As he does so,
MACBETH's effigy becomes visible again; beside it,
back to the audience, stands LADY MACBETH. As
MACDUFF raises his sword over the heap, LADY
MACBETH raises her instrument over the effigy's
head. As MACDUFF strikes, LADY MACBETH dashes
off the head of the effigy. The tight circle surrounding
MACBETH widens and opens. MACBETH is laying in a
heap, a black-sack over his head. All exit but three
WITCHES. WITCHES silently commune with each
other then slowly come downstage and take off their
stocking-masks.)*

1ST WITCH. *(Simply, conversationally)*
When shall we three meet again?
In thunder, lightning or in rain?

2ND WITCH. When the hurly-burly's done,
When the battle's lost and won.

3RD WITCH. That will be 'ere the set of sun.

*(WITCHES stand motionless. The battery of lights
that line the back of the stage slowly come to full
then fade to black.)*

END

The Shrew

CAST

BIANCA	GRUMIO
KATHERINE	PETRUCHIO
BAPTISTA	BOY
HORTENSIO	GIRL

A cry in the darkness. Lights up: BIANCA *tied to a pole, bound hand and foot.* KATE *holds the rope and slowly applies pressure by drawing it taut.*

BIANCA. Good sister, wrong me not nor wrong yourself
  To make a bondmaid and a slave of me.
  That I disdain. But for these other gawds,
  Unbind my hands, I'll pull them off myself,
  Yea, all my raiment, to my petticoat,
  Or what you command me will I do,
  So well I know my duty to my elders.

KATE. Of all thy suitors, here I charge thee, tell
  Whom thou lov'st best. See thou dissemble not.

BIANCA. Believe me, sister, of all the men alive
  I never yet beheld that special face
  Which I could fancy more than any other.

KATE. *(Pulls rope tighter)*
  Minion, thou liest. Is't not Hortensio?

BIANCA. If you affect him, sister, here I swear
  I'll plead for you myself but you shall have him.

KATE. O then, belike, you fancy riches more:
  You will have Grumio to keep you fair.

BIANCA. Is it for him you do envy me so?
  Nay, then you jest, and now I well perceive
  You have but jested with me all this while.
  I prithee, sister Kate, untie my hands.

KATE. If that be jest then all the rest was so.

  (Pulls rope tighter. BIANCA screams.)

133

(Enter BAPTISTA.*)*

BAPTISTA.   Why, how now, dame, whence grows this
           insolence?
     Poor girl, she weeps. Bianca, stand aside.
     For shame, thou hilding of a devilish spirit,
     Why dost thou wrong her that did ne'er wrong thee?
     When did she cross thee with a bitter word?

KATE.   Her silence flouts me and I'll be revenged.

BAPTISTA.   What, in my sight? Bianca, get thee in.

     (Taking BIANCA *round)*

     Go ply thy needle; meddle not with her.

     (BIANCA *exits crying)*

KATE.   Nay, now I see
     She is your treasure, she must have a husband;
     I must dance barefoot on her wedding day,
     And, for your love to her lead apes in hell.
     Talk not to me; I will go sit and weep
     Till I can find occasion of revenge.

     (Exit.)

BAPTISTA.   *(Regards rope with which* BIANCA *was tied)*
     Was ever gentleman thus grieved as I?

     Lights out.

     Lights up.

     PETRUCHIO *enters from left with* GRUMIO.
     HORTENSIO *from right. All have the look and manner
     of men involved in schemes and stratagems. A certain
     unsentimental practicality is common to all.*

HORTENSIO.   Petruchio.

PETRUCHIO.   My best beloved and approved friend.

HORTENSIO.   My old friend Grumio.
     And tell me now, sweet friend, what happy gale
     Blows you to Padua from old Verona?

PETRUCHIO.   Such wind as scatters young men through
           the world
     To seek their fortunes farther than at home,

Where small experience grows. But in a few,
Signior Hortensio, thus it stands with me:
Antonio my father is deceased.

(PETRUCHIO pauses for a moment as if recalling his loss. GRUMIO sympathises; HORTENSIO feels obliged to join in the mood then abruptly PETRUCHIO shatters it with a mocking laugh which GRUMIO shares. HORTENSIO, suddenly the butt of the joke, is taken aback.)

Crowns in my purse I have and goods at home
And so am come abroad to see the world.
Happily to wive and thrive as best I may.

HORTENSIO.   Petruchio, shall I then come roundly to thee
And wish thee to a shrewd ill-favoured wife?

PETRUCHIO.   Signior Hortensio, 'twixt such friends as we
Few words suffice; and therefore if thou know
One rich enough to be Petruchio's wife—
As wealth is burthen of my wooing dance—
Be she as foul as was Florentius' love,
As old as Sibyl, and as curst and shrewd
As Socrates' Xanthippe or a worse,
She moves me not, or not removes, at least,
Affection's edge in me, were she as rough
As are the swelling Adriatic seas.
I come to wive it wealthily in Padua;
If wealthily, then happily in Padua.

HORTENSIO.   Thou'ldst thank me but a little for my counsel—
And yet I'll promise thee she *shall* be rich,
And very rich—
Her house within the city
Is richly furnished with plate and gold,
Costly apparel, tents, and canopies,
Fine linen, Turkey cushions bossed with pearl,
Pewter and brass, and all things that belong
To house or housekeeping.
Tis known her father hath no less
Then three argosies, besides two galliases
and twelve tight galleys . . .
But thou'rt too much my friend,
And I'll not wish thee to her.

(Moving off; stopped by GRUMIO.*)*

GRUMIO. *(Close, threatening)* Nay, look you, sir, he tells
you flatly what his mind is. Why, give him gold
enough and marry him to a puppet or an anglet-baby
or an old trot with ne'er a tooth in her head, though
she has as many diseases as two-and-fifty horses. Why,
nothing comes amiss so money comes withal.

HORTENSIO. *(Reconsidering)*
I can, Petruchio, help thee to a wife
With wealth enough and young and beauteous,
Brought up as best becomes a gentlewoman.
Her only fault—and that is faults enough—
Is that she is intolerable curst
And shrewd and froward, so beyond all measure
That were my state far worser than it is,
I would not wed her for a mine of gold.

PETRUCHIO. Hortensio, peace. Thou know'st not gold's
effect.
And therefore let me be thus bold with you.
Tell me her father's name and 'tis enough,
For I will board her though she chide as loud
As thunder when the clouds in Autumn crack.
I will not sleep Hortensio till I see her.

*(*PETRUCHIO *and* GRUMIO, *now threateningly close
to* HORTENSIO.*)*

HORTENSIO. Her father is Baptista Minola,
An affable and courteous gentleman.
Her name is Katherina Minola.

*(*PETRUCHIO *smiles at* GRUMIO, *then at* HORTENSIO,
who looks at him uncertainly.)

Black out.

Lights up.

BAPTISTA, *richly dressed, stands tentatively before*
PETRUCHIO, HORTENSIO *and* GRUMIO.

BAPTISTA. Good morrow, sirs.

PETRUCHIO. And you, good sir. Pray, have you not a
daughter

Called Katherina, fair and virtuous?

BAPTISTA. I have a daughter, sir, called Katherina.

PETRUCHIO. *(Jovially, to* BAPTISTA*)*
I am a gentleman of Verona, sir,
That, hearing of her beauty and her wit,
Her affability and bashful modesty,
Her wondrous qualities and mild behaviour,
Am bold to show myself a forward guest
Within your house, to make mine eye the witness
Of that report which I so oft have heard.
And, for an entrance to my entertainment,
I do present you with a man of mine,

(Presenting HORTENSIO*)*

Cunning in music and the mathematics,
To instruct her fully in those sciences,
Whereof I know she is not ignorant.
Accept of him, or else you do me wrong.
His name is . . . *(faltering)*

HORTENSIO. Litio, born in . . . *(faltering)*

PETRUCHIO. . . . Mantua!
And by good fortune I have lighted well
On this young man; for learning and behaviour
Fit for her turn, well read in poetry
And other books—good ones, I warrant ye.

BAPTISTA. Y'are welcome, sir, and they for your good
          sake.
But for my daughter Katherine, this I know,
She is not for your turn, the more my grief.

(A threatening silence ensues. Gradually, BAPTISTA
becomes aware of it, and turns to find a grim, dead-eyed
PETRUCHIO, *who begins to speak slowly and
menacingly.)*

PETRUCHIO. I see you do not mean to part with her,
Or else you like not of my company.

BAPTISTA. Mistake me not; I speak but as I find.
Whence are you sir? What may I call your name?

PETRUCHIO. Petruchio is my name, Antonio's son,

A man well known throughout all Italy.

BAPTISTA.   I . . . know him well. You are welcome for his
sake.

*(PETRUCHIO suddenly restores an air of bonhomie.
HORTENSIO and GRUMIO place BAPTISTA on a stool
alongside PETRUCHIO then gather round the two men—
rather too closely to BAPTISTA.)*

PETRUCHIO.   Signior Baptista, my business asketh haste,
And every day I cannot come to woo.
You knew my father, and in him me,
Left solely heir to all his lands and goods,
Which I have bettered rather than decreased.
Then tell me, if I get your daughter's love
What dowry shall I have with her to wife?

BAPTISTA.   After my death the one half of my lands,

*(PETRUCHIO looks to HORTENSIO to see if this is
enough. HORTENSIO casually rubs a finger against his
nose. In the pause, BAPTISTA decides to up the ante.)*

And in possession twenty thousand crowns.

PETRUCHIO.   And, for that dowry, I'll assure her of
Her widowhood, be it that she survive me,
In all my lands and leases whatsoever.
Let specialities be therefore drawn between us
That covenants may be kept on either hand.

BAPTISTA.   Ay, when the special thing is well obtained,
That is, her love, for that is all in all.

PETRUCHIO.   Why, that is nothing, for I tell you, father,
I am as peremptory as she proud-minded.
And where two raging fires meet together
They do consume the thing that feeds their fury.
Though little fire grows great with little wind,
Yet extreme gusts will blow out fire and all.
So I to her, and so she yields to me,
For I am rough and woo not like a babe.

BAPTISTA.   Well mayst thou woo, and happy to be thy
speed!
But be thou armed for some unhappy words.

PETRUCHIO. Ay, to the proof, as mountains are for winds
That shake not, though they blow perpetually.

BAPTISTA. *(Coolly, under-cutting* PETRUCHIO's *rhetoric)*
Signior Petruchio, will you go with us
Or shall I send my daughter Kate to you?

PETRUCHIO. I pray you do. I'll attend her here
And woo her with some spirit when she comes.

*(*BAPTISTA *exits.)*

*(The three men laugh together, feeling they have success-
fully jumped the first hurdle; then, as if taking
PETRUCHIO through his catechisms, HORTENSIO and
GRUMIO begin to fire questions at him—clearly testing
his grasp of previously learnt information.)*

HORTENSIO. Say that she rail?

PETRUCHIO. Why then I'll tell her plain
She sings as sweetly as a nightingale.

GRUMIO. Say that she frown?

PETRUCHIO. I'll say she looks as clear
As morning roses nearly washed with dew.

HORTENSIO. Say she be mute and will not speak a word?

PETRUCHIO. Then I'll command her volubility
And say she uttereth piercing eloquence.

GRUMIO. If she do bid thee pack?

PETRUCHIO. *(Momentarily stumped, consults rolled-up
piece of paper in his boot)*
I'll give her thanks
As though she bid me stay by her a week.

HORTENSIO. If she deny to wed?

PETRUCHIO. I'll crave the day
When I shall ask the bans and when be married.
But here she comes . . .

*(*HORTENSIO *and* GRUMIO *exit quickly.)*

. . . and now, Petruchio, speak.

(KATE enters; very regal, very composed.
PETRUCHIO is in a self-induced state of contemplation.
KATE waits for him to acknowledge her; as he does not
do so, she begins to leave.)

(After a step or two, PETRUCHIO turns and begins.)

PETRUCHIO. *(Brightly)* Good morrow, Kate, for that's
your name, I hear.

KATE. Well have you heard, but something hard of hearing.
They call me Katherine that do talk of me.

PETRUCHIO. *(Insolently)* You lie, in faith, for you are
called plain Kate,
And bonny Kate, and sometimes Kate the curst.
But *(bright)* Kate, the prettiest Kate in Christendom,
Kate of Kate Hall, my super-dainty Kate,
For dainties are all Kates, and therefore, Kate,
Take this of me, Kate of my consolation.
Hearing thy mildness praised in every town,
Thy virtues spoke of, and thy beauty sounded—
Yet not so deeply as to thee belongs—
Myself am moved to woo thee for my wife.

KATE. Moved! In good time, let him that moved you hither
Remove you hence. I knew you at the first
You were a moveable.

PETRUCHIO. Why, what's a moveable?

KATE. A joint stool.

PETRUCHIO. *(Sitting, jovial)*
Thou hast hit it; come sit on me.

KATE. *(Clever)* Asses are made to bear and so are you.

PETRUCHIO. *(Hard, offensive)*
Women are made to bear and so are you.

KATE. No such jade as you, if me you mean.

PETRUCHIO. *(Lightening)*
Alas, good Kate, I will not burden thee,
For, knowing thee to be but young and light—

KATE. Too light for such a swain as you to catch
And yet as heavy as my weight should be.

PETRUCHIO.   Come, come, you wasp, i' faith you are too
  angry.

KATE.   If I be waspish, best beware my sting.

PETRUCHIO.   My remedy is then to pluck it out.

KATE.   Ay, if the fool could find it where it lies.

PETRUCHIO.   Who knows not where a wasp does wear
  his sting?

  (Vulgarly) In his tail.

KATE.   In his tongue.

PETRUCHIO.   Whose tongue?

KATE.   Yours if you talk of tales and so farewell.

PETRUCHIO.   What, with my tongue in your tail? Nay,
    come again.
  Good Kate, I am a gentleman—

KATE.   That I'll try. *(She strikes him.)*

  *(The slap dissolves all banter. PETRUCHIO looks KATE
  coldly in the eye and begins to speak quietly, in dead
  earnest.)*

PETRUCHIO.   I swear I'll cuff you if you strike again.

KATE.   *(Wary)* So may you lose your arms: If you strike me
    you are no gentleman,
  And if no gentleman, why then no arms.

PETRUCHIO.   *(Makes enormous effort to banish his emnity
  and impose gaiety; kneeling)*
  A herald, Kate? O, put me in thy books.

KATE.   What is your crest? A coxcomb?

PETRUCHIO.   *(Making a straight pass)*
  A combless cock, so Kate will be my hen.

KATE.   No cock of mine; you crow too like a craven.

PETRUCHIO.   Nay, come, Kate, come, you must not look
  so sour.

KATE.   It is my fashion when I see a crab.

PETRUCHIO. *(Finding it difficult to play the game)*
Why, here's no crab, and therefore look not sour.

KATE. There is, there is.

PETRUCHIO. Then show it me.

KATE. Had I a glass I would.

PETRUCHIO. *(Slowly, menacingly, first threat of physical violence)*
What, you mean my face?

KATE. Well aimed of such a young one.

PETRUCHIO. *(Inspecting her hair-line)* Now, by Saint George, I am too young for you.

KATE. Yet you are withered.

PETRUCHIO. 'Tis with cares.

KATE. I care not. *(Starts to go)*

PETRUCHIO. Nay, hear you, Kate, in sooth you scape not so. *(Blocking her way)*

KATE. I chafe you if I tarry. Let me go.

PETRUCHIO. No, not a whit.

(There is a pause during which KATE assesses her situation. Since her path is barred she resolutely decides to remain; turns and sits.)

I find you passing gentle.
'Twas told me you were rough and coy and sullen,
And now I find report a very liar,
For thou art pleasant, gamesome, passing courteous,
But slow in speech, yet sweet as springtime flowers.
Thou canst not frown, thou canst not look askance,
Nor bite the lip as angry wenches will,
Nor hast thou pleasure to be cross in talk,
But thou with mildness entertain'st thy wooers,
With gentle conference, soft and affable.
Why does the world report that Kate doth limp?
O sland'rous world! Kate like the hazel-twig
Is straight and slender, and as brown in hue
As hazelnuts and sweeter than the kernels.
O, let me see thee walk. Thou does't not halt.

KATE. Go, fool and whom thou keep'st command.

PETRUCHIO. *(Falsely cynical)*
Did ever Dian so become a grove
As Kate this chamber with her princely gait?
O, be thou Dian and let her be Kate,
And then let Kate be chaste and Dian sportful!

KATE. Where did you study all this goodly speech?

PETRUCHIO. It is extempore, from my mother-wit.

KATE. A witty mother! Witless else her son.

PETRUCHIO. Am I not wise?

KATE. Yes, keep you warm.
(Starts to go)

PETRUCHIO. Marry, so I mean, sweet Katherine, in thy bed.

(PETRUCHIO grabs KATE's crotch. She is momentarily stunned by the suddennes of this brutish move. Slowly PETRUCHIO takes firm hold of her wrists. There is visible pressure.)

And therefore, setting all this chat aside,
Thus in plain terms: your father hath consented
That you shall be my wife, your dowry 'greed on,
And will you, nill you, I will marry you.

(Enter BAPTISTA, HORTENSIO, GRUMIO)

For I am he am born to tame you, Kate,
And bring you from a wild Kate to a Kate
Conformable as other household Kates.
Here comes your father. Never make denial.
I must and will have Katherine to my wife.

BAPTISTA. Now, Signior Petruchio, how speed you with
my daughter?

PETRUCHIO. *(Suddenly jovial; eyes telling another story to KATE)*
How but well, sir? How but well?
It were impossible I should speed amiss.

BAPTISTA. Why, how now, daughter Katherine, in your
dumps?

KATE. Call you me daughter? Now I promise you
    You have showed a tender fatherly regard
    To wish me wed to one half lunatic,
    A madcap ruffian and a swearing Jack
    That thinks with oaths to face the matter out.

PETRUCHIO. Father, 'tis thus: yourself and all the world
    That talked of her have talked amiss of her.
    If she be curst it is for policy,
    For she's not froward but modest as the dove.
    She is not hot but temperate as the morn;
    For patience she will prove a second Grissel
    And Roman Lucrece for her chastity.
    And to conclude, we have 'greed so well together
    That upon Sunday is the wedding day.

KATE. I'll see thee hanged on Sunday first.

PETRUCHIO. *(Taking* BAPTISTA *round; playing down*
    KATE'*s visible opposition to the match)*
    I tell you, 'tis incredible to believe
    How much she loves me. O, the kindest Kate,
    She hung about my neck, and kiss on kiss
    She vied so fast, protesting oath on oath,
    That in a twink she won me to her love.
    O you are novices. 'Tis a world to see
    How tame, when men and women are alone,
    A meacock wretch can make the curstest shrew.
    Give me thy hand, Kate.

(Holds out hand.)

*(*GRUMIO, *who has worked his way round to* KATE'*s
side, forcibly takes her hand and plants it into*
PETRUCHIO'*s.)*

I will unto Venice
    To buy apparel 'gainst the wedding day.
    Provide the feast, father, and bid the guests;
    I will be sure my Katherine shall be fine

(Hand out to BAPTISTA*)*

BAPTISTA. I know not what to say.

*(*HORTENSIO, *who has worked his way round to*
BAPTISTA'*s side, takes his hand and clamps it*

into PETRUCHIO's.*)*

God send you joy, Petruchio! 'Tis a match.

HORTENSIO and GRUMIO.   Amen, say we.

PETRUCHIO.   Father, and wife, and gentlemen, adieu.
I will to Venice; Sunday comes apace.
We will have rings and things and fine array,
And kiss me Kate; we will be married 'a Sunday.

*(PETRUCHIO moves to kiss KATE. She draws back
instinctively. GRUMIO takes hold of her arms which
prevents her from moving any further back.
PETRUCHIO moves forward, takes KATE's face in his
hands. She goes limp and lifeless as he firmly plants a
kiss on her mouth. When he removes his lips, KATE's
barely perceptible smile suggests that although he can
take things by force, he will never get her willingly to
yield.)*

*(PETRUCHIO receives KATE's look, sensing the
hollowness of his victory.)*

Fade out.

GIRL *(BIANCA now dressed contemporary) strolls out from
centre-doorway. She is smoking a cigarette. Stands looking
off. In a moment,* BOY *(HORTENSIO now dressed in
modern clothes) appears at doorway.* GIRL *turns her head
to register his appearance then turns again and smokes.
Gradually, the* BOY *moves in.*

HE.   You knew I was watching you in there, didn't you?

SHE.   *(Aloof)* Were you?

HE.   Didn't you feel it?

SHE.   Not really.

HE.   I thought you did.

SHE.   Perhaps.

HE.   That's an elusive reply.

SHE.   Elusive?

HE. You're not very easy to pin down.

SHE. Do you want to?

HE. It's an idea.

(Pause. SHE smokes. HE looks for a ploy.)

It's bloody boring in there, isn't it?

SHE. It always is.

HE. Why do you go?

SHE. I don't know. I always expect it to improve.

HE. You're an optimist.

SHE. Why did you come?

HE. *(Suddenly improvising)* My astrology chart said something big was in store for me. 'Expect something strong and fiery to happen that will last a long time.'

SHE. It could be heartburn.

HE. *(Hyping)* Where's your romanticism, your sense of mystery. Don't you believe it's all written in the stars?

SHE. Do you?

HE. Yes, but in very small print. And I'm not even sure it's in English.

SHE. Doesn't seem worth all the trouble then, does it?

HE. Not if you're not a romantic.

SHE. And you are.

HE. President of the Club.

SHE. Very large membership?

HE. Enormous, and lots of celebrities as well. Wasn't it Oscar Wilde, one of our fully paid-up members by the way, who said, I may be lying in the gutter but I'm looking at the stars.

SHE. *Was* he lying in the gutter?

HE. No, I expect he was in a posh Mayfair club with objets d'art on every side and a five-course dinner on the boil. What a charlatan!

SHE. Exactly.

HE. *(Losing the thread)* What do you mean, exactly?

(SHE smiles at him, continues to smoke, and moves a little further off.)

(After a moment, HE takes her hand and begins to study it. This goes on for a while.)

SHE. Do you read palms as well?

HE. Oh yes, and Tarot cards, tea leaves, bumps-on-the-head and, on a good day, even cigarette ash. *(Continues to study hand)*

SHE. Do I pass inspection?

HE. *(Close)* Flying colours.

(They look at each other. SHE touches his cheek. HE makes a move toward her for the embrace. She breaks and walks away casually.)

HE. *(After registering the rebuff)* What do you do?

SHE. As I like. Usually.

HE. Are you doing what you like at the moment?

SHE. At this very moment?

HE. Yes.

SHE. I think so.

HE. And what's that?

SHE. Not very much of anything in particular.

HE. *(Mock-offended)* Is that really the way you'd describe our conversation?

SHE. It's how I'd describe yours.

HE. I think that's what the social psychologists call 'holding your own'.

SHE. I never read them.

HE. *You* don't have to.

(Pause)

SHE.   And you? Are you doing as you like?

HE.   *(A motto)* I never do as I like. I always do as I must.

SHE.   How dreary for you.

HE.   Not at all. It's very good for the soul to 'do as one must'. It develops all kinds of traits like discipline, pride, shrewdness, self-sufficiency . . .

SHE.   Egotism?

HE.   *(Caught)* That's a by-product, I suppose.

SHE.   In rather plentiful supply.

HE.   *(Mask away)* Well, I have to impress you with something. Language is all I have.

SHE.   And even that's somewhat impoverished.

(Pause)

HE.   *(At a loss; tries a new tack)* You know, when you're watching someone for something like two hours across a crowded room, you tend to make up little stories about them. I've got quite a file of stuff about you.

SHE.   Really?

HE.   Born in Surrey—or possibly Hampshire. Father hunts and shoots, dabbles in real estate, wears plus fours. Sent you through boarding school, a year on the continent and then Girton, finishing with a bevy of firsts in lots of esoteric subjects like medieval epistemology or 12th century ceramics. Flat in Kensington, credit account in Dickens and Jones, and a supercharged Fiat all of your very own. Am I getting warm?

SHE.   You're not even tepid.

HE.   I should think the main difference between us is purely economic.

SHE.   Do you mean money?

HE.   Yes.

SHE.   Why don't you say so. 'Economic' is a kind of camouflage-word, isn't it.

HE. 'Money' is so crude.

SHE. Only if you haven't got any.

HE. Touché.

SHE. Were we fencing?

HE. I thought I felt a little nick.

SHE. I'm sorry.

HE. Oh, I don't mind.

SHE. Good. Then I don't have to apologise.

(Pause. HE approaches her, touches her hair, gradually kisses her. SHE yields in the kiss then, as his kiss becomes more familiar, breaks.)

SHE. *(Holding him slightly off. Quietly)* Do you expect sex as a matter of course?

HE. *(Surprised)* Were we talking about sex?

SHE. Weren't you?

HE. *(Admitting it)* I suppose I was.

SHE. Do you?

HE. As a matter of course. No. Of course not. It never is a matter of course.

SHE. It isn't with me. I thought it would be fairer to let you know.

HE. *(Dryly)* Thanks.

SHE. You're welcome. *(SHE kisses him hard. HE reels slightly recovering from the clinch)* You're very nice. Even if you are a bit of a clot. *(Moves away)*

HE. I suppose I had better take that as a compliment.

SHE. The one thing that all men have in common is the ability to produce great billowing waves of boredom. Lately, one way and another, I seem to have got quite drenched.

HE. Now, women are never boring. Being beautiful, they never risk boredom by ever using their minds.

SHE.   But not all women are beautiful. Some are quite plain.

HE.   *(Off-hand)* Yes, those are the boring ones.

SHE.   Doesn't beauty ever get boring?

HE.   Never.

SHE.   Not even ten years afterward—twenty, thirty years afterward?

HE.   Not if it's *real* beauty.

SHE.   Real beauty, as you call it, has the alarming tendency to turn into *real* old age, and there's nothing beautiful about that.

HE.   But why should you be worrying about that, being as beautiful as you are.

SHE.   *(Regards him wryly for a moment)* You get to the pictures quite a bit, don't you?

HE.   *(Assuming the ice is now broken; levelling)* I watched you all night long in there. Staring like a bloody owl. Don't tell me you didn't notice.

SHE.   I'm not sure.

HE.   You don't kiss like you're not sure.

SHE.   Are you sure you're not jumping to conclusions?

HE.   Do you think I am?

SHE.   I think . . . *(Suddenly playing the grand lady)* you're a very forward youth.

HE.   *(Playing the game, curtsies)* Your humble servant, m'lady.

SHE.   You may kiss my foot.

(In character, HE *does so.* SHE *then extends hand, he kisses that. She extends finger, he kisses that.)*

That will do, thank you.

HE.   Thank you, m'lady. Much obliged, m'lady. *(Jumps up)* Look, I've got a 1964 Austin outside and a back-and-doubles route to Paddington where a bottle of vintage bubbly is cooling in the fridge. *(Displays keys)* How say you?

SHE.   *(Remote, but not aggressive)* I've got to be going.

HE. What?

(SHE goes.)

Why? Look, can I ring you? Can I have your number?

SHE. *(At doorway)* I'm sorry. I have to make a very early start in the morning.

(SHE leaves. HE stands flustered facing doorway.)

Black out.

A bell tolls grimly in the distance.

Lights up on KATE, standing motionless like a doll, wearing a simple white shift; eyes straight ahead; a vague sense of being the victim of some grim, unwanted social ceremony.

Upstage right of her stands BIANCA holding bridal veil. Upstage left, GRUMIO. Downstage left, BAPTISTA, supervising the ceremony. As the bell tolls mournfully, HORTENSIO slowly comes forward holding KATE's bridal gown open before him. He stops in front of her; GRUMIO steps behind her; KATE's arms are lifted straight out as if they were those of a mechanical doll. Together HORTENSIO and GRUMIO slip her into the bridal gown. When this is done, BIANCA comes forward and places the bridal veil over KATE's head. All four then regard her from their respective corners. KATE turns her head to BAPTISTA who nods his approval. The bell stops tolling, full lights come up and the formality of the previous scene suddenly evaporates. BIANCA and GRUMIO exit. BAPTISTA crosses angrily downstage and KATE, irritably upstage.

BAPTISTA. *(To GRUMIO)* This is the 'pointed day
    That Katherine and Petruchio should be married,
    And yet we hear not of our son-in-law.
    What will be said? What mockery will it be
    To want the bridegroom when the priest attends
    To speak the ceremonial rites of marriage!
    What says Litio to this shame of ours?

KATE. No shame but mine. I must, forsooth, be forced
    To give my hand opposed against my heart
    Unto a mad-brain rudesby, full of spleen,
    Who wooed in haste and means to wed at leisure.
    I told you, I, he was a frantic fool,

Hiding his bitter jests in blunt behaviour.
And to be noted for a merry man,
He'll woo a thousand, 'point the day of marriage,
Make friends, invite, and proclaim the banns,
Yet never means to wed where he hath wooed.

HORTENSIO.   Patience, good Katherine, and Baptista too.
Upon my life, Petruchio means but well,
Whatever fortune stays him from his word
Though he be blunt, I know him passing wise;
Though he be merry, yet withal he's honest.

KATE.   Would Katherine had never seen him though!

(Exit)

GRUMIO.   *(Entering, pretending shock)*
Why, Petruchio is coming.

*(PETRUCHIO enters, dressed in a sumptuous female
bridal gown, similar to KATE's. No female wig; no hat;
masculine head on female form.)*

PETRUCHIO.   Come, where be these gallants? Who's at home?

BAPTISTA.   You are welcome, sir.

PETRUCHIO.   And yet I come not well.

GRUMIO.   And yet you halt not.

BAPTISTA.   Not so well appareled
As I wish you were.

PETRUCHIO.   But where is Kate? Where is my lovely bride?
Gentles, methinks you frown.
And wherefore gaze this goodly company
As if they saw some wondrous monument,
Some comet or unusual prodigy?
How does my father?

BAPTISTA.   Why, sir, you know this is your wedding day.
First were we sad, fearing you would not come,
Now sadder that you come so unprovided.
Fie, doff this habit, shame to your estate,
An eyesore to our solemn festival.

GRUMIO.   *(Faking outrage)*

> And tell us what occasion of import
> Hath all so long detained you from your wife
> And sent you hither so unlike yourself.

PETRUCHIO.   Tedious it were to tell and harsh to hear.
Sufficeth, I am come to keep my word
But where is Kate? I stay too long from her.
The morning wears, 'tis time we were at church.

HORTENSIO.   *(Faking outrage)* See not your bride in
these unreverent robes.

GRUMIO.   Go to my chamber; put on clothes of mine.

PETRUCHIO.   Not I, believe me; thus I'll visit her.

BAPTISTA.   But thus, I trust, you will not marry her.

PETRUCHIO.   *(Sudden outburst)*
Good sooth, even thus; therefore ha' done with words.
To me she's married, not unto my clothes.
But what a fool am I to chat with you
When I should bid good morrow to my bride
And seal the title with a lovely kiss.

*(KATE re-enters followed by bridesmaid—BIANCA.
She stops as she sees PETRUCHIO in dress. All stand
anticipating her reaction. PETRUCHIO slowly turns
and confronts KATE. Then, making no attempt to
conceal the male within the female attire, walks very
slowly towards KATE. When he arrives before her, he
suddenly performs an unexpected female curtsey,
abruptly defuses the charged atmosphere and places
himself beside his bride.)*

PETRUCHIO.   Gentlemen and friends, I thank you for your pains.
I know you think to dine with me today
And have prepared great store of wedding cheer,
But so it is, my haste doth call me hence
And therefore here I mean to take my leave.

BAPTISTA.   Is't possible you will away tonight?

PETRUCHIO.   I must away today, before night come.
Make it no wonder; if you knew my business,
You would entreat me rather go than stay.
And, honest company, I thank you all

That have beheld me give myself away
To this most patient, sweet, and virtuous wife.
Dine with my father, drink a health to me,
For I must hence, and farewell to you all.

(Shakes hands with HORTENSIO, GRUMIO,
BAPTISTA *and begins to move off.)*

GRUMIO.   Let us entreat you stay till after dinner.

PETRUCHIO.   It may not be.

HORTENSIO.   Let me entreat you.

PETRUCHIO.   It cannot be.

KATE.   Let me entreat you.

*(*PETRUCHIO *still facing away, halts.)*

PETRUCHIO.   I am content.

KATE.   Are you content to stay?

PETRUCHIO.   *(Turning to* KATE*)*
I am content you shall entreat me stay,
But yet not stay, entreat me how you can.

KATE.   Now if you love me, stay.

*(*PETRUCHIO *approaches* KATE *slowly and, when
close, pretends to call to* GRUMIO *for horse—although
the double-entendre insult to* KATE *is registered by
all.)*

PETRUCHIO.   My horse!

KATE.   *(Fiery-hot)* Nay, then
Do what thou canst, I will not go today,
No, nor tomorrow, not till I please myself.
The door is open, sir, there lies your way.
You may be jogging whilst your boots are green;
For me, I'll not be gone until I please myself.

PETRUCHIO.   O Kate, content thee; prithee, be not angry.

KATE.   I will be angry. What hast thou to do?
Father, be quiet; he shall stay my leisure.
Gentlemen, forward to the bridal dinner.
I see a woman may be made a fool
If she had not a spirit to resist.

THE SHREW

PETRUCHIO. They shall go forward, Kate, at thy
              command.
  Obey the bride, you that attend on her.
  Go to the feast, revel and domineer,
  Carouse full measure to her maidenhead,
  Be mad and marry, or go hang yourselves.
  But for my bonny Kate, she must with me.
  I will be master of what is mine own.

(During the following speech, PETRUCHIO *slowly
strips off bridal gown, revealing his male attire
underneath.)*

  She is my goods, my chattels; she is my house,
  My household stuff, my field, my barn,
  My horse, my ox, my ass, my anything,
  And here she stands. Touch her whoever dare,
  I'll bring mine action on the proudest he
  That stops my way in Padua.

*(*PETRUCHIO *grabs* KATE's *arm and starts to usher
her out. She manages a momentary halt at the
doorway during which she glowers at a helpless
*BAPTISTA *and then is briskly removed.*

BAPTISTA *makes an instinctive move towards the
doorway to come to* KATE's *aid but* GRUMIO
steps down to bar his path. BAPTISTA *thinks better
of it and moves to* BIANCA. *She turns away from him
coldly. Visibly drenched with guilt and uncertain,
*BAPTISTA *moves to opposite exit and out.* GRUMIO
turns upstage and looks to where KATE *and*
PETRUCHIO *have exited.*
HORTENSIO *steps down and coolly addresses
BIANCA.)

HORTENSIO. Mistress, what's your opinion of your sister?

BIANCA. *(Grimly, but secretly pleased)* That being mad
  herself, she is madly mated.

(An inscrutable look to HORTENSIO.*)*

Black out.

Lights up. The BOY *and* GIRL *confronting each other.*

HE. Were you just trying it on?

SHE. Trying what on?

HE. Come on, don't play games.

SHE. I don't know what you're on about.

HE. You were cooped up with that guy for almost three hours. I might just as well have been the hatstand.

SHE. Oh for God's sake. You're not going to get up tight because of that.

HE. How would you like to hang around at a party for over three hours, drinking lousy wine, and making small talk while the person you're supposed to be with is snuggling in some remote corner of the room. That's your idea of companionship, is it?

SHE. We weren't snuggling—we were discussing. You make it sound as if he was having me on the carpet.

HE. He might just as well have done.

SHE. Oh come on . . . we're both out of kindergarten.

HE. That's not the point.

SHE. Well it escapes me.

HE. Lots of things seem to escape you these days.

SHE. Look. The boy had read a book I'd just finished. He had opinions about it. They were interesting, different from mine, and we just discussed it. Now since when did that become a capital offence?

HE. And my line of conversation is just too dreary to bother about.

SHE. We're always conversing. You don't go to a party to pick up the threads of pillow talk from the night before, do you? I thought you seemed quite interested in that bleached blonde. How did I know you were suffering?

HE. She wasn't bleached and I wasn't suffering. If a guy brings a girl to a party, there's usually some kind of vague understanding that they're together.

SHE. Thanks for the tip. Next time I'll wear a sign: 'Property of . . .'

HE. I don't mean that.

SHE. I know exactly what you mean. It's just that grotty old background exerting its traditional pull, isn't it? 'She's mine. I'm hers.' Public, neon-lit togetherness.

HE. You make it sound like some horrible crime to want to be with the girl you're engaged to.

SHE. Not a horrible crime—just a niggling little lapse of taste.

HE. Are we engaged or aren't we?

SHE. Yes, I suppose we are.

HE. That's not the kind of thing that's usually up in the air. Either we are or we aren't.

SHE. We are, but I don't like to make a public issue out of it.

HE. What's that supposed to mean?

SHE. I mean 'engaged' 'betrothed' 'spoken for' . . . they're words that make me wriggle inside. Like being stamped with a branding iron.

HE. You mean we're not engaged.

SHE. We're in love, isn't that enough?

HE. People in love usually get engaged.

SHE. All right, we're engaged.

HE. *(Exasperated)* I don't know where I am with you.

SHE. *(Goes to him; a peace-making move)* Don't let's quarrel about something as silly as this.

HE. *(In her arms)* If I didn't love you, I wouldn't give two hoots who you were holed up in a corner with; don't you see that?

SHE. I do. You're really sweet.

HE. *(Breaking away)* Now I feel like I'm being bribed with candy.

SHE. *(Irritable)* Nothing seems to satisfy you tonight.

HE. *(Hot)* Are you trying to tell me you were only fascinated by that guy's brains.

SHE. No, I was helplessly infatuated with his physique. In between quotations from Freud and Adler, he told me he had a camel parked outside and invited me to spend the rest of my life as a slave in his harem.

HE. Very funny.

SHE. Not as funny as the look on your face.

HE. The way I was brought up, if you loved someone, you thought of spending at least part of your life with her.

SHE. *(Wearying)* It's a little late for nostalgia about 'the good old days' and the 'little old shack by the railway track'.

HE. Every time I bring up the subject you just shy away. I mean are we or aren't we. Are we together or just . . .

SHE. If you say 'ships passing in the night' I'll scream.

HE. You don't want to be tied down. Admit it.

SHE. Does anyone? I mean besides heiffers and bondage-pervs?

HE. What the hell are we doing with each other?

SHE. *(Taking him round)* Why do you keep demanding answers all the time?

HE. Because I'm bothered by questions. You don't seem to be bothered by anything.

SHE. I'm bothered by seeing you tied up in knots like this. Look, I'm sorry if I offended you tonight. I didn't mean to. I got involved in a conversation that interested me, and, well, I suppose I neglected you. I'm sorry about that. Really.

HE *(Contrite, back in her arms)* I'm just being a grouch—as usual.

SHE. *(Baby-talking)* Big bad grouch.

HE. I heard little flashes of all that hyper-intellectual stuff all night, and I suppose I just got angry because I was, well, barred.

SHE.   We have much more interesting things to do.

HE.   I'm just being a clot.

SHE.   Big grouchy clot. *(They kiss, then remain in each other's arms)*

HE.   *(Quietly)* Can you stay tonight?

SHE.   I've got to be at dad's in the morning.

HE.   I can run you back. Before work.

SHE.   Do you think you'll have the energy?

HE.   That's up to you.

SHE.   Then I doubt it.

HE.   I'm sorry about all that stupid stuff . . .

SHE.   Shh . . . *(Kisses him quiet.)*

HE.   I was just being. . .

SHE.   A clot. I know. *(Kisses him.)*

HE.   Is everything okay?

SHE.   *(Taking his hand)* Come on.

(Fade out.)

Lights up.

PETRUCHIO's *house. Very dark. Very Gothic. Sparse wooden table. Three stools.*

PETRUCHIO's *voice is heard offstage.*

PETRUCHIO.   Where be these knaves?

(PETRUCHIO, dusty from his travels, enters; KATE behind.)

What, no man at door
To hold my stirrup nor to take my horse?
Where is Nathaniel, Gregory, Philip?

159

What, no attendance? No regard? No duty?
Where is the foolish knave I sent before?

GRUMIO. *(Wearing mask of gnarled brutish servant)*
Here sir, as foolish as I was before.

PETRUCHIO. You peasant swain! You whoreson malt-horse
drudge!
Go, rascal, go and fetch my supper in.

(Exit GRUMIO.)

Sit down, Kate, and welcome.

*(PETRUCHIO sits at head of table awaiting service. A
long pause during which his irritation grows then erupts
suddenly and pounds table.)*

Food, Food, FOOD!!!

*(HORTENSIO, also wearing ugly, gnarled servant's mask,
enters.)*

Why, when I say?—Nay, good sweet Kate, sit down.
Off with my boots, you rogue, you villain!

(HORTENSIO goes to remove PETRUCHIO's boot.)

(Sings) 'It was the friar of orders, gray,
As he forth walked on his way'—
Out, you rogue, you pluck my foot awry!

*(PETRUCHIO kicks HORTENSIO and sends him
sprawling. Eventually exits.)*

Be merry, Kate. Some water here! What ho!

(Suddenly aware of absence, looking about furtively)

Where are my slippers? Shall I have some water?

(HORTENSIO re-enters with bowl.)

Come, Kate, and wash, and welcome heartily.

(HORTENSIO drops bowl.)

You whoreson villain, will you let it fall?

*(PETRUCHIO twists HORTENSIO's arm behind his
back, visibly inflicting severe pain.)*

KATE. Patience, I pray you. 'Twas a fault unwilling.

PETRUCHIO. A whoreson, beetle-headed, flap-eared
knave!

GRUMIO. *(Off)* The tailor now stays thy leisure.

*(GRUMIO, now dressed as tailor and without
servant's mask, enters carrying garments.
HORTENSIO scampers out.)*

PETRUCHIO. Come, tailor, let us see these ornaments.
What news with you, sir?

GRUMIO. Here is the cap your worship did bespeak.

PETRUCHIO. *(Taking the hat in his hand and examining
it; slowly developing dissatisfaction)*
Why, this was moulded on a porringer—
A velvet dish. Fie, fie, 'tis lewd and filthy.
Why, 'tis a cockle or a walnut shell,
A knack, a toy, a trick, a baby's cap.
Away with it. *(Tosses hat aside)* Come, let me have
bigger.

KATE. *(Picking up hat)* I'll have no bigger.
This doth fit the time,
And gentlewomen wear such caps as these.

PETRUCHIO. When you are gentle you shall have one too
And not till then.

KATE. *(Suddenly brazen)*
Why, sir, I trust I may have leave to speak,
And speak I will. I am no child, no babe.
Your betters have endured me say my mind,
And if you cannot, best you stop your ears.
My tongue will tell the anger of my heart,
Or else my heart, concealing it, will break,
And rather than it shall I will be free
Even to the uttermost, as I please, in words.

PETRUCHIO. Why, thou sayest true. It is a paltry cap,
I love thee well in that thou lik'st it not.

KATE. Love me or love me not, I like the cap,
And it I will have or I will have none.

PETRUCHIO. *(Tearing hat in two)*
> Thy gown? Why, aye. Come, let us see't.

(Examining the dress; slowly turning critical)

> O mercy, God! What masking stuff is here?
> What's this? A sleeve? Tis like a demi-cannon.
> What, up and down, carved like an apple-tart?
> Why, what, a devil's name tailor, call'st thou this?

GRUMIO. You bid me make it orderly and well,
> According to the fashion and the time.

PETRUCHIO. I did not bid you mar it to the time.
> Go, hop me over every kennel home,
> For you shall hop without my custom.
> I'll none of it. Hence, make your best of it.
> *(Throws dress down)*

KATE. *(Picks up dress)*
> I never saw a better-fashioned gown.
> More quaint, more pleasing, nor more commendable.
> Belike you mean to make a puppet of me.

PETRUCHIO. *(Suddenly aware of the tailor's diabolical
> purpose, turns on him threateningly)*
> Why true, he means to make a puppet of thee.

GRUMIO. *(Cowering at PETRUCHIO's approach)*
> She says your worship means to make a puppet of her.

PETRUCHIO. O monstrous arrogance!
> Braved in my own house with a skein of thread!
> Away, thou rag, thou quantity, thou remnant
> Or I shall so bemete thee with thy yard
> As thou shalt think on prating whilst thou liv'st.
> I tell thee, I, that thou hast marred her gown.

GRUMIO. Your worship is deceived. The gown is made
> Just as my master had direction.

PETRUCHIO. Go take it hence; be gone and say no
more.

*(GRUMIO, as tailor, fearfully snatches gown and
hurriedly exits.)*

PETRUCHIO. *(Pleasantly)* Come, come, Kate, sit down.

(KATE does not stir. PETRUCHIO, no longer pleasant, icily repeats.)

S i t   d o w n.

(KATE stands glowering for a moment and then sits. Immediately PETRUCHIO becomes genial once more.)

Some food here! Ho! I know you have a stomach.

(HORTENSIO, wearing mask of servant, enters with platter, places it on table and steps back. KATE, who is clearly hungry, makes a move towards the platter. PETRUCHIO's hand reaches it first, preventing KATE from removing the lid.)

Will you give thanks, sweet Kate, or else shall I?

(Proceeds to say grace while KATE waits. After a moment, he raises the lid of the platter.)

What's this? Mutton?

HORTENSIO. Ay.

PETRUCHIO. 'Tis burnt, and so is all the meat.
What dogs are these! Where is the rascal cook?
How durst you, villains, bring it from the dresser,
And serve it thus to me that love it not?
There, take it to you, trenchers, cups, and all.

(Sweeps the platter off the table and then turns the table over in one swift, violent movement. HORTENSIO picks up all the pieces and exits hurriedly.)

KATE. I pray you, husband, be not so disquiet,
The meat was well if you were so contented.

PETRUCHIO. I tell thee, Kate, 'twas burnt and dried away.
And I expressly am forbid to touch it,
For it engenders choler, planteth anger,
And better 'twere that both of us did fast—
Since of ourselves, ourselves are choleric—
Than feed it with such over-roasted flesh.
Be patient. Tomorrow't shall be mended,
And for this night we'll fast for company.
Come, I will show thee to thy bridal chamber.

*(PETRUCHIO claps his hands twice and after a
moment, HORTENSIO and GRUMIO, still disguised as
servants, enter and stand waiting by the door.
PETRUCHIO gestures in the direction of the bridal
chamber. KATE hesitates for a moment and then, still
composed, moves slowly towards the exit. As she
nears the servants, she stops and peers into their faces;
i.e. HORTENSIO's and GRUMIO's masks. Then holding
her head erect, she continues her progress out. The two
servants look up to PETRUCHIO and smile slowly.
PETRUCHIO returns their smile. Slowly, they turn and
follow in the direction of KATE.)*

*PETRUCHIO then turns to the audience and, revealing
for the first time an overt psychopathic manner, begins
to speak.*

PETRUCHIO.   Thus have I politicly begun my reign,
    And 'tis my hope to end successfully.
    My falcon now is sharp and passing empty,
    And till she stoop she must not be full gorged,
    For then she never looks upon her lure.
    Another way I have to man my haggard,
    To make her come and know her keeper's call,
    That is, to watch her as we watch these kites
    That bate and beat and will not be obedient.
    She eat no meat today, nor none shall eat.
    Last night she slept not, nor tonight she shall not.
    As with the meat, some undeserved fault
    I'll find about the making of the bed,
    And here I'll fling the pillow, there the bolster,
    This way the coverlet, another way the sheets.
    Ay, and amid this hurly I intend
    That all is done in reverent care of her,
    And in conclusion she shall watch all night.
    And if she chance to nod I'll rail and brawl
    And with the clamour keep her still awake.
    And thus I'll curb her mad and headstrong humour.
    He that knows better how to tame a shrew,
    Now let him speak—'tis charity to show.

(Fade out.)

THE SHREW

Lights up: BOY *and* GIRL *shouting simultaneously.*

HE.   For Christ's sake, will you shut up!

SHE.   Why? Afraid of what the neighbours might say?
Typical working-class angst.

HE.   Don't start all that psychoanalytical crap. My id, my
ego, my angst. My ass!

SHE.   *(In check)* You wouldn't be you without the spite
and the four letter words.

HE.   Cunt!

SHE.   *(Patronizing)* Go on . . . go on.

HE.   Shithead! That's eight letters.

SHE.   *(Objective)* God, are you pathetic.

HE.   And here comes the patronization—right on schedule.
You're so logical, I'm so infantile . . .

SHE.   And obnoxious!
HE.   . . . obnoxious.

SHE.   and a bore!⟩
HE.   . . . a bore. ⟨—Why don't you put it on tape. All you'd
have to do is flip a switch.

(Pause. SHE *withdraws.)*

SHE.   You really enjoy these sessions, don't you? Your
perversity feeds on them.

HE.   *(On the true subject)* Get the fucking halter off my neck.
If I want serfdom, I'll go to Siberia. I'll put my head
on the block. I can see anyone I like!

SHE.   And sleep with anyone you like!?

HE.   Look baby, if you walked into a room and saw me
holding hands with a nun, you'd assume I just polished
her off on the font.

SHE.   *(Cold)* How odious can you get?

HE.   I don't know. Depends how long I live.

SHE.   You can soil yourself as much as you like—with

whomever you like—all I ask is that you don't lie and play the innocent.

HE. No, but you can screw around as much as you like.

SHE. I may see men; I may even get to like them, but I don't, in your elegant phrase, 'screw around'. I'm not that ravenous—nor that indiscriminate.

HE. No, you just have mind-fucks.

SHE. *(Close to tears)* I don't betray you with every pimply youth that whistles at me in the street.

HE. *(Defending himself)* I tell you that kid is . . . just a kid. She's just cokes, joke-books and bad rock music.

SHE. Then why let her do this to us?

HE. Do what, for Christ's sake? You're the only one that's doing anything, and you've been doing it for months. *(A beat. Self-recognition.)* Do you have any idea how ridiculous you make me feel? Forcing me to adopt attitudes that are just . . . assinine!

SHE. Do you think I enjoy this? Do you think I want my eyes to look like plum-puddings every morning?

HE. *(Takes her round)* Oh, for God's sake, baby.

SHE. *(Yielding)* Why do you do it, why?

HE. *(Trying to cool it)* Look, we can't live in each other's pockets. You don't want the kind of love where people melt into each other like grilled cheese. There's you and there's me. That's one and one.

SHE. But that makes two, doesn't it?

HE. Look, baby, you know what I feel about you.

SHE. *(Coldly, breaking away)* Let's not recite the catechisms, shall we? I know what *you* feel and you know what *I* feel—so where does that leave us? I want something I can hold on to. Something I can be sure of. Something I can put in the bank.

HE. *(Not wanting to start again)* Banks fail.

SHE. And us? Have we failed too?

HE. *(After a tell-tale moment, hugs her close)* No, for Christ's sake, we'll go on forever, like The Merry Widow.

(Physical contact gradually relaxes both of them.)

SHE. *(In the embrace)* Promise me you won't see her again.

(HE tightens the embrace desperately to avoid the issue.)

SHE. Please. Promise.

HE. *(Bursting away)* Can't you see what you're doing?

SHE. *(Hurt by the suddenness of the rupture)* What am I doing that's so horrible? Asking for a show of loyalty while you insist everything be taken on trust!?

HE. Why the hell can't you take it on trust?

SHE. Why should I? If you mean what you say, why should I?

HE. There's that sound again. That bloody rack winching away!

SHE. If you had any real decency in you . . .

HE. *(Roused)* You mean 'breeding', don't you? I know all your bloody euphemisms by heart.

SHE. All right, breeding. Is that such a liability in a person? A little breeding; a little sense of honour; a little sense of, yes laugh your head off, chivalry. Respect for things, for people, for vows. Is it so outrageous to want a life with a little dignity attached.

HE. *(Calm)* I can just see your father singing 'God Save the Queen' with that constipated look of patriotism twisting the muscles in his stupid face.

SHE. *(Objective)* You are such filth.

HE. Shit, baby, not filth! You can wash filth, but shit stains and smells and corrodes, and that's what you mean isn't it. I'm the Old Shit-Shoveller From The Smelly Suburbs and you're the Fine Lady that's getting her skirts all messed up.

SHE. *(Studying him)* You do this deliberately. You come close just so you can take aim. Just so you can kick me in the teeth.

HE. *(Repentant)* No . . . no . . . no . . .

SHE. That's your pleasure. That's your high. *(Cries.)*

HE. *(Comforting)* Please, please—don't turn me into the ogre you have in your head. It's not me. It's not. I'm trying to love you. I am.

SHE. *(Through tears)* You're not. You're sick of it. You want it dead. You want me dead.

HE. *(In her arms)* No, no baby. I love you; I love you.

SHE. *(Through tears)* No respect.

HE. *(Trying to jolly her out of it)* Come on; come on. Baby, baby.

(HE kisses her—forcing her to return. The embrace becomes hot, frantic. They move to the floor. Then in a respite . . .)

SHE. Will you promise? Will you?

(To obliterate his reaction, HE pushes further into the kiss; into the physical reality of The Girl. SHE stiffens, fights him off. They struggle between passion and contempt. She pulls more forcibly out of the embrace. Instinctively, he slaps her hard. There is a moment of nothing. SHE on the floor, looking into his eyes. He tries to make it up with more physical contact. She is an iceberg. Eventually, he releases himself from her. She gathers herself together, moves away from him and lights a cigarette.)

SHE. *(Incongruously sensible)* Look, this is silly. I mean apart from being hurtful and miserable, it's also silly. What's the point? The biggest waste in the world is trying to change people You don't want it. I don't want it. Why go on?

HE. *(Clocking the inference)* Sometimes you talk as if we met ten minutes ago—the result of some hideous computer-dating system—and all we have to do is shake hands and say goodnight, and that's it. I know we don't go back to the Flood, but we do have a kind of history. Things have happened between us. We're not strangers.

SHE. *(After a puff)* Aren't we?

HE. *(Hot)* No, we're not! I know you inside out.

SHE. *(Refusing to fall into the pattern)* I think we should give it a rest.

HE. Stop talking as if we were a bloody dance-act.

SHE. We just confuse each other. *You* don't understand; *I* don't understand. It's just one big bloody misunderstanding. Let's take some time out. Maybe it will clear itself up.

HE. *(Pause)* Is that your gracious way of saying bugger off.

SHE. No. It's trying to deal sensibly with a situation that's becoming nonsensical. You have to admit it is.

HE. I don't have to admit anything, and don't hose me down with all that 'sweet reason' like I was some kind of head-case.

SHE. You see what I mean. You *think* that but I don't *mean* that.

HE. Look . . .

SHE. One of us has to be sensible.

HE. And sure enough, it'll be you. Your reliable old level-headedness will come galloping to the rescue.

SHE' *(Non-combative)* I'm not going to fight with you.

HE. *(Getting close)* Look, I'm sorry about that. *(Referring to the slap)* And as for the other thing, it's not what you think at all. Not at all.

SHE. *(Pacific)* It doesn't matter. Really.

HE. *(Despising her cool)* It mattered a helluva lot five minutes ago.

SHE. *(Unemotional)* I'm sorry. I was a little hysterical.

HE. Let's not play The Sorry Game because you know

I always wind up sorrier than you.

SHE. *(Utterly reasonable)* I don't want to play any game. *(Checks watch.)* I have to make an early start tomorrow.

(HE scoffs to himself, remembering when he heard that line before.)

HE. *(Hungry)* Stay tonight.

SHE. *(Not wanting to be cruel)* No, not tonight.

HE. *(Sorry he weakened)* I'm not going to beg, dammit.

SHE. I don't expect you to. *(Pause. Cigarette out.)* I'd better go.

HE. *(Tries to stop her with a move)* Look . . .

(SHE stops, fully composed, looks.)

HE. *(After a pause; no more moves to play)* You better go.

(SHE kisses him lightly, meaninglessly on the cheek, and moves off.)

HE. *(When she's gone)* I'll call you.

(Fade out.)

Lights up. KATE, *her head on her arm, slumped over table.* GRUMIO *sits whittling across from her. After a moment,* KATE *awakens, looks around, remembers where she is. Her face is white with hunger. Her wedding-dress, in tatters.*

KATE. What, did he marry me to famish me?
Beggars that come unto my father's door,
Upon entreaty have at present alms;
If not, elsewhere they meet with charity.
But I, who never knew how to entreat
Nor never needed that I should entreat,
Am starved for meat, giddy for lack of sleep,
With oaths kept waking and with brawling fed.

(Suddenly sees GRUMIO *sitting opposite.)*

I prithee go and get me some repast,
I care not what, so it be wholesome food.

GRUMIO. *(Facing away from her)*
What say you to a neat's foot?

KATE. I prithee let me have it.

GRUMIO. I fear it is too choleric a meat.
How say you to a fat tripe finely broiled?

KATE. I like it well. Good Grumio, fetch it me.

GRUMIO. I cannot tell, I fear 'tis choleric.
What say you to a piece of beef and mustard?

KATE. A dish that I do love to feed upon.

GRUMIO. Ay, but the mustard is too hot a little.

KATE. Why then, the beef, and let the mustard rest.

GRUMIO. Nay then, I will not. You shall have the
mustard
Or else you get no beef of Grumio.

KATE. Then both or one, or anything thou wilt.

GRUMIO. *(Turns full to* KATE*)*
Why then, the mustard without the beef.

KATE. *(Realizing she has been cruelly toyed with)*
Go, get thee gone, thou false deluding slave,
Thou feed'st me with the very name of meat.
Sorrow on thee and all the pack of you
That triumph thus upon my misery.
Go, get thee gone, I say.

(Enter PETRUCHIO *and* HORTENSIO *with meat.)*

PETRUCHIO. How fares my Kate? What, sweeting, all amort?

*(*PETRUCHIO *gives* GRUMIO *his next disguise, a wig
and stick.* GRUMIO *nods and quietly slips out.)*

HORTENSIO. Mistress, what cheer?

KATE. Faith, as cold as can be.

PETRUCHIO. Pluck up thy spirits; look cheerfully upon me.
Here, love, thou seest how diligent I am
To dress thy meat myself and bring it thee.
I am sure, sweet Kate, this kindness merits thanks

171

What, not a word? Nay then, thou lov'st it not,
And all my pains is sorted to no proof.
Here, take away this dish.

*(HORTENSIO begins to remove dish; KATE
desperately lurches towards it.)*

KATE. I pray you, let it stand.

PETRUCHIO.   The poorest service is repaid with thanks,
And so shall mine before you touch the meat.

KATE.   *(Glowering, consumed with hatred, forcing herself
to mouth the words)*
I thank you, sir.

HORTENSIO.   Signior Petruchio, fie, you are to blame.
Come, Mistress Kate, I'll bear you company.

*(Sits and begins eating. KATE suddenly pulled up and
away from table by PETRUCHIO.)*

PETRUCHIO.   And now, my honey love,
Will we return unto thy father's house
And revel it as bravely as the best,
With silken coats and caps and golden rings,
With ruffs and cuffs and fardingales and things,
With scarves and fans and double change of brav'ry,
With amber bracelets, beads, and all this knav'ry.

*(HORTENSIO having consumed chicken leg tosses it to
floor. It lands at PETRUCHIO's feet.)*

PETRUCHIO.   What, hast thou dined?

*(PETRUCHIO kicks the bone off just as a desperate
KATE makes a lurch to pick it up.)*

PETRUCHIO.   Well, come, my Kate, we will unto your father's,
Even in these honest mean habilments.
Our purses shall be proud, our garments poor,
For 'tis the mind that makes the body rich,
And as the sun breaks through the darkest clouds
So honour peereth in the meanest habit.
(To HORTENSIO) Go call my men, and let us
straight to him;
And bring our horses unto Long-lane end.

There will we mount and thither walk on foot.
Let's see, I think 'tis now some seven o'clock,
And well we may come there by dinnertime.

KATE.   I do assure you, sir, 'tis almost two,
And 'twill be suppertime ere you come there.

PETRUCHIO.   It shall be seven ere I go to horse.
Look what I speak or do or think to do.
You are still crossing it. Sirs, let't alone:
I will not go today, and ere I do,
It shall be what o'clock I say it is.

*(PETRUCHIO deliberately sits himself down and
stubbornly stares straight ahead. HORTENSIO,
realizing his master must be humoured, does likewise.
KATE regards the two immobile men sitting stock
still and facing outward. It all becomes too much for
her. She slumps onto her stool, her head falling onto
her arm on the table. PETRUCHIO, retaining his
posture, darts a look at her from the corner of his eye,
then returns to his obdurate pose. Then, without
warning, jumps up gaily and begins trotting as if he
were on horseback.)*

PETRUCHIO.   Come on, in God's name, once more to
our father's.

*(HORTENSIO rises, pulls KATE up from her stool,
and places her between PETRUCHIO and himself.
Then HORTENSIO also begins to trot in place as if
on horseback. KATE, bewildered, regards both men.
HORTENSIO makes a sign to her that she should
humour PETRUCHIO by trotting as well. After a
moment, KATE, who is confused and exhausted,
makes a feeble effort to trot along with the two
men.)*

PETRUCHIO.   Good Lord, how bright and goodly shines the
moon.

KATE.   The moon? The sun. It is not moonlight now.

PETRUCHIO.   I say it is the moon that shines so bright.

KATE.   I know it is the sun that shines so bright.

PETRUCHIO. *(Frantic outburst)*
> Now, by my mother's son, and that's myself,
> It shall be moon or star or what I list,
> Or ere I journey to your father's house.
> *(To* HORTENSIO*)*
> Go on and fetch our horses back again.

> *(Stops trotting and angrily walks off brooding and smouldering.)*

> Evermore crossed and crossed, nothing but crossed!

HORTENSIO. *(To* KATE*)* Say as he says or we shall never go.

KATE. *(Confused)*
> Forward, I pray, since we have come so far,
> And be it moon or sun or what you please.

> *(*PETRUCHIO *debates silently for a moment, then trots back to his position and continues to trot in place.* HORTENSIO *and* KATE *restored to their imaginary horses beside him.)*

PETRUCHIO. I say it is the moon.

KATE. I know it is the moon.

PETRUCHIO. Nay, then you lie. It is the blessed sun.

KATE. Then God be blessed, it is the blessed sun.
> But sun it is not when you say it is not,
> And the moon changes even as your mind.
> What you will have it named, even that it is,
> And so it shall be so for Katherine.

PETRUCHIO. Well, forward, forward! Thus the bowl should run
> And not unluckily against the bias.

> *(The three continue to trot in place;* KATE, *painfully, heavily.)*

> But soft, company is coming here.

> *(Enter* GRUMIO *now disguised as an old man.)*

> Good morrow, gentle mistress; where away?
> Tell me, Sweet Kate, and tell me truly too,
> Hast thou beheld a fresher gentlewoman?

Such war of white and red within her cheeks!
What stars do spangle heaven with such beauty
As those two eyes become that heavenly face?
Fair lovely maid, once more good day to thee.
Sweet Kate, embrace her for her beauty's sake.

KATE. *(To* GRUMIO, *after a helpless look to*
HORTENSIO*)*
Young budding virgin, fair and fresh and sweet,
Whither away, or where is thy abode?
Happy the parents of so fair a child!
Happier the man whom favourable stars
Allots thee for his lovely bedfellow!

PETRUCHIO. Why, how now Kate, I hope thou are
not mad.
This is a man, old, wrinkled, faded, withered,
And not a maiden, as thou sayst he is.

KATE. Pardon, old father, my mistaking eyes
That have been so bedazzled with the sun
That everything I look on seemeth green.
Now I perceive thou art a reverend father;
Pardon, I pray thee, for my mad mistaking.
(Falls to her knees, weeping.)

PETRUCHIO. Do, good old grandsire, and withal make
known
Which way thou travelest. If along with us,
We shall be joyful of thy company.

GRUMIO. Fair sir, and you my merry mistress,
That with your strange encounter much amazed me,
My name is called Antonio, my dwelling, Verona.

(To PETRUCHIO, *while stripping off his wig and
beard, unseen by* KATE *who is at his feet.)*

And bound I am to Padua, there to visit
A son of mine which long I have not seen.

PETRUCHIO. What is his name?

GRUMIO. Petruchio, gentle sir.

PETRUCHIO. Happily met. Come ride with us.

*(*PETRUCHIO, HORTENSIO *and* GRUMIO *proceed*

to trot in place, facing straight out. Slowly,
PETRUCHIO *turns to the trotting* GRUMIO *and smiles
at him;* GRUMIO *smiles back.* PETRUCHIO *then turns
and smiles to* HORTENSIO, *who also smiles back. The
three continue trotting in place and then trot out.*
KATE, *on the floor, pathetically paddles her hands on
the floor, as if accompanying them in their trot.)*

(Slowly, KATE *draws herself up. A high-pitched
crescendo whistle is heard inside her head which the
audience also hears. It builds to an impossible pitch
and then something snaps. All lights go red.)*

BAPTISTA.   Poor girl, she weeps.

(Takes KATE *round consolingly.)*

Seeing too much sadness hath congealed your blood
And melancholy is the nurse of frenzy.
Until the tears that thou hath lately shed,
Like envious flood o'errun thy lovely face,
Thou wast the finest creature in the world.

GRUMIO.   *(Kindly, as servant)*
Will't please you drink a cup of sack?

HORTENSIO.   *(Kindly, as servant)*
Will't please you taste of these conserves?

GRUMIO.   What raiment will my mistress wear today?
(Puts golden raiment around her shoulders.)

KATE.   *(Looking around)*
Or do I dream or have I dreamed till now?

GRUMIO.   Will't thou have music. Hark Apollo plays.

(Harp music faintly in the background.)

And twenty caged nightingales do sing.

HORTENSIO.   Or will't thou sleep? We'll have thee to a
            couch
Softer and sweeter than the lustful bed
On purpose trimmed up for Semiramis.

BAPTISTA.   *(Taking her in his arms)*
Call home thy ancient thoughts from banishment
And banish hence these abject lowly dreams.

Look how thy servants do attend on thee,
Each in his office ready at thy beck.

GRUMIO.   Say thou wilt walk, we will bestrow the ground.

HORTENSIO.   Or wilt thou ride? Thy horses shall be
trapped
Their harness studded with all gold and pearl.

GRUMIO.   Dost thou love pictures? We will fetch thee
straight
Adonis painted by a running brook
And Cytherea all in sedges hid,
Which seems to move and wanton with her breath
Even as the waving sedges play with the wind.

KATE.   I do not sleep. I see, I hear, I speak.
I smell sweet savors and I feel soft things.

BAPTISTA.   O how we joy to see your wit restored.
O that once more you knew but what you are.

KATE.   *(Tearful in gratitude)*
The Lord be thanked for thy good amends.

(Enter PETRUCHIO*)*

PETRUCHIO.   *(Kindly)* Where is my wife?

KATE.   Here, noble lord. What is thy will with her?

PETRUCHIO.   *(Kindly)* Are you my wife and will not call
me husband?
My men call me 'lord'; I am your goodman.

KATE.   My husband and my lord, my lord and husband.
I am your wife in all obedience.

PETRUCHIO.   *(Comes forward, takes her in his arms and
kisses her tenderly)*
Madam, undress you and come now to bed.

KATE.   *(Suddenly fearful)*
Let me entreat of you
To pardon me yet for a night or two,
Or, if not so, until the sun be set.
My physicians have expressly charged
In peril to incur a former malady,
That I should yet absent me from your bed.

I hope this reason stands for my excuse.

*(There is a pause as PETRUCHIO's kindliness slowly
evaporates, and everyone else follows suit. Slowly,
KATE turns from one to the other seeing only grim and
cruel faces on all sides.)*

BAPTISTA. *(Suddenly fierce)* O monstrous arrogance!

*(KATE is backed over to the table and then thrown down
over it. Her servants and BAPTISTA hold her wrists to
keep her secure. PETRUCHIO looms up behind her and
whips up her skirts ready to do buggery. As he inserts,
an ear-piercing, electronic whistle rises to a crescendo
pitch. KATE's mouth is wild and open, and it appears
as if the impossible sound is issuing from her lungs.)*

Black out

*Lights up on a surreal tribunal-setting. PETRUCHIO sits
behind a high tribunal-desk. He is looking straight ahead. In
the background, there is the unmistakeable murmur of
women's voices; chatting, gossiping, conniving. After a
moment GRUMIO, dressed in a black gown like an official
of the Court, bangs his staff three times. The whispering
stops.*

*KATE is ushered in by BAPTISTA. She is wearing a
simple, shapeless institutional-like garment. She stares
straight ahead and gives the impression of being
mesmerized. Her face is white; her hair drawn back, her
eyes wide and blank.*

KATE. *(Weakly)*
What is your will, sir, that you send for me?

PETRUCHIO.   Katherine, I charge thee, tell these headstrong women
What duty they owe to their lords and husbands.

*(KATE does not reply. After a moment, BAPTISTA,
who is beside her, touches her shoulder comfortingly.
Eventually, KATE begins to mouthe words. Obviously,
she has learned this speech by rote and is delivering
it as if the words were being spoken by another.)*

KATE.   *(Beginning mechanically)*
Fie, fie, unknit that threatening unkind brow
And dart not scornful glances from those eyes
To wound thy lord, thy king, thy governor.
A woman moved is like a fountain troubled,
Muddy, ill-seeming, thick, bereft of beauty,
And while it is so, none so dry or thirsty
Will deign to sip or touch one drop of it.
Thy husband is thy lord, thy life, thy keeper,
Thy head, thy sovereign . . .

*(KATE comes to a dead halt. Her head slumped
onto her chest. BAPTISTA steps forward and shakes
her back to life. As soon as she has resumed, he steps
back.)*

. . . one that cares for thee,
And for thy maintenance commits his body
To painful labour both by sea and land,
To watch the night in storms, the day in cold
Whilst thou li'st warm at home, secure and safe.
Such duty as the subject owes the prince . . .

*(KATE cannot complete the phrase; after a moment,
PETRUCHIO prompts her.)*

PETRUCHIO.   Even such a woman oweth . . .

KATE.   *(Forcing herself on)*
Even such a woman oweth to her husband,
And when she is froward, peevish, sullen, sour,
And not obedient to his honest will,
What is she but a foul contending rebel
And graceless traitor to her loving lord?

*(A thump on the table from PETRUCHIO brings
KATE, who has reached an hysterical point, back
to some semblance of calm.)*

I am ashamed that women are so simple
To offer war where they should kneel for peace,
Or seek for rule, supremacy and sway,
When they are bound to serve, love and . . .

(Again, KATE cannot frame the word.)

PETRUCHIO.   *(Quietly)* . . . obey.

KATE. *(Suddenly frantic)*
Come, come you froward and unable worms,
My mind hath been as big as one of yours,
My heart as great, my reason haply more,
To bandy word for word and frown for frown.
But now I see our lances are but straws,
Our strength, as weak, our weaknesses, past compare,
That seeming to be most which we indeed least are.

(From the background, the BOY *and* GIRL, *now
dressed in formal wedding attire—he in a dress-suit, she in
gleaming white—begin to move toward each other,
between* PETRUCHIO's *tribunal table and* KATE's
downstage position.)

KATE. Then vail your stomachs, for it is no boot,
And place your hands below your husband's foot,
In token of which duty, if he please,
My hand is ready, may it do him ease.

*(The bride and bridegroom, now beside each other and
framed just behind* KATE, *incline their heads to one
another and smile out to invisible photographers for a
wedding picture.)*

Black out.

END

Measure for Measure

CAST

DUKE	BISHOP
ESCALUS	CLAUDIO
ANGELO	LUCIO
PROVOST	ISABELLA

In Blackout. Sound of the DUKE*'s trumpet.*

Lights up.

ESCALUS, *whose back is to the audience, is examining the Duke's medallion-of-state, which rests on the Throne. After a moment, the* BISHOP *arrives, catches* ESCALUS *in the act.* BISHOP *smiles knowingly to* ESCALUS, *suggesting that he knows, as does* ESCALUS, *this authority will soon be vested on him.* ESCALUS *returns the smile, looks off as he hears someone coming, and takes up a formal position beside the Throne—as does the* BISHOP.
The PROVOST *arrives very smartly and takes up his formal position. He is followed, at once, by the* DUKE *who strides on, nods, takes the medallion and hat from a cushion now held by* ESCALUS, *and then sits.*

DUKE. Escalus.

ESCALUS. My lord.

DUKE. Of government the properties to unfold
Would seem in me t'affect speech and discourse,
Since I am put to know that your own science
Exceeds, in that, the lists of all advice
My strength can give you. Then no more remains
But that, to your sufficiency, as your worth is able,

You do those worthy faculties engage
And let them work. The nature of our people,
Our city's institutions, and the terms
For common justice, y'are as pregnant in
As art and practice hath enriched any
That we remember. There is our commission,

From which we would not have you warp. Call hither,
I say, bid come before us Angelo.
What figure of us think you he will bear?
For you must know, we have with special soul
Elected him our absence to supply,
Lent him our terror, dressed him with our love,
And given his deputation all the organs
Of our own power. What think you of it?

ESCALUS. *(Concealing his disappointment)*
If any in Vienna be of worth
To undergo such ample grace and honour,
It is Lord Angelo.

(Enter ANGELO)

DUKE.   Look where he comes.

*(*BISHOP *and* ESCALUS *exchange fretful looks.)*

ANGELO.   Always obedient to your grace's will,
I come to know your pleasure.

DUKE.   Angelo,
There is a kind of character in thy life
That to th'observer doth thy history
Fully unfold. Thyself and thy belongings
Are not thine own so proper as to waste
Thyself upon thy virtues, they on thee.
Heaven doth with us as we with torches do,
Not light them for themselves: for if our virtues
Did not go forth of us, 'twere all alike
As if we had them not. Spirits are not finely touched
But to fine issues, nor Nature never lends
The smallest scruple of her excellence
But, like a thrifty goddess, she determines
Herself the glory of a creditor,
Both thanks and use. But I do spend my speech
To one that can my part in him advertise.
Hold therefore, Angelo:

*(Removes his Judge's cap and medallion; placing both
on velvet cushion held by* ESCALUS.*)*

In our remove be thou at full ourself.
Mortality and mercy in Vienna
Live in thy tongue and heart. Good Escalus,

Though first in question, is thy secondary.
Take thy commission.

ANGELO. ˙Now, good my lord,
Let there be some more test made of my metal
Before so noble and so great a figure
Be stamped upon't.

DUKE. No more evasion.
We have with leavened and prepared choice
Proceeded to you; therefore take your honours,
Our haste from hence is of so quick condition
That it prefers itself, and leaves unquestioned
Matters of needful value. We shall write to you,
As time and our concernings shall importune,
How it goes with us, and do look to know
What doth befall you here. So fare you well.
To th'hopeful execution do I leave you
Of your commissions.

ANGELO. Yet give leave, my Lord,
That we may bring you something on the way.

DUKE. My haste may not admit it;
Nor need you, on mine honour, have to do
With any scruple. Your scope is as mine own,
So to enforce or qualify the laws
As to your soul seems good. Give me your hand.
I'll privily away: I love the people,
But do not like to stage me to their eyes;
Though it do well, I do not relish well
Their loud applause and Aves vehement,
Nor do I think the man of safe discretion
That does affect it. Once more, fare you well.

ANGELO. The heavens give safety to your purposes!

ESCALUS. Lead forth and bring you back in happiness!

DUKE. I thank you. Fare you well.

(ANGELO and ESCALUS exit.)

(BISHOP, visibly irate, moves angrily to DUKE.)

BISHOP. I shall desire you sir to give me leave
To have free speech with you,
And it concerns me to look into . . .

DUKE. No, holy Father, throw away that thought.

(Taking drink from concealed bar in arm of Throne.)

Nor let thy strictures fall upon my head
Until my greater purpose yet be known.

BISHOP. May your Grace speak of it?

DUKE. My holy Sir, none better knows than you
How I have ever loved the life removed
And held in idle price to haunt assemblies
Where youth and cost a witless bravery keeps.
I have delivered to Lord Angelo,
A man of stricture and firm abstinence,
My absolute power and place here in Vienna,
And he supposes me travelled to Poland,
For so I have strewed it in the common ear,
And so it is received.
Now, you will demand of me why I do this.

BISHOP. Gladly, my lord.

DUKE. We have strict statutes and most biting laws,
The needful bits and curbs to headstrong steeds,
Which for this fourteen years we have let slip;
Even like an o'ergrown lion in a cave,
That goes not out to prey. Now, as fond fathers,
Having bound up the threatening twigs of birch,
Only to stick it in their children's sight
For terror, not to use, in time the rod
Becomes more mocked than feared, so our decrees,
Dead to infliction, to themselves are dead,
And liberty plucks justice by the nose;
The baby beats the nurse, and quite athwart
Goes all decorum.

BISHOP. It rests in your grace
To unloose this tied-up justice when you please,
And it in you more dreadful would have seemed
Than in Lord Angelo.

DUKE. I do fear, too dreadful.
Sith 'twas my fault to give the people scope,
'Twould be my tyranny to strike and gall them
For what I bid them do; for we bid this be done

When evil deeds have their permissive pass
And not the punishment. Therefore, bethinking this
I have on Angelo imposed the office,
Who may, in th'ambush of my name, strike home,
And yet my nature never in the sight
To do it slander. Lord Angelo is precise,
Stands at a guard with envy, scarce confesses
That his blood flows, or that his appetite
Is more to bread than stone. Hence shall we see,
If power change purpose, what our seemers be.

DUKE *offers drink to* BISHOP *who refuses disdainfully.)*

(Fade out:)

(Enter PROVOST, CLAUDIO *(Bound) and* LUCIO.)

CLAUDIO.   Fellow, why dost thou show me thus to th'world?
Bear me to prison, where I am committed.

PROVOST.   I do it not in evil disposition,
But from Lord Angelo by special charge.

CLAUDIO.   Thus can the demigod Authority
Make us pay down for our offence by weight
The words of heaven. On whom it will, it will;
On whom it will not, so: Yet still 'tis just.

LUCIO.   Why, how now, Claudio? Whence comes this restraint?

CLAUDIO.   From too much liberty, my Lucio, liberty.
As surfeit is the father of much fast,
So every scope by the immoderate use
Turns to restraint. Our natures do pursue,
Like rats that ravin down their proper bane,
A thirsty evil, and when we drink we die.

LUCIO.   If I could speak so wisely under an arrest, I would
send for certain of my creditors. And yet, to say the
truth, I had as lief have the foppery of freedom as the
mortality of imprisonment. What's thy offence, Claudio?

CLAUDIO.   What but to speak of would offend again.

LUCIO.   What, is't murder?

CLAUDIO.   No.

LUCIO. Lechery?

CLAUDIO. Call it so.

PROVOST. Away, sir, you must go.

CLAUDIO. One word, good friend. Lucio, a word with you.

LUCIO. A hundred, if they'll do you any good.
Is lechery so looked after?

CLAUDIO. Thus stands it with me: upon a true contract
I got possession of Julietta's bed.
You know the lady. She is fast my wife
Save that we do denunciation lack
Of outward order. This we came not to,
Only for propagation of a dower
Remaining in the coffer of her friends,
From whom we thought it meet to hide our love
Till time had made them for us. But it chances
The stealth of our most mutual entertainment
With character too gross is writ on Juliet.

LUCIO. With child, perhaps?

CLAUDIO. Unhappily, even so.
And the new deputy now for the Duke —
Whether it be the fault and glimpse of newness,
Or whether that the body public be
A horse whereon the governor doth ride,
Who, newly in the seat, that it may know
He can command, lets it straight feel the spur;
Whether the tyranny be in his place,
Or in his eminence that fills it up,
I stagger in—but this new governor
Awakes me all the enrolled penalties
Which have, like unscoured armour, hung by th'wall
So long that fourteen zodiacs have gone round
And none of them been worn, and for a name
Now puts the drowsy and neglected act
Freshly on me. 'Tis surely for a name.

LUCIO. I warrant it is, and thy head stands so tickle on
thy shoulders that a milkmaid, if she be in love, may
sigh it off. Send after the Duke and appeal to him.

CLAUDIO. I have done so, but he's not to be found.

I prithee, Lucio, do me this kind service:
This day my sister should the cloister enter,
And there receive her approbation.
Acquaint her with the danger of my state,
Implore her, in my voice, that she makes friends
To the strict deputy, bid herself assay him.
I have great hope in that, for in her youth
There is a prone and speechless dialect,
Such as move men; beside, she hath prosperous art
When she will play with reason and discourse,
And well she can persuade.

LUCIO. I pray she may, as well for the encouragement of the like, which else would stand under grievous imposition, as for the enjoying of thy life, who I would be sorry should be thus foolishly lost at a game of tick-tack. I'll to her.

CLAUDIO. I thank you, good friend Lucio.

LUCIO. Within two hours.

CLAUDIO. Come, officer, away.

(They exit.)

(Enter ANGELO *and* ESCALUS.*)*

(During scene, ANGELO *dons the Duke's garments of authority: cap and medallion.)*

ANGELO. We must not make a scarecrow of the law,
Setting it up to fear the birds of prey,
And let it keep one shape, till custom make it
Their perch and not their terror.

ESCALUS. Ay, but yet
Let us be keen and rather cut a little
Than fall, and bruise to death. Alas this gentleman,
Whom I would save, had a most noble father.
Let but your honour know,
Whom I believe to be most strait in virtue,
That, in the working of your own affections,
Had time cohered with place or place with wishing,
Or that the resolute acting of your blood
Could have attained th'effect of your own purpose,
Whether you had not sometime in your life
Erred in this point which now you censure him,
And pulled the law upon you.

ANGELO.   'Tis one thing to be tempted, Escalus,
    Another thing to fall. I not deny,
    The jury, passing on the prisoner's life,
    May in the sworn twelve have a thief or two
    Guiltier than him they try; what's open made to justice,
    That justice seizes; what knows the laws
    That thieves do pass on thieves? 'Tis very pregnant,
    The jewel that we find, we stoop and take't
    Because we see it; but what we do not see
    We tread upon, and never think of it.
    You may not so extenuate his offence
    For I have had such faults; but rather tell me,
    When I, that censure him, do so offend,
    Let mine own judgement pattern out my death
    And nothing come in partial. Sir, he must die.

(Enter PROVOST.)

ESCALUS.   Be it as your wisdom will.

ANGELO.   Where is the provost?

PROVOST.   Here, if it like your honour.

ANGELO.   See that Claudio
    Be executed by tomorrow morning:
    Bring his confessor, let him be prepared;
    For that's the utmost of his pilgrimage.

*(As ANGELO goes to give execution order to PROVOST,
he turns to see PROVOST looking darkly at ESCALUS.
ANGELO notes the smouldering atmosphere between
PROVOST and ESCALUS, briskly places the order into
the PROVOST's hands and exits. The PROVOST studies
the order for a moment then looks up at ESCALUS.)*

ESCALUS.   Well, heaven forgive him, and forgive us all.
    Some rise by sin, and some by virtue fall:
    Some run from brakes of office, and answer none,
    And some condemned for a fault alone.

*(ESCALUS looks back at the order in his hand. 'Hmph's'
sarcastically.)*

Fade out.

Lights up:

ISABELLA *with prayer-book.*

LUCIO *arrives briskly. Sees nun with back to him, sidles up and begins seductively.*

LUCIO. Hail, virgin, if you be, as those cheek-roses
　　　　Proclaim you are no less. Can you so stead me
　　　　As bring me to the sight of Isabella,
　　　　A novice of this place, and the fair sister
　　　　To her unhappy brother, Claudio?

ISABELLA. Why 'her unhappy brother'? Let me ask,
　　　　The rather for I now must make you know
　　　　I am that Isabella, and his sister.

LUCIO. *(Caught, now respectfully doffing his cap.)*
　　　　Gentle and fair, your brother kindly greets you.
　　　　Not to be weary with you, he's in prison.

ISABELLA. Woe me, for what?

LUCIO. For that which, if myself might be his judge,
　　　　He should receive his punishment in thanks.
　　　　He hath got his friend with child.

ISABELLA. Sir, make me not your story.

LUCIO. It is true.
　　　　I would not, though 'tis my familiar sin
　　　　With maids to seem the lapwing and to jest,
　　　　Tongue far from heart, play with all virgins so.
　　　　I hold you as a thing enskied and sainted,
　　　　By your renouncement an immortal spirit
　　　　And to be talked with in sincerity,
　　　　As with a saint.

ISABELLA. You do blaspheme the good in mocking me.

LUCIO. Do not believe it. Fewness and truth, 'tis thus:
　　　　Your brother and his lover have embraced.
　　　　As those that feed grow full, as blossoming time
　　　　That from the seedness the bare fallow brings
　　　　To teeming fusion even so her plenteous womb
　　　　Expresseth his full tilth and husbandry.

ISABELLA. Someone with child by him? My cousin Juliet?

LUCIO.   Is she your cousin?

ISABELLA.   Adoptedly, as school-maids change their names
By vain though apt affection.

LUCIO.   She it is.

ISABELLA.   O, let him marry her.

LUCIO.   This is the point.
The Duke is very strangely gone from hence.
Upon his place,
And with full line of his authority,
Governs Lord Angelo, a man whose blood
Is very snow-broth, one who never feels
The wanton stings and motions of the sense,
But doth rebate and blunt his natural edge
With profits of the mind, study, and fast.
He, to give fear to use and liberty,
Which have for long run by the hideous law,
As mice by lions, hath picked out an act,
Under whose heavy sense your brother's life
Falls into forfeit; he arrests him on it,
And follows close the rigour of the statute
To make him an example. All hope is gone,
Unless you have the grace by your fair prayer
To soften Angelo. And that's my pith of business
'Twixt you and your poor brother.

ISABELLA.   Doth he so seek his life?

LUCIO.   Has censured him
Already and, as I hear, the provost hath
A warrant for his execution.

ISABELLA.   Alas, what poor ability's in me
To do him good.

LUCIO.   Assay the power you have.

ISABELLA.   My power? Alas, I doubt.

LUCIO.   Our doubts are traitors
And make us lose the good we oft might win,
By fearing to attempt. Go to Lord Angelo,
And let him learn to know, when maidens sue,
Men give like gods; but when they weep and kneel,

All their petitions are as freely theirs
As they themselves would owe them.

ISABELLA. I'll see what I can do.

LUCIO. But speedily.

ISABELLA. I will about it straight,
No longer staying but to give the Mother
Notice of my affair. I humbly thank you.
Commend me to my brother. Soon at night
I'll send him certain word of my success.

*(LUCIO and ISABELLA exit opposite sides
on Blackout.)*

ANGELO's *chamber—high judicial desk.*

PROVOST. I'll know
His pleasure; maybe he'll relent. Alas,
He hath but as offended in a dream.
All sects, all ages smack of this vice, and he
To die for it!

(Enter ANGELO.)

ANGELO. Now, what's the matter, provost?

PROVOST. Is it your will Claudio shall die tomorrow?

ANGELO. Did not I tell thee, yea? Hadst thou not order?
Why dost thou ask again?

PROVOST. Lest I might be too rash.
Under your good correction, I have seen
When, after execution, judgement hath
Repented o'er his doom.

ANGELO. Go to; let that be mine.
Do you your office, or give up your place,
And you shall well be spared.

(ANGELO crosses and sits behind desk.)

PROVOST. I crave your honour's pardon.
What shall be done, sir, with the groaning Juliet?
She's very near her hour.

192

ANGELO.   Dispose of her
        To some more fitter place, and that with speed.

PROVOST.   Here is the sister of the man condemned
        Desires access to you.

ANGELO.   Hath he a sister?

PROVOST.   Ay, my good lord, a very virtuous maid,
        And to be shortly of a sisterhood,
        If not already.

ANGELO.   Well, let her be admitted. And,
        See you the fornicatress be removed;
        Let her have needful, but not lavish, means.
        There shall be order for't.

PROVOST.   God save your honour. *(He exits.)*

        (Enter ISABELLA.)

ANGELO.   *(to* ISABELLA*)* Y'are welcome. What's your will?

ISABELLA.   I am a woeful suitor to your honour,
        Please but your honour hear me.

ANGELO.   Well, what's your suit?

ISABELLA.   There is a vice that most I do abhor,
        And most desire should meet the blow of justice,
        For which I would not plead, but that I must,
        For which I must not plead, but that I am
        At war 'twixt will and will not.

ANGELO.   Well: the matter?

ISABELLA.   I have a brother is condemned to die.
        I do beseech, you, let it be his fault,
        And not my brother.

        *(ANGELO looks up for first time. Sees ISABELLA.
        Registers her. Pause.)*

ANGELO.   Condemn the fault, and not the actor of it?
        Why, every fault's condemned ere it be done.
        Mine were the very cipher of a function,
        To fine the faults whose fine stands in record,
        And let go by the actor.

ISABELLA.   O just, but severe law!

I had a brother then; heaven keep your honour.
(Begins to go: stops.) Must he needs die?

ANGELO.   Maiden, no remedy.

ISABELLA.   Yes, I do think that you might pardon him,
And neither heaven nor man grieve at the mercy.

ANGELO.   I will not do't.

ISABELLA.   But can you if you would?

ANGELO.   Look what I will not, that I cannot do.

ISABELLA.   But might you do't, and do the world no wrong,
If so your heart were touched with that remorse
As mine is to him?

ANGELO.   He's sentenced: 'tis too late.

ISABELLA.   Too late? Why, no. I that do speak a word
May call it back again. Well, believe this,
No ceremony that to great ones longs,
Not the king's crown, nor the deputed sword,
The marshal's truncheon, nor the judge's robe,
Become them with one half so good a grace
As mercy does.
If he had been as you, and you as he,
You would have slipped like him; but he, like you
Would not have been so stern.

ANGELO.   Pray you, be gone.

ISABELLA.   *(Riled)* I would to heaven I had your potency,
And you were Isabel; should it then be thus?
No, I would tell what 'twere to be a judge,
And what a prisoner.

ANGELO.   Your brother is a forfeit of the law,
And you but waste your words.

ISABELLA.   Alas, alas;
Why, all the souls that were were forfeit once,
And He that might the vantage best have took
Found out the remedy. How would you be,
If He, which is the top of judgement, should
But judge you as you are? O think on that,
And mercy then will breathe within your lips,
Like man new made.

(Pause as ANGELO *eyes* ISABELLA *curiously.*
ISABELLA, *nervous under his scrutiny.)*

ANGELO.   Be you content, fair maid,
It is the law, not I, condemns your brother;
Were he my kinsman, brother, or my son,
It should be thus with him. He must die tomorrow.

ISABELLA.   Tomorrow? Oh, that's sudden; spare him, spare
him.
He's not prepared for death. Even for our kitchens
We kill the fowl of season. Shall we serve heaven
With less respect than we do minister
To our gross selves? Good, good my lord, bethink you:
Who is it that hath died for this offence?
There's many have committed it.
Yet show some pity.

ANGELO.   I show it most of all when I show justice,
For then I pity those I do not know,
Which a dismissed offence would after gall,
And do him right that, answering one foul wrong,
Lives not to act another. Be satisfied
Your brother dies tomorrow. Be content.

ISABELLA.   *(Hot, angry)*
So you must be the first that gives this sentence
And he, that suffers. O, 'tis excellent
To have a giant's strength, but it is tyrannous
To use it like a giant.
Could great men thunder
As Jove himself does, Jove would ne'er be quiet,
For every pelting, petty officer
Would use his heaven for thunder,
Nothing but thunder. Merciful heaven,
Thou rather with thy sharp and sulphurous bolt
Splits the unwedgeable and gnarled oak
Than the soft myrtle; but man, proud man,
Dressed in a little brief authority,
Most ignorant of what he's most assured,
His glassy essence, like an angry ape
Plays such fantastic tricks before high heaven
As makes the angels weep; who, with our spleens,
Would all themselves laugh mortal.
We cannot weigh our brother with ourself,

195

Great men may jest with saints: 'tis wit in them,
But in the less, foul profanation.
That in the captain's but a choleric word
Which in the soldier is flat blasphemy.

ANGELO.   Why do you put these sayings upon me?

ISABELLA.   Because authority, though it err like others,
Hath yet a kind of medicine in itself
That skins the vice o'th'top. Go to your bosom,
Knock there, and ask your heart what it doth know
That's like my brother's fault; if it confess
A natural guiltiness such as is his,
Let it not sound a thought upon your tongue
Against my brother's life.

ANGELO.   *(Aside)* She speaks, and 'tis
Such sense that my sense breeds with it.
Fare you well. *(Leaves desk, begins to go.)*

ISABELLA.   Gentle my lord, turn back.

ANGELO.   I will bethink me. Come again tomorrow.

ISABELLA.   Hark how I'll bribe you. Good my lord, turn back.

ANGELO.   How? Bribe me?

ISABELLA.   Ay, with such gifts that heaven shall share with
you
Not with fond shekels of the tested gold,
Or stones whose rate are either rich or poor
As fancy values them; but with true prayers
That shall be up at heaven and enter there
Ere sunrise: prayers from preserved souls,
From fasting maids whose minds are dedicate
To nothing temporal.

ANGELO.   Well, come to me tomorrow.

ISABELLA.   Heaven keep your honour safe.

ANGELO.   Amen.

ISABELLA.   At what hour tomorrow
Shall I attend your lordship?

ANGELO.   At any time 'forenoon.

ISABELLA.   God save your honour.

(Exit ISABELLA: *spot on* ANGELO.*)*

ANGELO.   From thee: even from thy virtue.
    What's this? What's this? Is this her fault or mine
    The tempter, or the tempted, who sins most?
    Ha?
    Not she, nor doth she tempt; but it is I
    That, lying by the violet in the sun,
    Do as the carrion does, not as the flower,
    Corrupt with virtuous season. Can it be
    That modesty may more betray our sense
    Than woman's lightness? Having waste ground enough
    Shall we desire to raze the sanctuary
    And pitch our evils there? O fie, fie, fie!
    What dost thou? Or what art thou, Angelo?
    Dost thou desire her foully for those things
    That make her good? O, let her brother live:
    Thieves for their robbery have authority
    When judges steal themselves. What, do I love her,
    That I desire to hear her speak again,
    And feast upon her eyes? What is't I dream on?
    O cunning enemy that, to catch a saint,
    With saints dost bait thy hook. Most dangerous
    Is that temptation that doth goad us on
    To sin in loving virtue. Never could the strumpet
    With all her double vigour, art and nature,
    Once stir my temper; but this virtuous maid
    Subdues me quite. Ever till now,
    When men were fond, I smiled and wondered how.

(Looks down at execution order in his hand at Fade out.)

CLAUDIO*'s cell.*

PROVOST.
    So then you hope of pardon from Lord Angelo?

CLAUDIO.   The miserable have no other medicine
    But only hope;
    I have hope to live, and am prepared to die.

(Exit CLAUDIO *and* PROVOST.*)*

LUCIO.   Marry, this Claudio is condemned for untrussing! A
          little more leniency to lechery would do no harm, say I.
          'Tis a general vice, and impossible to extirp it quite til
          eating and drinking be put down.

          It was a mad fantastical trick of the Duke to steal from
          the State, and usurp the beggary he was never born to.
          Some say he is with the Emperor of Russia; other some,
          he is in Rome. Lord Angelo dukes it well in his absence.
          They say this Angelo was not made by man and woman
          after this downright way of creation. Some report a sea-
          maid spawned him. Some that he was begot between two
          stock-fishes. But it is certain when he makes water his
          urine is congealed ice.

          Why what a ruthless thing is this in him, for the rebellion
          of a cod-piece to take away the life of a man!
          Would the Duke that is absent have done this? Ere he
          would have hanged a man for the getting of a hundred
          bastards, he would have paid for the nursing of a thousand.
          He had some feeling of the sport. The Duke had crotchets
          in him. He's not past it yet. Why, he would mouth with a
          beggar though she smelt brown bread and garlic. I would
          the Duke were returned again.

          This ungenitured agent will unpeople the province with
          continency. Sparrows must not build in his house-eaves
          because they are lecherous. The Duke yet would have
          dark deeds darkly answered. He would never bring them
          to light. Would he were returned.

ANGELO's *chamber.*

ANGELO.   O heavens,
          Why does my blood thus muster to my heart,
          Making both it unable for itself,
          And dispossessing all my other parts
          Of necessary fitness?
          So play the foolish throngs with one that swoons,
          Come all to help him, and so stop the air
          By which he should revive; and even so
          The general, subject to a well-wished king,

Quit their own part, and in obsequious fondness
Crowd to his presence, where their untaught love
Must needs appear offence.

(Enter ISABELLA.*)*

How now, fair maid!

ISABELLA.   I am come to know your pleasure.

ANGELO.   That you might know it, would much better please
    me
Than to demand what 'tis. Your brother cannot live.

ISABELLA.   Even so. Heaven keep your honour. *(Begins to go.)*

ANGELO.   Yet may he live a while; and it may be
    As long as you or I, yet he must die.

ISABELLA.   Under your sentence?

ANGELO.   Yea.

ISABELLA.   When, I beseech you? That in his reprieve,
    Longer or shorter, he may be so fitted
    That his soul sicken not.

ANGELO.   Ha! Fie, these filthy vices! *(Coming down from
    behind desk.)* It were as good
    To pardon him that hath from nature stol'n
    A man already made as to remit
    Their saucy sweetness that do coin God's image
    In stamps that are forbid: 'tis all as easy
    Falsely to take away a life true made
    As to put metal in restrained means
    To make a false one.

ISABELLA.   'Tis set down so in heaven, but not in earth.

ANGELO.
    Say you so? Then I shall pose you quickly.
    Which had you rather, that the most just law
    Now took your brother's life, or to redeem him
    Give up your body to such sweet uncleanness
    As she that he hath stained?

ISABELLA.   Sir, believe this,
    I had rather give my body than my soul.

ANGELO.   I talk not of your soul. Our compelled sins
    Stand more for number than accompt.

ISABELLA.   How say you?

ANGELO.   Nay, I'll not warrant that, for I can speak
    Against the thing I say. Answer to this:
    I, now the voice of the recorded law,
    Pronounce a sentence on your brother's life;
    Might there not be a charity in sin
    To save this brother's life?

ISABELLA.   Please you to do't,
    I'll take it as a peril to my soul;
    It is no sin at all, but charity.

ANGELO.   Pleased you to do't, at peril of your soul.
    Were equal poise of sin and charity.

ISABELLA.   That I do beg his life, if it be sin,
    Heaven let me bear it: you granting of my suit,
    If that be sin, I'll make it my morning prayer
    To have it added to the faults of mine
    And nothing of your answer.

ANGELO.   Nay, but hear me;
    Your sense pursues not mine. Either you are ignorant,
    Or seem so craftily; and that's not good.

ISABELLA.   Let me be ignorant, and in nothing good
    But graciously to know I am not better.

ANGELO.   Thus wisdom wishes to appear most bright
    When it doth tax itself, as these black masks
    Proclaim an enshield beauty ten times louder
    Than beauty could, displayed. But mark me;
    To be received plain, I'll speak more gross:
    Your brother is to die.

ISABELLA.   So.

ANGELO.   And his offence is so, as it appears,
    Accountant to the law upon that pain.

ISABELLA.   True.

ANGELO.   Admit no other way to save his life—
    As I subscribe not that, nor any other,
    But in the loss of question—that you, his sister

Finding yourself desired of such a person
Whose credit with the judge, or own great place,
Could fetch your brother from the manacles
Of the all-binding law; and that there were
No earthly mean to save him, but that either
You must lay down the treasures of your body,
To this supposed, or else to let him suffer,
What would you do?

ISABELLA.   As much for my poor brother as myself:
That is, were I under the terms of death,
Th' impression of keen whips I'd wear as rubies,
And strip myself to death as to a bed
That long I have been sick for, ere I'd yield
My body up to shame.

ANGELO.   Then must your brother die.

ISABELLA.   And 'twere the cheaper way.
Better it were a brother died at once
Than that a sister, by redeeming him,
Should die for ever.

ANGELO.   Were not you then as cruel as the sentence
That you have slandered so?

ISABELLA.   Ignomy in ransom and free pardon
Are of two houses: lawful mercy is
nothing kin to foul redemption

ANGELO.   You seemed of late to make the law a tyrant,
And rather proved the sliding of your brother
A merriment than a vice.

ISABELLA.   O pardon me, my lord; it oft falls out
To have what we would have, to speak not what we
mean,
I something do excuse the thing I hate
For his advantage that I dearly love.

ANGELO.   We are all frail.

ISABELLA.   Else let my brother die
If he alone this sin doth owe and none
Succeed him in that weakness.

ANGELO.   Nay, women are frail too.

ISABELLA.   Ay, as the glasses where they view themselves,
   Which are as easy broke as they make forms,
   Women, help heaven! Men their creation mar
   In profiting by them. Nay, call us ten times frail,
   For we are soft as our complexions are,
   And credulous to false prints.

ANGELO.   I think it well,
   And from this testimony of your own sex—
   Since I suppose we are made to be no stronger
   Than faults may shake our frames—let me be bold
   I do arrest your words. Be that you are,
   That is, a woman; if you be more, you're none.
   If you be one, as you are well expressed
   By all external warrants, show it now,
   By putting on the destined livery.

ISABELLA.   I have no tongue but one. Gentle my lord,
   Let me entreat you speak the former language.

ANGELO.   Plainly conceive, I love you.

ISABELLA.   My brother did love Juliet,
   And you tell me that he shall die for't.

ANGELO.   He shall not, Isabel, if you give me love.
   (Takes ISABELLA*'s hand.)*

ISABELLA.   *(Pulling away)* I know your virtue hath a licence
    in't,
   Which seems a little fouler than it is,
   To pluck on others.

ANGELO.   Believe me, on mine honour,
   My words express my purpose.

ISABELLA.   Ha! Little honour to be much believed,
   And most pernicious purpose. Seeming, seeming!
   I will proclaim thee, Angelo, look for't!
   Sign me a present pardon for my brother,
   Or with an outstretched throat I'll tell the world
   What man thou art.

ANGELO.   Who will believe thee, Isabel?
   My unsoiled name, th'austereness of my life,
   My vouch against you, and my place i'th'state,
   Will so your accusation overweigh

That you shall stifle in your own report
And smell of calumny. I have begun,
And now I give my sensual race the rein.
Fit thy consent to my sharp appetite,
Lay by all nicety and prolixious blushes,
That banish what they sue for. Redeem thy brother
By yielding up thy body to my will,
Or else he must not only die the death,
But thy unkindness shall his death draw out
To lingering sufferance. Answer me tomorrow
Or, by the affection that now guides me most,
I'll prove a tyrant to him. As for you,
Say what you can, my false o'erweighs your true

*(ANGELO takes ISABELLA's hand, despite her
resistance, and kisses it fondly in the palm. As she pulls
away from the kiss ANGELO exits and simultaneously a
single spot picks up ISABELLA.)*

ISABELLA.   To whom should I complain. Did I tell this,
Who would believe me? O perilous mouths,
That bear in them one and the selfsame tongue,
Either of condemnation or approof,
Bidding the law make curtsy to their will,
Hooking both right and wrong to th'appetite,
To follow as it draws. I'll to my brother.
Though he hath fall'n by prompture of the blood,
Yet hath he in him such a mind of honour
That, had he twenty heads to tender down
On twenty bloody blocks, he'd yield them up,
Before his sister should her body stoop
To such abhorred pollution.
Then, Isabel, live chaste, and, brother, die.
More than our brother is our chastity.

Blackout

Lights up

CLAUDIO.   Now, sister, what's the comfort?

ISABELLA.   Why?
As all comforts are: most good, most good indeed.
Lord Angelo, having affairs to heaven
Intends you for his swift ambassador,

Where you shall be an everlasting Leiger.
Therefore your best appointment make with speed;
Tomorrow you set on.

CLAUDIO.   Is there no remedy?

ISABELLA.   None, but such remedy as, to save a head,
To cleave a heart in twain.

CLAUDIO.   But is there any?

ISABELLA.   Yes, brother, you may live;
There is a devilish mercy in the judge,
If you'll implore it, that will free your life,
But fetter you till death.

CLAUDIO.   Perpetual durance?

ISABELLA.   Ay just. Perpetual durance, a restraint,
Though all the world's vastidity you had,
To a determined scope.

CLAUDIO.   But in what nature?

ISABELLA.   In such a one as, you consenting to't,
Would bark your honour from that trunk you bear,
And leave you naked.

CLAUDIO.   Let me know the point.

ISABELLA.   O, I do fear thee, Claudio, and I quake
Lest thou a feverous life shouldst entertain,
And six or seven winters more respect
Than a perpetual honour. Dar'st thou die?
The sense of death is most in apprehension,
And the poor beetle that we tread upon
In corporal sufference finds a pang as great
As when a giant dies.

CLAUDIO.   Why give you me this shame?
Think you I can a resolution fetch
From flowery tenderness? If I must die,
I will encounter darkness as a bride,
And hug it in mine arms.

ISABELLA.   There spake my brother. There my father's grave
Did utter forth a voice. Yes, thou must die.
Thou art too noble to conserve a life
In base appliances. This outward-sainted deputy,

Whose settled visage and deliberate word
Nips youth i'th'head, and follies doth enew
As falcon doth the fowl, is yet a devil
His filth within being cast, he would appear
A pond as deep as hell.

CLAUDIO.   The precise Angelo?

ISABELLA.   Oh, tis the cunning livery of hell,
The damned'st body to invest and cover
In precious guards. Dost thou think, Claudio,
If I would yield him my virginity,
Thou might'st be freed?

CLAUDIO.   O heavens, it cannot be.

ISABELLA.   Yes, he would give't thee, from this rank offence,
So to offend him still. This night's the time
That I should do what I abhor to name,
Or else thou diest tomorrow.

CLAUDIO.   Thou shalt not do't.

ISABELLA.   O, were it but my life
I'd throw it down for your deliverance
As frankly as a pin. Be ready, Claudio,
For your death tomorrow.

CLAUDIO.   Yes. Has he affections in him
That thus can make him bite the law by th'nose
When he would force it? Sure it is no sin,
Or of the deadly seven it is the least.

ISABELLA.   Which is the least?

CLAUDIO.   If it were damnable, he being so wise,
Why would he for the momentary trick
Be perdurably fined? O Isabel?

ISABELLA.   What says my brother?

CLAUDIO.   Death is a fearful thing.

ISABELLA.   And shamed life a hateful.

CLAUDIO.   Ay, but to die, and go we know not where,
To lie in cold obstruction and to rot;
This sensible warm motion to become
A kneaded clod; and the delighted spirit

To bathe in fiery floods, or to reside
In thrilling region of thick-ribbed ice,
To be imprisoned in the viewless winds
And blown with restless violence round about
The pendent world; or to be worse than worst
Of those that lawless and incertain thought
Imagine howling, 'tis too horrible.
The weariest and most loathed wordly life
That age, ache, penury, and imprisonment
Can lay on nature is a paradise
To what we fear of death.

ISABELLA.   Alas, alas.

CLAUDIO.   Sweet sister, let me live.
What sin you do to save a brother's life,
Nature dispenses with the deed so far
That it becomes a virtue.

ISABELLA.   Wilt thou be made a man out of my vice?
Is't not a kind of incest to take life
From thine own sister's shame? What should I think?
Heaven shield my mother played my father fair,
For such a warped slip of wilderness
Ne'er issued from his blood. Take my defiance,
Die, perish. Might but my bending down
Reprieve thee from thy fate, it should proceed.
I'll pray a thousand prayers for thy death,
No word to save thee.

CLAUDIO.   Nay, hear me, Isabel.

ISABELLA.   O, fie, fie, fie!
Thy sin's not accidental, but a trade.
Mercy to thee would prove itself a bawd,
'Tis best that thou diest quickly.

CLAUDIO.   O hear me, Isabella.

(ISABELLA gone, CLAUDIO falls into LUCIO's arms, as he enters.)

Let me ask my sister pardon. I am so out of love
with life that I will sue to be rid of it.

Lights out.

ANGELO *standing uneasily with order.*

PROVOST *enters.*

ANGELO. Whatsoever you may hear to the contrary,
    Let Claudio be executed by four of the clock.
    For my better satisfaction,
    Let me have Claudio's head sent me by five.

PROVOST. My lord . . .

ANGELO. *(Sharply)* Let this be duly performed,
    With a thought that more depends on it then we must
        yet deliver.
    Thus fail not to do your office,
    As you will answer it at your peril.

    (PROVOST exits.)

    *(ANGELO crosses himself; tries to pray,
    breaks off.)*

ANGELO. *(contd)*
    When I would pray and think, I think and pray
    To several subjects: heaven hath my empty words,
    Whilst my invention, hearing not my tongue,
    Anchors on Isabel: God in my mouth,
    As if I did but only chew His name,
    And in my heart the strong and swelling evil
    Of my conception. The state, whereon I studied,
    Is like a good thing, being often read,
    Grown seared and tedious; yea, my gravity,
    Wherein, let no man hear me, I take pride,
    Could I, with boot, change for an idle plume
    Which the air beats for vain. O place, O form,
    How often dost thou with thy case, thy habit,
    Wrench awe from fools, and tie the wiser souls
    To thy false seeming! Blood, thou art blood;
    Let's write 'good Angel' on the devil's horn,
    'Tis not the devil's crest.

Blackout

PROVOST, LUCIO, ESCALUS.

As ESCALUS *enters* LUCIO *withdraws to listen in.*

PROVOST. What comfort is for Claudio.

ESCALUS. *(Hedging)* There's some in hope.

PROVOST. It is a bitter Deputy.

    (Pause.)

ESCALUS. *(acknowledging the inevitable)*
    Provost, my brother Angelo will not be altered;
    Claudio must die tomorrow. Let him be furnished
    With divines, and have all charitable preparation
    If my brother wrought by my pity, it should not be
    So with him. Let me desire to know how you find
    Claudio prepared?

PROVOST. *(To himself)*
    He professes to have received no sinister measure
    From his judge, but most willingly humbles himself
    To the determination of Justice.

ESCALUS. *(To himself)*
    I have laboured for the poor gentleman to the
    extremest shore of my modesty, but my brother—
    Justice I have found so severe that he hath forc'd
    me to tell him that he is indeed Justice.

PROVOST. *(To himself, grimly)*
    If his own life answer the straitness of his proceeding, it
    shall become him well; wherein if he chance to fail, he
    hath sentenc'd himself.

ESCALUS. *(to* PROVOST*)*
    Not so, not so; his life is parallel'd
    Even with the stroke and line of his great justice
    He doth with holy abstinence subdue
    That in himself which he spurs on his power
    To qualify in others, were he meal'd with that
    Which he corrects, then were he tyrannous;
    But this being so, he's just . . . *(PROVOST looks
    at* ESCALUS, *searching for irony; finds none)*
    I am going to visit the prisoner; fare you well.

PROVOST. Peace be with you.

ISABELLA. *(Off-stage)* Peace, ho, be here.

PROVOST. The tongue of Isabel. She's come to know
If yet her brother's pardon be come hither.

ISABELLA. Have you no countermand for Claudio yet?

PROVOST. None, maid, none.

ISABELLA. *(With a curious, self-deluding smile)*
As near the dawning, provost, as it is,
You shall hear more ere morning.

PROVOST. Happily.
You something know, yet I believe there comes
No countermand; no such example have we.
Besides, upon the very siege of justice
Lord Angelo hath to the public ear
Professed the contrary.

ISABELLA. *(Smile vanishes, forced to acknowledge the
truth, bursting into tears)* What a merit were it in death
to take this poor maid from the world! What a corruption
in this life that it will let this man live!

LUCIO. *(Embracing her)* O Pretty Isabella, I am pale at
mine heart to see thine eyes so red. Thou must be
patient. I am fain to dine and sup with water and bran.
I dare not for my head fill my belly; one fruitful
meal would set me to't. By my troth, Isabel, I love thy
brother. If the old fantastical Duke of dark corners had
been at home, he had lived.

PROVOST. It grieves me for the death of Claudio, but there
is no remedy.

*(ISABELLA forces herself away from LUCIO and
PROVOST and is suddenly alone. As she stands listening
intently, she (and we) hear a cacophony of indistinct
voices; echoes from CLAUDIO, ANGELO, LUCIO and
the PROVOST.)*

(Voices on tape)

ANGELO. *(As before)* Your brother is a forfeit of the law.

CLAUDIO. *(As before)* If I must die I will encounter
Darkness like a bride.

ISABELLA. *(Fierce)* And strip myself to death as to a bed

ANGELO. *(As before)* By yielding up thy body to my will.

ISABELLA. *(Modest)* God save your honour.

ANGELO. *(As before)* Or else he must not only die the death

ISABELLA. *(Modest)* Please but your honour hear me.

ANGELO. *(As before)* But thy unkindness shall his death draw out.

ISABELLA. *(Scoffing)* Ha! Little honour to be much believed!

PROVOST. *(As before)* Yet I believe there comes no countermand.

CLAUDIO. *(As before)* Sure it is no sin . . .

ANGELO. *(Cynical)* Or of the deadly seven it is the least.

PROVOST. *(As before)* There comes no countermand.

CLAUDIO. Sweet sister . . .

ANGELO. *(as before)* If you give me love

CLAUDIO. Let me live!

> *(Over the jumble of voices, we hear the PROVOST's voice loud and clear. As soon as he speaks, the lighting turns to red and we are clearly in a kind of surreal dream-sequence.)*

PROVOST. *(Facing away; as if to hangman)* Come hither sirrah, can you cut off a man's head?

ISABELLA. Good Provost, here is Claudio's pardon;
Purchased by such sin
For which the pardoner himself is in.

PROVOST. *(Faced away)* I believe there comes no countermand.

ISABELLA. By the vow of mine order, I warrant you, here is the pardon.

PROVOST. *(Faced away)* Lord Angelo hath to the public ear confessed to the contrary.

ISABELLA. *(Accusingly)* Claudio whom here you have

210

warrant to execute is no greater forfeit to the law than
Angelo who hath sentenced him. *(Pleadingly.)* If
anything fall to you upon this, more than thanks and
good fortune, by the saint whom I profess, I will plead
against it with my life.

PROVOST.   It is against my oath.

ISABELLA.   Were you sworn to the Duke or the Deputy?

PROVOST.   To him and to his substitutes.

ISABELLA.   You will then have made no offence, if the
Duke avouch the justice of your dealing?

PROVOST.   But what likelihood in that?

DUKE.   *(Suddenly appearing with* ANGELO *behind; back to
back)* Not a resemblance but a certainty.
Look you sir, here is the hand and seal of the Duke.
You know the character, I doubt not, and the signet
Is not strange to you.

PROVOST.   *(Suddenly respectful)* Pardon me, noble lord.

*(*CLAUDIO *appears and is unmanacled by the* PROVOST.
He goes to the DUKE *and kneels.)*

DUKE.   Thou'rt condemned.
But for those earthly faults, I quit them all.
And pray thee take this mercy to provide
For better times to come.

*(*ISABELLA, *full of gratitude, bows down before*
DUKE.*)*

ISABELLA.   My noble Lord!

DUKE.   *(To* ISABELLA*)* Put yourself not into amazement
how these things should be. All difficulties are but easy
when they are known.
Give me your hand and . . .

ANGELO.   *(Transformed from the* DUKE*)* Plainly conceive,
I love you.

ISABELLA.   *(Playfully)* My brother did love Juliet.
And you tell me he shall die for't.

ANGELO.   *(Fondly)* He shall not Isabel, if you give me love.

ISABELLA. I know your virtue hath a licence in't
Which seems a little fouler than it is,
To pluck on others.

ANGELO. Believe me, on mine honour,
My words express my purpose.

ISABELLA. Ha! Little honour to be much believed,
And most pernicious purpose, Seeming, seeming!
I will proclaim thee, Angelo, look for't,
Sign me a present pardon for my brother,
Or with an outstretched throat I'll tell the world
What man thou art.

ANGELO. *(Taking her in his arms)* Who will believe thee,
Isabel?

*(They kiss fondly. ANGELO suddenly vanishes and
ISABELLA is discovered kneeling before the
BISHOP.)*

BISHOP. Repent you, fair one, of the sin you carry?

ISABELLA. I do, and bear the shame most patiently.

BISHOP. I'll teach you how you shall arraign your
conscience
And try your penitence, if it be sound,
Or hollowly put on.

ISABELLA. I'll gladly learn.

BISHOP. Love you the man that wronged you?

ISABELLA. *(Pause)* Yes, as I love the woman that wronged
him.

BISHOP. So then it seems your most offenceful act
Was mutually committed?

ISABELLA. Mutually.

BISHOP. Then was your sin of heavier kind than his.

ISABELLA. I do confess it, and repent it, father.

BISHOP. 'Tis meet so, daughter, but lest you do repent
As that the sin hath brought you to this shame,
Which sorrow is always towards ourselves, not heaven,
Showing we would not spare heaven as we love it,
But as we stand in fear.

ISABELLA.   I do repent me as it is an evil,
  And take the shame with joy.

BISHOP.   There rest.

*(BISHOP bends down as if to bless ISABELLA but
instead, takes her by the scruff of the neck and hurls
her forward, away from him.)*

Harlot!

(The BISHOP vanishes.)

*(CLAUDIO suddenly materialized: smirking
seductively.)*

CLAUDIO.   Sure, it is no sin
  Or of the deadly seven it is the least.

ISABELLA.   Which is the least?

CLAUDIO.   If it were damnable, he being so wise
  Why would he for the momentary trick
  Be perdurably fin'd—O Isabel!

ISABELLA.   *(Fearful)* What says my brother?

CLAUDIO.   *(Archly)* Death is a fearful thing.

ISABELLA.   *(Frightened)* Alas, alas.

CLAUDIO.   *(Close)* Sweet sister, let me live.
  What sin you do to save a brother's life.
  Nature dispenses with the deed so far
  That it becomes a virtue.

*(There is momentary tension between them, then
CLAUDIO grabs her rudely and tries to close her in a
lecherous embrace. ISABELLA pushes him off. He
laughs obscenely through her next speech.)*

ISABELLA.   O you beast! O faithless coward.
  O dishonest wretch.
  Beast. Beast. Beast.

(Cacophony of sound on tape as follows.)

(Voices on tape.)

ANGELO.   Sure it is no sin—or of the deadly seven, it is the
  least.

BISHOP. You must lay down the treasures of your body.

CLAUDIO. We are all frail.

ANGELO. The treasures of your body.

ISABELLA. And strip myself to death as to a bed
That long I have been sick for.

ANGELO. Plainly conceive that I love you.

BISHOP. Love you the man that . . .

ANGELO.   love you

CLAUDIO. Let me live . . .

BISHOP.   wronged you?

*(BISHOP, ANGELO repeat: Love you.
Wronged you while CLAUDIO's voice
crescendoes above it.)*

CLAUDIO. Let me live. Let me live. Let me live!!!

*(All visions and sound disappear suddenly. ISABELLA
now alone in a single spot.)*

ISABELLA. Dissolve my life, let not my sense unsettle
Lest I should drown, or stab, or hang myself.
O state of Nature, fail together in me
Since the best props are warpt. So which way now?
The best way is the next way to a grave.
Each errant step beside is torment. Lo,
The moon is down, the crickets chirp, the screech-owl
Calls in the dawn. All offices are done
Save what I fail in.
An end, and that is all.

*Lights blend surreally. CLAUDIO suddenly appears.
ISABELLA rushes into his arms. They embrace
desperately. CLAUDIO takes her by the hand and leads
her towards the curtained-bed. There she is presented to
ANGELO who clasps CLAUDIO's hand as CLAUDIO
does his. ANGELO then motions for CLAUDIO to
depart. CLAUDIO begins to back out of the scene and
into the waiting arms of the PROVOST who smiles
curiously at CLAUDIO then, putting his arm around his
shoulder in a fraternal manner, leads him out.*

ISABELLA *stands mute and still.* ANGELO *approaches her and tenderly undoes her nun's headpiece.* ISABELLA's *short, cropped hair is revealed underneath. Then he undoes her nun's habit until she stands naked before him. She remains still and devoid of emotion. Then,* ANGELO *bends down, places his arms around her waist and his head in the pit of her stomach.*

Instinctively, ISABELLA *makes a move as if to embrace* ANGELO's *head, but the gesture is cut short, and she then resumes her neutral position.* ANGELO *lifts her into his arms, draws open the surrounding curtains, and disappears behind them with* ISABELLA.

Downstage, in a gloomy light, the BISHOP *appears before* CLAUDIO, *who is kneeling before him, and administers the last rites.*

BISHOP. *(As if intoning a prayer)*
Be absolute for death: either death or life
Shall thereby be the sweeter. Reason thus with life
If I do lose thee, I do lose a thing
That none but fools would keep; a breath thou art
Servile to all the skyey influences
That does this habitation where thou keep'st
Hourly afflict. Merely, thou art death's fool,
For him thou labour'st by thy flight to shun,
And yet runn'st toward him still. Thou art not noble,
For all th'accommodations that thou bear'st
Are nursed by baseness. Thou'rt by no means valiant
For thou dost fear the soft and tender fork
Of a poor worm. The best of rest is sleep,
And that thou oft provok'st, yet grossly fear'st
Thy death, which is no more. Thou art not thyself,
For thou exists on many a thousand grains
That issue out of dust. Happy thou art not,
For what thou hast not, still thou striv'st to get,
And what thou hast, forget'st. Thou art not certain
For thy complexion shifts to strange effects,
After the moon. If thou art rich, thou'rt poor,
For, like an ass, whose back with ingots bows,
Thou bear'st thy heavy riches but a journey,
And death unloads thee. Friend hast thou none,
For thine own bowels, which do call thee sire,

215

The mere effusion of thy proper loins,
Do curse the gout, serpigo, and the rheum
For ending thee no sooner. Thou hast nor youth nor
    age,
But as it were an after-dinner's sleep,
Dreaming on both, for all thy blessed youth
Becomes as aged, and doth beg the alms
Of palsied eld: and when thou art old and rich,
Thou hast neither heat, affection, limb, nor beauty
To make thy riches pleasant. What's yet in this
That bears the name of life? Yet in this life
Lie hid more thousand deaths; yet death we fear,
That makes these odds all even.

*(BISHOP gives benediction over CLAUDIO and both
characters fade out.)*

(Lights up by bed.)

*(ISABELLA slowly extricates herself from behind the
curtains, stumbles upon a desk on which sits a covered
object. She trembles for a moment then whips away the
cover revealing severed head of CLAUDIO. There is an
ear-splitting scream.)*

*(Lights up downstage where BISHOP is now hearing
ANGELO in confession. ANGELO, on his knees, before
him.)*

ANGELO. O my dread Lord,
    I should be guiltier than my guiltiness
    To think I can be undiscernible
    When I perceive your grace, like power divine,
    Hath looked upon my passes.

BISHOP. *(Harshly)* He who the sword of heaven will bear
    Should be as holy as severe;
    Pattern in himself to know
    Grace to stand, and virtue, go:
    More not less to others paying
    Than by self offences weighing.
    Shame to him whose cruel striking
    Kills for faults of his own liking.

ANGELO. No longer session hold upon my shame,
    But let my trial be mine own confession.

Immediate sentence then, and sequent death
Is all the grace I beg.

*(BISHOP raises him up sternly; looks him squarely in
the face, and then smiles kindly.)*

BISHOP.   Grace go with you. Benedicte. *(Exit.)*

ANGELO.   *(For a moment relieved, then his face darkening
with memory.)* He should have lived,
Save that his riotous youth with dangerous sense
Might in the times to come have ta'en revenge,
By so receiving a dishonoured life
With ransom of such shame. Would yet he had lived.
Alack, when once our grace we have forgot,
Nothing goes right. We would, and we would not.

(Exits.)

LUCIO.   *(Who has watched ANGELO's confession with mock
contempt)*
Hark how the villain would close now, after his treason-
able abuses. Such a fellow is not to be talked about
withal. Away with him to prison. Where is the Provost?
Away with him to prison, I say. Lay bolts upon him.
Let him speak no more.

Being criminal, in double violation
Of sacred chastity, and of promise-breach,
The very mercy of the law cries out,
Most audible, even from his proper tongue,
'An Angelo for Claudio, death for death!'
Haste still pays haste, and leisure answers leisure,
Like doth quit like and Measure still for Measure.
Then, Angelo, thy faults thus manifested,
'We do condemn thee to the very block
Where Claudio stooped to death, and with like haste.'
Away with him.
Take him hence.
To th'rack with him.
Touse him joint by joint!

*(Drops his facetiously vengeful mask and confronts
the audience head-on)*
 The business of my state
Made me a looker-on here in Vienna,

Where I have seen corruption boil and bubble
Till it o'errun the stew. Laws for all faults,
But faults so countenanced that the strong statutes
Stand like the forfeits in a barber's shop,
As much in mock as mark.

(ISABELLA enters fierce and resolute.)

ISABELLA. O, I will to him and pluck out his eyes!
Unhappy Claudio! Wretched Isabel!
Injurious world! Most damned Angelo!
(Bursts into tears.)

LUCIO.   This nor hurts him nor profits you a jot.
Forbear it therefore; give your cause to heaven.
Mark what I say which you shall find
By every syllable a faithful verity.
The Duke comes home tomorrow—nay, dry your eyes—
Already he hath carried
Notice to Escalus and Angelo
Who do prepare to meet him at the gates
There to give up their power.
I have found you out a stand most fit
Where you may have such vantage on the Duke
He shall not pass you.
If you can pace your wisdom
In that good path that I would wish it go,
And you shall have your bosom
On this wretch,
Grace of the Duke, revenges to your heart,
And general honour.

*(ISABELLA stops crying, and grimly tears the crucifix
from round her neck.)*

Blackout

PROVOST *enters carrying* CLAUDIO'*s clothes and an empty
sack. During following speech, he stuffs clothes into sack.*

PROVOST.   What a merry world it is, since, of two crimes,
the merrier was put down and the worser allowed,
by order of law a furred gown to keep him warm;
and furred with fox and lambskin too, to signify
that craft be richer than innocence!

Here's a change indeed in the common wealth!
Why, there is so great a fever on goodness that
only its dissolution will cure it. Novelty is
only in request, and it is as dangerous to be aged
in any kind of course as it is to be virtuous in
any undertaking. There is scarce truth enough to
make societies secure—but security enough to
make fellowships accurst.
Much upon this riddle runs the wisdom of the world.
This news is old enough—yet it is every day's news.

*(Pulls drawstring tightly around sack for a moment,
hauls it onto his back and exits on fade out.)*

Sound of the DUKE's trumpet as at start of play.

Lights up.

*DUKE enters from one side; ANGELO, ESCALUS and
BISHOP from the other.*

DUKE.   My very worthy cousin, fairly met.
Our old and faithful friend, we are glad to see you.

ESCALUS.   Happy return be to your royal grace.

DUKE.   Many and hearty thankings to you both.
We have made inquiry of you, and we hear
Such goodness of your justice that our soul
Cannot but yield you forth to public thanks,
Forerunning more requital.

ANGELO.   You make my bonds still greater.

DUKE.   O, your desert speaks loud, and I should wrong it
To lock it in the wards of covert bosom,
When it deserves with characters of brass
A forted residence 'gainst the tooth of time
and razure of oblivion. Give me your hand,
And let the subjects see, to make them know
that outward courtesies would fain proclaim
Favours that keep within.

LUCIO   *(Entering with ISABELLA and PROVOST)* Now is
your time. Speak loud and kneel before him.

DUKE. Come Escalus, you must walk by us on our other hand
    And good supporters are you.

ISABELLA. Justice, O royal Duke! Vail your regard
    Upon a wronged—I would fain have said, a maid.
    O worthy prince, dishonour not your eye
    By throwing it on any other object
    Till you have heard me in my true complaint
    And given me justice, justice, justice, justice!

DUKE. Relate your wrongs. In what? By whom? Be brief.
    Here is Lord Angelo shall give you justice.
    Reveal yourself to him.

ISABELLA. O worthy Duke,
    You bid me seek redemption of the devil.
    Hear me yourself, for that which I must speak
    Must either punish me, not being believed,
    Or wring redress from you. Hear me, O hear me, hear.

ANGELO. My lord, her wits, I fear me, are not firm.
    She hath been a suitor to me for her brother,
    Cut off by course of justice—

ISABELLA. By course of justice!

ANGELO. And she will speak most bitterly and strange.

ISABELLA. Most strange, but yet most truly, will I speak.
    That Angelo's foresworn, is it not strange?
    That Angelo's a murderer, is't not strange?
    That Angelo is an adulterous thief,
    An hypocrite, a virgin-violator,
    Is it not strange, and strange?

DUKE. Nay, it is ten times strange.

ISABELLA. Is it not truer he is Angelo
    Than this is all as true as it is strange.
    Nay, it is ten times true, for truth is truth
    To th'end of reck'ning;

    *(Pause. LUCIO steps forward giving support to
    ISABELLA.)*

DUKE. Away with her. Poor soul,
    She speaks this in th'infirmity of sense.

ISABELLA. O prince, I conjure thee, as thou believ'st
    There is another comfort than this world,
    That thou neglect me not with that opinion
    That I am touched with madness. Make not impossible
    That which but seems unlike. 'Tis not impossible
    But one, the wicked'st caitiff on the ground,
    May seem as shy, as grave, as just, as absolute
    As Angelo. Even so may Angelo,
    In all his dressings, characts, titles, forms,
    Be an arch-villain. Believe it, royal prince.
    If he be less, he's nothing: but he's more,
    Had I more name for badness.

DUKE. By mine honesty,
    If she be mad, as I believe no other,
    Her madness hath the oddest frame of sense,
    Such a dependency of thing on thing,
    As e'er I heard in madness.

ISABELLA. O gracious Duke,
    Harp not on that, nor do not banish reason
    For inequality, but let your reason serve
    To make the truth appear where it seems hid.

DUKE. Many that are not mad
    Have sure more lack of reason. What would you say?

ISABELLA. I am the sister of one Claudio,
    Condemned upon the act of fornication
    To lose his head, condemned by Angelo.
    I, in probation of a sisterhood,
    Was sent to by my brother. One Lucio
    As then the messenger—

LUCIO. That's I, an't like your grace,
    I came to her from Claudio, and desired her
    To try her gracious fortune with Lord Angelo
    For her poor brother's pardon.

ISABELLA. That's he indeed.

DUKE. You were not bid to speak.

LUCIO. No, my good Lord,
    Nor wished to hold my peace.

DUKE. I wish you now, then.

Pray you, take note of it, and when you have
A business for yourself, pray heaven you then
Be perfect.

LUCIO. I warrant your honour.

DUKE. The warrant's for yourself: take heed to't.
Proceed.

ISABELLA. I went
To this pernicous caitiff deputy—

DUKE. That's somewhat madly spoken.

ISABELLA. Pardon it,
The phrase is to the matter.

DUKE. The matter then, proceed.

ISABELLA. In brief, to set the needless process by,
How I persuaded, how I prayed, and kneeled,
How he refelled me, and how I replied—
For this was of much length—the vile conclusion
I now begin with grief and shame to utter.
He would not, but by gift of my chaste body
To his concup'scible intemperate lust
Release my brother, and after much debatement
My sisterly remorse confutes mine honour,
And I did yield to him. But the next morn betimes,
His purpose surfeiting, he sends a warrant
For my poor brother's head.

(Long pause. DUKE turns slowly and regards the
BISHOP, *then turns to* ESCALUS, *and finally to*
ANGELO *who, without expression, returns the*
DUKE's *look. After a goodly pause, the* DUKE *begins*
to speak—still facing ANGELO.)

DUKE. By heaven fond wretch *(then turning towards*
ISABELLA) thou knowest not what thou speak'st.
Or else thou art suborned against his honour
In hateful practice. First, his integrity
Stands without blemish. Next, it imports no reason
That with such vehemency he should pursue
Faults proper to himself. If he had so offended,
He would have weighed thy brother by himself,
And not have cut him off. Someone hath set you on.

Confess the truth, and say by whose advice
Thou cam'st here to complain.

*(ISABELLA dumbstruck, steps back and turns
slowly from the DUKE to the BISHOP to
ESCALUS to ANGELO, seeing them all anew.)*

ISABELLA. And is this all?
Then, O you blessed ministers above,
Keep me in patience, and with ripened time
Unfold the evil which is here wrapped up
In countenance. Heaven shield your grace from woe,
As I thus wronged hence unbelieved go.

DUKE. I know you'd fain be gone. Yet stay awhile.
(Turning to his own.) Shall we thus permit
A blasting and a scandalous breath to fall
On him so near us?
No might nor greatness in mortality
Can censure 'scape; back-wounding calumny
The whitest virtue strikes. What king so strong
Can tie the gall up in the slanderous tongue?
Do you not smile at this, Lord Angelo?
O heaven, the vanity of wretched fools!

ANGELO. I did but smile till now.
Now, good my lord, give me the scope of justice.
My patience here is touched. I do perceive
These poor informal wretches are no more
But instruments of some more mightier member
That sets them on.

DUKE. Thou foolish knave, and thou pernicious woman,
Think'st thou thy oaths,
Though they would swear down each particular saint,
Were testimonies against his worth and credit
That's sealed in approbation?
Thy slanders now shall by our laws be weighed
And by their Justice priz'd. Take her to prison
And see our pleasure herein executed. To prison
with her! *(Turning front.)*
And all about that can hear, now hear this:
The law hath not been dead, though it hath slept.
Those many had not dared to do that evil

223

If that the first that did th'edict infringe
Had answered for his deed. Now 'tis awake,
Take note of what is done, and like a prophet
Looks in a glass that shows what future evils,
Either now, or by remissness new, conceived,
Are now to have no successive degrees,
But, ere they live, to end.

(DUKE *gestures to suggest formal ceremony is ended.*
ISABELLA *is escorted out by* PROVOST *while tables
are set up, and formal gowns are laid to one side. Before
she exits,* ANGELO *approaches* ISABELLA *and whispers
for her hearing alone.)*

ANGELO. *(Taking her arm)*
I have a motion much imports your good,
Whereto if you'll a willing ear incline,
What's mine is yours, and what is yours is mine.

*(ISABELLA expressionlessly shoves away ANGELO's hand,
turns and moves off swiftly, conducted by the PROVOST.)*

*(The table is now set. The DUKE, now in gay private
attire, in stark contrast to his judicial robes, sits at one
place; ESCALUS and ANGELO beside him; they too
are now dressed casually. Food and drink is brought.)*

*(The following dialogue is permeated with a gaiety and
crudity that belies all we know of these characters.)*

DUKE. *(Mimicking the lower-classes)* What news abroad
i' the world?

ANGELO. *(Mock guiltily, also with put-on voice)* Sir,
I have been an unlawful bawd time out of mind,
but yet I will be content to be a lawful hangman.
I would be glad to receive some instruction from
me fellow partner.

ESCALUS. *(Laughing at* ANGELO's *imitation; mock-
astonished)* A bawd, sir? *(To* DUKE.) Fie upon him, he
will discredit our mystery.

ANGELO. 'Faith, my lord, I spoke it but according to the
trick. If you will hang me for it, you may. But I had
rather it would please you I might be whipped.

(All fall about with laughter.)

DUKE.   Whipped first, sir, and hanged after. *(This tops last joke and all explode with even greater laughter.)* Proclaim it, Provost, round about the city,
If any woman wronged by this lewd fellow,
As I have heard him swear himself there's one
Whom he begot with child—let her appear,
And he shall marry her.

ANGELO.   *(Acting craven)* I beseech your highness, do not marry me to a whore. Marrying a punk, my Lord, is pressing to death, whipping *and* hanging.

DUKE.   *(Pouring wine over* ANGELO's *head)*
Slandering a prince deserves it.

(All laugh uproariously and carry on clowning, eating and drinking through.)

(Fade out)

Variations on The Merchant of Venice

CAST

SHYLOCK	SALANIO
CHUS	LORENZO
TUBAL	DUKE
JESSICA	BALTHAZAR
ANTONIO	GAOLER
BASSANIO	MESSENGER
GRATIANO	PORTIA
SALERIO	NERISSA

Sound of explosion followed by pandemonium.

VOICE OVER.   *(Slides illustrating events:)*
  Jerusalem, July 22nd, 1946. At 12.30 p.m. today a
  tremendous explosion ripped off an entire wing of the
  King David Hotel destroying seven floors and 25 rooms
  occupied by the Secretariat of the Palestine Government and the Defence Security office of British
  Military Headquarters. There are 91 known dead,
  47 injured and 43 persons including senior government
  officials missing. Ambulance men are passing water to
  injured victims still lying buried under concrete blocks
  and fallen masonry while a way is being cut for their
  rescue. Across the road, on the white stone wall of
  the recreation hall of the YMCA building, a huge
  bloody patch shows where one man had been blown
  across the road against the wall 50 yards away. The
  Jewish Underground Terrorist organisation, Irgun, has
  claimed responsibility for the atrocity which has been
  widely condemned by, among others, the executive
  of the Jewish Agency, Dr. Chaim Weitzman and
  President Harry S. Truman. Known Zionist terrorists
  are being rounded up throughout Jerusalem. Several
  have been shot in skirmishes with British Patrols in the
  old part of the city.

  *(Lights up on dead body covered with khaki blanket:
  group of Jews huddled around,* SHYLOCK, TUBAL,
  CHUS, JESSICA, *etc.)*

227

SHYLOCK. *(After silent prayer)*
    The plagues of Egypt and the curse of heaven,
    Earth's barrenness, and all men's hated
    Inflict upon them, thou great Primus Motor.
    And here upon my knees, striking the earth,
    I ban their souls to everlasting pains
    And extreme tortures of the fiery deep
    Thus thus have dealt with me in my distress.

    O wretched brethren, born to see this day!
    Why stand you thus unmov'd with my laments?
    Why weep you not to think upon these wrongs?

TUBAL. Know Shylock, as hardly can we brook
    The cruel handling of ourselves in this.
    Thou see'st how they ravine all our land.

SHYLOCK. Why do we yield to their extortion!
    We are a multitude, and they but few
    That now encompasseth what is our own.

CHUS. Good Shylock, be patient.

SHYLOCK. Aye, I prithee leave me in my patience.
    You that were ne'ere possess't of wealth are pleased
        with want.
    But give him liberty at least to mourn
    That in a field amidst his enemies,
    Doth see his soldiers slain, himself disarm'd
    And knows no means of his recovery.
    Henceforth, I'll wish but for eternal night,
    That clouds of darkness may enclose my flesh,
    And hide these extreme sorrows from mine eyes.
    For cruelly we have toiled to inherit here
    And painful nights have been appointed me,
    Great injuries are not soon forgot.

TUBAL. Come, let us leave him in his ireful mood.
    Our words will but increase his ecstasy.

CHUS. On then, but trust me, 'tis a misery
    To see a man in such affliction

TUBAL. Farewell Shylock.

    (CHUS and TUBAL and OTHERS pick up DEAD MAN

and carry him out on stretcher. JESSICA *comes forward to* SHYLOCK.)

JESSICA. Here is the letter, writ as thou command'st.

SHYLOCK. *(Reads it, returns it to* JESSICA)
Entertain Lorenzo as you will
With all the courtesy you can afford,
Provided that you keep your maidenhead.
Use him as if he were a Philistine.
Dissemble, swear, protest, vow to love him.
In's company canst thou intercept
Those fateful tidings which the governor's tongue
Jealously would guard from others ears.

JESSICA. What, shall I suffer him to be betrothed?

SHYLOCK. *(Impatiently)*
It's no sin to deceive a Christian
For they themselves hold it a principle,
Faith is not to be held with heretics,
But all are heretics that are not Jews.
This follows well and therefore fear it not.

JESSICA. *(Subduing her anger)*
I cannot choose, seeing my father bids.

SHYLOCK. *(Making amends)*
Daughter, thou perceivst the plight
Wherein these Christians have oppressed us.
Be ruled by me; for in extremity,
We ought to make bar of no policy.

JESSICA. Shall we thus debase our ancient faith,
And violate our vows?

SHYLOCK. We serve our god
When, with our guile we strike his enemies
And like the holy warriors of old
We must test our faith upon the field.
Thy courage now must forage in thy blood.

JESSICA. What'ere it be to injure them
That have so manifestly wrong'd us,
I shall, for thy sake, attempt.

SHYLOCK. Then Jessica, think upon thy ways,
Entreat him fair and give him friendly looks,

So shall he slubber thee with heedless speech.
(looks down at armband of slain man in hand)
They say we are a scatter'd Nation,
I cannot tell, but we have scrambled up
Our wealth from every foreign shore,
And soon our many tribes shall be as one.
We'll be reveng'd on this accursed town
And with our Brother's blood shall cleanse its sin.

JESSICA.   Not for myself, but gentle Shylock,
Father, for thee lamenteth Jessica.
But I will learn to leave these fruitless tears
And urg'd thereto with my afflictions,
With fierce exclaims run to the Senate-house
And in the Senate reprehend them all,
And rend their hearts with tearing of my hair
Till they remove the wrongs they have invok'd.

SHYLOCK.   No, Jessica, things past recovery
Are hardly cur'd with exclamations.
Attend me close and I'll instruct thy woe.
First be thou void of these affections:
Compassion, love, vain hope and heartless fear.
Be mov'd at nothing, see thou pity none,
But to thyself smile when the Christians moan.
This is the life we Jews are us'd to lead
And reason too, for Christians do the like.

(JESSICA goes to speak, SHYLOCK puts finger to her lips.)

SHYLOCK.   Be silent daughter, sufferance breeds ease
And time shall yield us an occasion
Which on the sudden cannot serve the turn.

(JESSICA tries to stifle sobs, falls into SHYLOCK's arms. He holds her close on Blackout.)

Lights up:

Background rumble of distant explosions, and occasional rifle-fire.

BASSANIO, *in the uniform of an English Lieutenant enters with* ANTONIO *who is dressed in 40s English attire suggestive of the Foreign Office.* BASSANIO *looks towards the distant rumble, shakes his head sadly—as does* ANTONIO. *They sit by table of outdoor cafe, order drinks. Both staring straight ahead as din gradually subsides in the distance.*

ANTONIO. In sooth, I know not why I am so sad.
 It wearies me, you say it wearies you
 But how I caught it, found it or came by it,
 What stuff 'tis made of, whereof it is born,
 I am to learn:
 And such a want-wit sadness makes of me
 That I have much ado to know myself.

BASSANIO. Your mind is tossing on the ocean,
 There, where your argosies with portly sail,
 Like Signiors and rich burghers on the flood,
 Or as it were the pageants of the sea—
 Do overpeer the petty traffickers,
 That curtsy to them, do them reverence.
 As they fly by with them with their woven wings.
 Believe me sir, had I such venture forth,
 The better part of my affections would
 Be with my hopes abroad.

ANTONIO. Believe me no—I thank my fortune for it
 My ventures are not in one bottom trusted,
 Nor to one place; nor is my whole estate
 Upon the fortune of this present year.
 Therefore my merchandise makes me not sad.
 (Suddenly bitter) O these monstrous times
 Put bars between the owners and their rights,
 And so, though yours, not yours. *(Broods)*

BASSANIO. You have too much respect on the world
 They do lose it who buy it with much care.

 ANTONIO *brushes away his dark thoughts and turns anew to* BASSANIO.

ANTONIO. Well, tell me now what lady is the same
 To whom you swore a secret pilgrimage,
 That you today promised to tell me of?

BASSANIO. 'Tis not unknown to you, Antonio,
 How much I have disabled mine estate,
 By somewhat showing a more swelling port

Than my faint means would grant continuance:
Nor do I now make moan to be abridged
From such a noble rate, but my chief care
Is to come fairly off from the great debts
Wherein my time, something too prodigal,
Hath left me gaged. To you, Antonio,
I owe the most in money and in love,
And from your love I have a warranty
To unburthen all my plots and purposes
How to clear of all the debts I owe.

ANTONIO. I pray you, good Bassanio, let me know it,
And if it stands, as you yourself still do,
Within the eye of honour, be assured,
My purse, my person, my extremest means,
Lie all unlocked to your occasions.

BASSANIO. In my schooldays, when I had lost one shaft,
I shot his fellow of the self-same flight
The self-same way, with more advised watch,
To find the other forth, and by adventuring both,
I oft found both: I urge this childhood proof,
Because what follows is pure innocence . . .
I owe you much, and, like a wilful youth,
That which I owe is lost—but if you please
To shoot another arrow that self way
Which you did shoot the first, I do not doubt,
As I will watch the aim, or to find both,
Or bring your letter hazard back again,
And thankfully rest debtor for the first.

ANTONIO. You know me well, and herein spend but time
To wind about my love with circumstance,
And out of doubt you do me now more wrong
In making question of my uttermost
Than if you had made waste of all I have:
Then do but say to me what I should do
That in your knowledge may by me be done,
And I am prest unto it: therefore, speak.

BASSANIO. In Belmont is a lady richly left,
And she is fair, and fairer than that word,
Of wondrous virtues—sometimes from her eyes
I did receive fair speechless messages.

(Half lights up on PORTIA *in peignoir, attended by* NERISSA, *lolling on divan.)*

Her name is Portia, nothing undervalued
To Cato's daughter, Brutus' Portia;
Nor is the wide world ignorant of her worth
For the four winds blow in from every coast
Renowned suitors, and her sunny locks
Hang on her temples like a golden fleece,
Which makes her seat of Belmont Colchos' strand
And many Jasons come in quest of her.

(Full lights up. PORTIA *recumbent on divan with makeup pads over her eyes,* NERISSA, *her black companion massaging her neck.)*

PORTIA. By my troth, Nerissa, my little body is aweary of this great world.

NERISSA. You would be, sweet madam, if your miseries were in the same abundance as your good fortunes are: and yet for aught I see, they are as sick that surfeit with too much as they that starve with nothing; it is no mean happiness therefore to be seated in the mean.

PORTIA. Good sentences and well pronounced.

NERISSA. They would be better if well followed.

PORTIA. If to do were as easy as to know what were good to do, Chapels had been churches, and poor men's cottages prince's palaces. It is a good divine that follows his own instructions. I can easier teach twenty what were good to be done, than be one of the twenty to follow mine own teaching . . . But this reasoning is not in the fashion to choose me a husband. O me, the word "choose"! I may neither choose whom I would nor refuse whom I dislike—so is the will of a living daughter curbed by the will of a dead father . . . Is it not hard, Nerissa, that I cannot choose one, nor refuse none?

NERISSA. Your father was ever virtuous, and holy men at their death have good inspirations, therefore the lottery that he hath devised in these three chests of gold silver and lead, whereof who chooses his meaning chooses

233

you, will no doubt never be chosen by any rightly but one whom you shall rightly love. But what warmth is there in your affection towards any of these princely suitors that are already come?

PORTIA.   There is not one among them but I dote on his very absence. No, if I live to be as old as Sibylla, I will die as chaste as Diana unless I be obtained by the manner of my father's will.

NERISSA.   Do you not remember lady, in your father's time, a Venetian, a scholar and a soldier that came hither in the company of the Marquis of Montferrat?

PORTIA.   Yes, yes, it was Bassanio, as I think so was he called.

NERISSA.   True, madam, he of all the men that ever my foolish eyes looked upon, was the best deserving a fair lady.

PORTIA.   *(Consulting picture file)* I remember him well, and I remember him worthy of thy praise.

(Lights fade to reveal former scene.)

BASSANIO.   O my Antonio, had I but the means
To hold a rival place with one of them,
I have a mind presages me such thrift,
That I should questionless be fortunate.

ANTONIO.   Thou know'st that all my fortunes are at sea,
Neither have I money nor commodity
To raise a present sum, therefore go forth,
Try what my credit can in Venice do—
That shall be racked, even to the uttermost,
To furnish thee to Belmont, to fair Portia.
Go, presently inquire, and so will I,
Where money is, and I no question make
To have it of my trust or for my sake.

*(WAITER brings check, places on table beside
BASSANIO who surreptitiously slides it over to
ANTONIO. ANTONIO discovers cheque, signs for it,
and rises to go.)*

ANTONIO.   I am presently called forth to supper.

(BASSANIO, presuming a bargain has been made, gives ANTONIO a firm handshake. ANTONIO, somewhat confused, leaves as GRATIANO, obviously having overheard end of last scene, appears.)

GRATIANO. *(Appearing suddenly, having overheard tail end of last scene)* Signior Bassanio.

BASSANIO. Gratiano!

GRATIANO. I have a suit to you.

BASSANIO. You have obtained it. *(Starts to go)*

GRATIANO. *(Stops him)* I must go with you to Belmont.

BASSANIO. Why then you must. *(Starts to go again.)*

GRATIANO. You must not deny me.

BASSANIO. *(Levelling with him)* Hear thee, Gratiano.
Thou art too wild, too rude, and bold of voice;
Parts that become thee happily enough
And in such eyes as ours appear not faults
But where thou art not known, why, there they show
Somewhat too illiberal.

GRATIANO. *(Deliberately clowning)* Let me play the fool,
With mirth and laughter let old wrinkles come . . .

BASSANIO. Pray thee, take pain
To allay with some cold drops of modesty
Thy skipping spirit, lest through thy wild
    behaviour,
I be misconstrued in the place I go to
And lose my hopes.

GRATIANO. If I do not put on a sober habit,
Talk with respect, and swear but now and then,
Wear prayer-books in my pocket, look demurely;
Nay more, while grace is saying, hood mine eyes
Thus with my hat, and sigh and say amen,
Use all the observance of civility,
Like one well-studied in a sad ostent
To please his grandam—never trust me more.

BASSANIO. *(Suspicious)* Well, we shall see your bearing.

235

GRATIANO. *(Suddenly whipping fifth of whiskey from back pocket)* Nay, but I bar tonight. You shall not gauge me by what we do tonight .

BASSANIO. Fare you well: I have some business.

GRATIANO. You must not deny me.

(GRATIANO suddenly looks hurt, drops down beside BASSANIO like a doleful pup and barks mournfully. BASSANIO, despite himself, laughs and leaves, saying good naturedly.

BASSANIO. Fare you well.

(GRATIANO, content and still playing the pup, exits.)

Fade out.)

Music: Lights up.

LORENZO and JESSICA enter hand in hand. They are outdoors.

LORENZO. How sweet the moonlight sleeps upon this bank!
Here will we sit and let the sounds of music
Creep in our ears—soft stillness and the night
Become the touches of sweet harmony.
Sit, Jessica. Look how the floor of heaven
Is thick inlaid with patons of bright gold.
There's not the smallest orb which thou behold'st
But in his motion like an angel sings,
Still choiring to the young-eyed cherubims;
Such harmony is in immortal souls!
But whilst this muddy vesture of decay
Doth grossly close it in, we cannot hear it.

JESSICA. I am never merry when I hear sweet music.

LORENZO. The reason is, your spirits are attentive;
For do but note a wild and wanton herd,
Or race of youthful and unhandled colts,
Fetching mad bounds, bellowing and neighing loud—
Which is the hot condition of their blood
If they but hear perchance a trumpet sound,
Or any air of music touch their ears,
You shall perceive them make a mutual stand,

Their savage eyes turned to a modest gaze
By the sweet power of music; therefore, the poet
Did feign that Orpheus drew trees, stones, and floods,
Since naught so stockish, hard, and full of rage,
But music for the time doth change his nature.
The man that hath no music in himself,
Nor is not moved with concord of sweet sounds,
Is fit for treasons, stratagems, and spoils,
The motions of his spirit are dull as night,
And his affections dark as Erebus:
Let no such man be trusted. Mark the music.

(He draws her close hungrily. She suddenly starts as if hearing someone approach. Then she dashes off. GRATIANO appears to LORENZO who, entirely out of character, beams out a broad, lewd smile.)

GRATIANO. *(Also smiling)*
O what a goodly outside falsehood hath.

(LORENZO makes a gesture to suggest he is almost "in" to JESSICA and both men laugh coarsely.)

(Fade out.)

SHYLOCK, TUBAL *and* BASSANIO.

TUBAL. *(With small notebook and pencil)*
Three thousand ducats—well.

BASSANIO. *(Talking to SHYLOCK)* Ay sir, for three months.

TUBAL. For three months—well.

BASSANIO. For the which, as I told you, Antonio shall be bound.

TUBAL. Antonio shall become bound—well.

BASSANIO. May you stead me? Will you pleasure me? Shall I know your answer?

TUBAL. Three thousand ducats for three months—and Antonio bound.

BASSANIO. Your answer to that!

SHYLOCK. Antonio is a good man.

BASSANIO. Have you heard any imputation to the contrary?

SHYLOCK. My meaning in saying he is a good man is to
have you understand me that he is sufficient.

TUBAL. Yet his means are in supposition. He hath an argosy
bound to Tripolis, another to the Indies; I understand
moreover upon the Rialto, he hath a third at Mexico, a
fourth for England and other ventures he hath
squander'd abroad.

SHYLOCK. *(To* TUBAL*)* But ships are but boards, sailors but
men . . .

TUBAL. And there be land-thieves . . .

SHYLOCK. And water-thieves . . .

TUBAL. Land-rats . . .

SHYLOCK. And water-rats . . .

TUBAL. Water-rats?

SHYLOCK. I mean pi-rates.

TUBAL. And then there is the peril of waters,

SHYLOCK. Winds,

TUBAL. And rocks . . .

SHYLOCK. *(To* BASSANIO*)* The man is, notwithstanding,
sufficient.

TUBAL. Three thousand ducats?

SHYLOCK. I think I may take his bond.

BASSANIO. Be assured you may.

SHYLOCK. I will be assured I may, and that I may be
assured, I will bethink me . . .

BASSANIO. Here is Signior Antonio.

SHYLOCK. Rest you fair, good signior,
Your worship was the last man in our mouths.

ANTONIO. Shylock, albeit I neither lend nor borrow
By taking nor giving of excess,
Yet to supply the ripe wants of my friend

I'll break a custom. *(to* BASSANIO*)* Is he yet
    possessed
How much ye would?

SHYLOCK. Ay, ay, three thousand ducats.

ANTONIO. And for three months.

SHYLOCK. I had forgot—three months—you told me so.
    Well then, your bond: and let me see—but hear you,
    Methoughts you said you neither lend nor borrow
    Upon advantage.

ANTONIO. I do never use it.

SHYLOCK. When Jacob grazed his uncle Laban's sheep
    This Jacob from our holy Abram was
    (As his wise mother wrought in his behalf)
    The third possessor; ay, he was the third—

ANTONIO. And what of him? did he take interest?

SHYLOCK. No, not take interest—not as you would say
    Directly interest. Mark what Jacob did.
    When Laban and himself were compromised
    That all the eanlings which were streaked and pied
    Should fall as Jacob's hire, the ewes, being rank
    In end of autumn, turned to the rams,
    And when the work of generation was
    Between these woolly breeders in the act,
    The skilful shepherd pilled me certain wands,
    And, in the doing of the deed of kind,
    He stuck them up before the fulsome ewes,
    Who, then conceiving, did in aning time
    Fall parti-coloured lambs, and those were Jacob's.
    This was a way to thrive, and he was blest:
    And thrift is blessing if men steal it not.

ANTONIO. This was a venture, sir, that Jacob served for—
    A thing not in his power to bring to pass,
    But swayed and fashioned by the hand of heaven.
    Was this inserted to make interest good?
    Or is your gold and silver ewes and rams?

SHYLOCK. I cannot tell, I make it breed as fast!
    But note me, signior.

ANTONIO. Mark you this, Bassanio,
The devil can cite Scripture for his purpose.
An evil soul, producing holy witness,
Is like a villain with a smiling cheek,
A goodly apple rotten at the heart.

SHYLOCK. Three thousand ducats—'tis a good round sum
(Consulting notebook) Three months from twelve, then
let me see the rate.

ANTONIO. Well, Shylock, shall we be beholding to you?

SHYLOCK. Signior Antonio, many a time and oft
In the Rialto you have rated me
About my moneys and my usances:
Still have I borne it with a patient shrug,
For suff'rance is the badge of all our tribe.
You call me misbeliever, cut-throat dog,
And spit upon my Jewish gaberdine,
And all for use of that which is mine own.
Well then, it now appears you need my help:
Go to then, you come to me, and you say,
"Shylock, we would have moneys"—you say so!
You that did void your rheum upon my beard,
And foot me as you spurn a stranger cur
Over your threshold. Moneys is your suit.
What should I say to you? Should I not say
"Hath a dog money? Is it possible
A cur can lend three thousand ducats?" or
Shall I bend low, and in a bondman's key,
With bated breath and whisp'ring humbleness,
Say this:
"Fair sir, you spit on me on Wednesday last—
You Spurned me such a day—another time
You called me dog: and for these courtesies
I'll lend you thus much moneys"?

ANTONIO. I am as like to call thee so again,
To spit on thee again, to spurn thee too.
If thou wilt lend this money, lend it not
As to thy friends—for when did friendship take
A breed for barren metal of his friend?—
But lend it rather to thine enemy,
Who if he break, thou mayst with better face
Exact the penalty.

SHYLOCK.   Why, look you, how you storm!
    I would be friends with you, and have your love,
    Forget the shames that you have stained me with,
    Supply your present wants, and take no doit
    Of usance for my moneys, and you'll not hear me:
    This is kind I offer.

TUBAL.   This were kindness!

SHYLOCK.   This kindness will I show.
    Go with me to a notary, seal me there
    Your single bond, and, in merry sport,
    If you repay me not on such a day,
    In such a place, such sum or sums as are
    Expressed in the condition, let the forfeit
    Be nominated for an equal pound
    Of your fair flesh, to be cut off and taken
    In what part of your body pleaseth me.

ANTONIO.   Content, in faith—I'll seal to such a bond,
    And say there is much kindness in the Jew.

BASSANIO.   You shall not seal to such a bond for me,
    I'll rather dwell in my necessity.

ANTONIO.   Why, fear not man, I will not forfeit it.
    Within these two months, that's a month before
    This bond expires, I do expect return
    Of thrice three times the value of this bond.

TUBAL.   O father Abram! what these Christians are,
    Whose own hard dealing teaches them suspect
    The thoughts of others.

SHYLOCK.   Pray you, tell me this—
    If he should break his day, what should I gain
    By the exaction of the forfeiture?
    A pound of a man's flesh, taken from a man,
    Is not so estimable, profitable neither,
    As flesh of muttons, beefs, or goats. I say,
    To buy his favour, I extend this friendship.
    If he will take it, so—if not, adieu,
    And, for my love, I pray you wrong me not.

ANTONIO.   Yes, Shylock, I will seal unto this bond.

SHYLOCK.   Then meet me forthwith at the notary's

Give him directions for this merry bond,
And I will go and purse the ducats straight,
And presently I will be with you.

ANTONIO. The Hebrew will turn' Christian—he grows kind.

BASSANIO. I like not fair terms and a villain's mind.

ANTONIO. Come on—in this there can be no dismay,
My ships come home a month before the day.

*(SHYLOCK, TUBAL and CHUS watch ANTONIO and
BASSANIO exit.)*

SHYLOCK. See the simplicity of these base slaves
Who for the villains have not wit themselves
Think me to be a senseless lump of clay
That will with every water wash to dirt.
No, we are born methinks, to better chance
And fram'd of finer mould than common men
That measure naught but by the present time.
A reaching thought will search our deepest wits
And cast with cunning for the time to come.

(Fade out to black)

Lights up

SALERIO, LORENZO, GRATIANO.

LORENZO. What's the news?

SALERIO. *(Takes a letter from his wallet)* And it shall
please you to break up this, it shall seem to signify

LORENZO. I know the hand. In faith 'tis a fair hand.
And whiter than the paper it writ on,
Is the fair hand that writ.

GRATIANO. Love-news, in faith.

LORENZO. Tell gentle Jessica I will not fail her—speak it
privately.
Go, and meet me and Gratiano
At Gratiano's lodging some hour hence.

SALERIO. Ay, marry, I'll be gone about it straight.

(SALERIO exits)

GRATIANO.   Was not that letter from fair Jessica?

LORENZO.   I must needs tell thee all. She hath directed
How I shall take her from her father's house,
What gold and jewels she is furnished with,
And how all is now at readiness. Gratiano, hear:
"My thoughts before were frail and unconfirmed
And I was chain'd to follies of the world,
But now experience, purchased with grief,
Has made me see the difference of things.
My sinful soul alas, hath pac'd too long
The fatal labyrinth of misbelief
Far from the Son that gives eternal life."

GRATIANO.   Now by my hood, a gentile and no Jew!

LORENZO.   Come, go with me, peruse this as thou goest.
Fair Jessica shall be my torchbearer.

(They exit.)

(Fade out.)

Lights up.

SHYLOCK's *house.*

SHYLOCK *enters with* SALERIO *reading note.*

SHYLOCK.   *(Calls)* Jessica!

(JESSICA appears at the door.)

JESSICA.   What is your will?

SHYLOCK.   I am bid forth to supper, Jessica.
There are my keys . . . But wherefore should I go?
I am not bid for love—they flatter me.
But yet I'll go in hate, to feed upon
The prodigal Christian. Jessica, my girl,
Look to my house. I am right loath to go;
There is some ill a-brewing towards my rest,
For I did dream of money-bags tonight.

SALERIO.   I beseech you sir, go. My young friend doth
expect your approach.

SHYLOCK.   So do I his.

SALERIO.   I will not say you shall see a masque, but if you
   do, then it was not for nothing that my nose fell
   a-bleeding on Black-Monday last.

SHYLOCK.   What are there masques? Hear you me Jessica—
   Lock up my doors, and when you hear the drum
   And the vile squealing of the wry-necked fife,
   Clamber not you up to the casements then,
   Nor thrust your head into the public street
   To gaze on Christian fools with varnished faces:
   But stop my House's ears, I mean my casements,
   Let not the sound of shallow fopp'ry enter
   My sober house. By Jacob's staff I swear
   I have no mind of feasting forth tonight:
   But I will go. Go you before me sirrah—
   Say I will come.

SALERIO.   I will go before, sir . . .

   (As he departs he passes by the door and whispers)

   Mistress, look out at window, for all this—
   There will come a Christian by,
   Will be worth a Jewess' eye.

SHYLOCK.   Well, Jessica, go in.
   Perhaps I will return immediately.
   Do as I bid you, shut doors after you.
   Fast bind, fast find,
   A proverb never stale in thrifty mind.

   *(SHYLOCK gives JESSICA a knowing look and exits
   with SALERIO.)*

   *At that moment, CHUS suddenly appears from behind
   curtain holding a black metal box. JESSICA starts.
   CHUS puts finger to his lips and shushes her into
   silence.*

   *Lights up on JESSICA and CHUS. CHUS checks
   outside windows, then stealthfully puts down black
   metal box and proceeds to cover JESSICA with a
   large male cloak. As soon as he does this, LORENZO's
   voice is heard without.*

LORENZO.   Ho! Who's within?

CHUS with a look, urges JESSICA to reply. During the course of next scene, CHUS proceeds to check contents of black box and wrap JESSICA in cloak.)

JESSICA. Who are you? Tell me, for more certainty,
Albeit I'll swear that I do know your tongue.

LORENZO. Lorenzo, and thy love.

JESSICA. Lorenzo, certain, and my love indeed,
For who love I so much? And now who knows
But you, Lorenzo, whether I am yours?

LORENZO. Heaven and thy thoughts are witness that thou
art.

JESSICA. I am glad 'tis night, you do not look on me,
For I am much ashamed of my exchange:
But love is blind, and lovers cannot see
The pretty follies that themselves commit.

LORENZO. Descend, for you must be my torch-bearer.

JESSICA. What, must I hold a candle to my shames?
They in themselves, good sooth, are too, too light.
Why, 'tis an office of discovery, love,
And I should be obscured.

LORENZO. But come at once,
For the close night doth play the runaway,
And we are stayed for at Bassanio's feast.

JESSICA. I will make fast the doors, and gild myself
With some more ducats, and be with you straight.
Here, catch this casket, it is worth the pains.

(Throws casket.)

(Fade out.)

Lights up.

Opposite side of stage.

LORENZO catches casket. Delivers next speech to it, rummaging around in its contents.

LORENZO. Beshrew me but I love her heartily,
For she is wise, if I can judge her,
And fair she is, if that mine eyes be true
And true she is, as she hath proved herself:
And therefore, like herself, wise, fair and true,
Shall she be placed in my constant soul.

GRATIANO. And yet . . .

LORENZO. And yet?

GRATIANO. Who riseth from a feast
With that keen appetite that he sits down?
Where is the horse that doth untread again
His tedious measures with the unbated fire
That he did pace them first? All things that are,
Are with more spirit chased than enjoyed.

(JESSICA comes from the house, looks uneasily from one to the other, then to LORENZO.)

LORENZO. What, art thou come? On, gentlemen, away—
Our masquing mates by this time for us stay.

(JESSICA, LORENZO, SALERIO and GRATIANO exit.)

(After a moment, TUBAL and CHUS appear and look in the direction in which they have all gone.)

(Fade out.)

Lights up.

PORTIA *at Belmont sitting with a 1940s* Vogue.
NERISSA *enters.*

PORTIA. How now, what news?

NERISSA. The four strangers seek for you, Madame, to take their leave. And there is a forerunner from a fifth, the Prince of Morocco who brings word, the Prince his master has now arrived.

PORTIA. If I could bid the fifth welcome with so good a heart as I can bid the other four farewell, I should be glad of his approach. Whiles we shut the gate upon one

wooer, another knocks at the door. Come Nerissa . . .
bid him enter.

*(NERISSA exits, PORTIA puts on final touches of
makeup and settles back on divan.)*

*(After a moment, BASSANIO, disguised as PRINCE
OF MOROCCO, enters, preceded by GRATIANO
also dressed as an Arab.)*

BASSANIO. Mislike me not for my complexion,
The shadowed livery of the burnished sun,
To whom I am a neighbour and near bred.
Bring me the fairest creature northward.born
Where Phoebus' fire scarce thaws the icicles,
And let us make incision for your love,
To prove whose blood is redder, his or mine.
I tell thee, lady, this aspect of mine
Hath feared the valiant. By my love, I swear
The best-regarded virgins of our clime
Have loved it too. I would not change this hue
Except to steal your thoughts, my gentle queen.

PORTIA. In terms of choice I am not solely led
By nice direction of a maiden's eyes:
Besides, the lott'ry of my destiny
Bars me the right of voluntary choosing:
But if my father had not scanted me
And hedged me by his wit, to yield myself
His wife who wins me by that means I told you,
Yourself, renowned prince, then stood as fair
As any comer I have looked on yet
For my affection.

BASSANIO. Even for that I thank you.
Therefore, I pray you, lead me to the caskets
To try my fortune. By this scimitar—.
That slew the Sophy and a Persian prince
That won three fields of Sultan Solyman—
I would o'erstare the sternest eyes that look:
Outbrave the heart most daring on the earth:
Pluck the young sucking cubs from the she-bear,
Yea, mock the lion when a'roars for prey
To win thee, lady. But alas the while!
If Hercules and Lichas play at dice . . . . . .

PORTIA. You must take your chance—
And either not attempt to choose at all,
Or swear, before you choose, if you choose wrong,
Never to speak to lady afterward
In way of marriage. Therefore be advised.

BASSANIO. Nor will not. Come, bring me unto my chance.

PORTIA. First, forward to the temple. After dinner
Your hazard shall be made.

BASSANIO. Good fortune then!
To make me blest or cursed'st among men.

*(PORTIA and NERISSA leave. As they pass, GRATIANO
disguised as an Arab, salaams before each. They file out
and as he begins to salaam a third time, BASSANIO
kicks him in the backside and both make a hasty exit.)*

(Fadeout.)

*(TUBAL and SHYLOCK enter and take up a waiting
position. They are shortly joined by CHUS who proceeds
to filter information into SHYLOCK's ear. CHUS on
one side of SHYLOCK, TUBAL on the other.)*

CHUS. I saw Bassanio under sail.
With him is Gratiano gone along
And in their ship I am sure Lorenzo is not.

TUBAL. I with raucous outcries raised the Duke
Who went with him to search Bassanio's ship.

CHUS. He came too late, the ship was under sail,
But there the Duke was given to understand
That in another craft were seen together
Lorenzo and his amorous Jessica.
Besides, Antonio certified the Duke
They were not with Bassanio in his ship.

TUBAL. Yet tis certain they are bound for Belmont
And others of their party gone along
To stead Lorenzo and his sudden bride.

CHUS. I saw Bassanio and Antonio part.

VARIATIONS ON THE MERCHANT OF VENICE

Bassanio told him he would make some speed
Of his return. He answered 'Do not go,
Slubber not business for my sake, Bassanio'
And even there, his eye big with tears,
Turning his face, he put his hand behind him,
And with affection wondrous sensible
He wrung Bassanio's hand, and so they parted.

TUBAL. *(Recollecting)*

Thou hast not heard a passion so confused
So strange, outrageous and so variable
As those that mock thy cries upon the street.
"My daughter! O my ducats! O my daughter!
Fled with a Christian! O my Christian ducats!
Justice! The law! My ducats and my daughter!

(Laughs with CHUS; SHYLOCK smiling thinly)

Let proud Antonio look he keep this day.

CHUS. Marry, well remembered,

I countered with a Frenchman yesterday
Who told me, in the narrow seas that part
The French and English, there miscarried
A vessel of our country richly fraught.
I prayed with all my heart that it were his.
Indeed, methought I saw the dangerous rocks
Which touching but his gentle vessel's side
Would scatter all her spices on the stream,
Enrobe the roaring waters with silks
And in word, but even now worth this,
And now worth nothing.

SHYLOCK. *(Looking straight ahead)*

If I can catch him once upon the hip,
I will feed fat the ancient grudge I bear him.
He hates our sacred nation, and he rails
Even there where merchants most do congregate,
On me, my bargains and my well-won thrift,
Which he calls interest. Cursed be my tribe.
If I forgive him.

(Blackout.)

Lights up.

The hall of PORTIA's *house at Belmont;*
PORTIA *enters, with* BASSANIO *as the Prince of Morocco.*

PORTIA.   Go, draw aside the curtains, and discover
The several caskets to this noble prince.
Now make your choice.

("MOROCCO" examines the caskets.)

BASSANIO.   The first, of gold, who this inscription bears:
"Who chooseth me shall gain what many men desire":
The second, silver, which this promise carries:
"Who chooseth me shall get as much as he deserves".
This third, dull lead, with warning all as blunt:
"Who chooseth me must give and hazard all he hath".
How shall I know if I do choose the right?

PORTIA.   The one of them contains my picture, prince.
If you choose that, then I am yours withal.

BASSANIO.   Some god direct my judgement! Let me see,
I will survey th'inscriptions back again.
What says this leaden casket?
"Who chooseth me must give and hazard all he hath".
Must give—for what? for lead? hazard for lead?
This casket threatens. Men that hazard all
Do it in hope of fair advantages:
A golden mind stoops not to shows of dross.
I'll then not give nor hazard aught for lead.
What says the silver with her virgin hue?
"Who chooseth me shall get as much as he deserves".
As much as he deserves! Pause there, Morocco,
And weigh thy value with an even hand.
If thou be'st rated by thy estimation,
Thou dost deserve enough—and yet enough
May not extend so far as to the lady:
And yet to be afeard of my deserving
Were but a weak disabling of myself.
As much as I deserve! Why, that's the Lady.
I do in birth deserve her, and in fortunes,
In graces, and in qualities of breeding:
But more than these, in love I do deserve.

VARIATIONS ON THE MERCHANT OF VENICE

What if I strayed no further, but chose here?
Let's see once more this saying graved in gold:
"Who chooseth me shall gain what many men desire".
Why, that's the lady—all the world desires her.
From the four corners of the earth they come,
To kiss this shrine, this mortal-breathing saint.
One of these three contains her heavenly picture.
Is't like that lead contains her? 'Twere damnation
To think so base a thought—it were too gross
To rib her cerecloth in the obscure grave.
Or shall I think in silver she's immured,
Being ten times undervalued to tried gold?
O sinful thought! Never so rich a gem
Was set in worse than gold. They have in England
A coin that bears the figure of an angel
Stamped in gold, but that's insculped upon;
But here an angel in a golden bed
Lies all within . . . Deliver me the key:
Here I do choose, and thrive I as I may!

PORTIA.   There, take it, prince, and if my form lie there,
Then I am yours.

(HE unlocks the golden casket.)

BASSANIO.   O hell! What have we here?
A carrion Death, within whose empty eye
There is a written scroll! I'll read the writing.

> "All that glitters is not gold,
> Often have you heard that told.
> Many a man his life hath sold,
> But my outside to behold.
> Gilden tombs do worms infold.
> Had you been as wise as bold,
> Young in limbs, in judgement old,
> Your answer had not been inscrolled—
> Fare you well, your suit is cold."

Cold, indeed, and labour lost.
Then, farewell heat, and welcome frost.
Portia, adieu! I have too grieved a heart
To take a tedious leave: thus losers part.

(HE departs.)

NERISSA *and* PORTIA *give a sigh of relief.*

PORTIA. A gentle riddance. Draw the curtains, go.
Let all of his complexion choose me so.

(NERISSA suddenly looks to PORTIA *and* PORTIA
to NERISSA, *registering the fact that* PORTIA *has
committed a faux pas in relation to her black
companion.)*

(Blackout.)

Lights up.

TUBAL *and* CHUS *meeting.*

TUBAL. How now, what news on the Rialto?

CHUS. Why, yet it lives there unchecked that Antonio
hath a ship of rich lading wracked on the narrow seas;
the Goodwins, I think they call the place—a very
dangerous flat and fatal, where the carcasses of many
a tall ship lie buried, as they say, if my gossip
Report be an honest woman of her word.

TUBAL. I would she were as lying a gossip in that,
as ever knapped ginger, or made her neighbours
believe she wept for the death of her third husband.
But is it true, without any slips of prolixity or crossing
the plain highway of talk, that the good Antonio, the
honest Antonio—O that I had a title good enough to keep
his name company . . .

CHUS. Come the full stop.

TUBAL. Why, the end is, he hath lost a ship. *(Both laugh
and embrace one another.)*

CHUS. *(Bitter)* I would it might prove the end of his losses.

(TUBAL gives a signal; SALERIO *and* SOLANIO *enter;
as does* SHYLOCK.)*

SALERIO. How now Shylock what news from Genoa? Hast
thou found thy Daughter?

SHYLOCK. I often came where I did hear of her, but cannot
find her.

SOLANIO. And what news among the merchants?

SHYLOCK. You knew, none so well, none so well as you, of my daughter's flight.

SALERIO. That's certain. I, for my part, knew the tailor that made the wings she flew withal.

SOLANIO. And Shylock for his own part, knew the bird was fledge, and then it is the complexion of them to leave the dam.

SHYLOCK. She is damned for it.

SALERIO. That's certain, if the devil may be her judge.

SHYLOCK. My own flesh and blood.

SALERIO. *(To* SOLANIO*)* There is more difference between his flesh and hers than between jet and ivory, more between their bloods, than there is between red wine and rhenish.

SHYLOCK. Why there, there, there, there—a diamond gone, cost me two thousand ducats in Frankfort—the curse never fell upon my nation till now—two thousand ducats in that, and other precious, precious jewels. I would my daughter were dead at my foot, and the jewels in her ear! Would she were hearsed at my foot, and the ducats in her coffin. And I know not what's spent in the search. Why, thou loss upon loss. The thief gone with so much and so much to find the thief, and no satisfaction, no revenge, nor no ill luck stirring but what lights on my shoulders, no sighs but o' my breathing, no tears but 'o my bidding. *(Feigns weeping.)*

*(*SALERIO *and* SOLANIO *pull faces and mock pity.)*

TUBAL. Yet, other men have ill luck too. Antonio, as I heard in Genoa . . .

SHYLOCK. What? Ill luck?

TUBAL. . . . hath an argosy cast away, coming from Tripolis.

SHYLOCK. I thank God, I thank God. Is it true?

TUBAL. I spoke with some of the sailors that escaped the wreck.

SHYLOCK. I thank thee Tubal, good news, good news. Ha, ha. Heard in Genoa.

SALERIO. Your daughter spent in Genoa, as I heard, one night, fourscore ducats.

SHYLOCK. Thou stick'st a dagger in me. I shall never see my gold again—fourscore ducats at a sitting! Fourscore ducats!

CHUS. There came divers of Antonio's creditors in my company to Venice, that swear he cannot choose but break.

SHYLOCK. I'm very glad of it, I'll plague him, I'll torture him, I am glad of it.

SALERIO. One of them brought a ring that he had of your daughter for a monkey.

SHYLOCK. Out upon me. Thou torturest me. *(To TUBAL.)* Tubal it was my turquoise—I had it of Leah when I was a bachelor: I would not have given it for a wilderness of monkeys.

CHUS. But Antonio is certainly undone.

SHYLOCK. Nay, that's very true. A bankrupt, a prodigal who dare scarce show his head on the Rialto, a beggar that was used to come so smug upon the mart. Let him look to his bond! He was wont to call me usurer, let him look to his bond! He was wont to lend money for a Christian courtesy, let him look to his bond!

SALERIO. Why, I am sure, if he forfeit, thou wilt not take his flesh—*(Laughs with SOLANIO)* what's that good for?

SHYLOCK. To bait fish withal. *(This stops their laughter.)* If it will feed nothing else, it will feed my revenge. I will have the heart of him if he forfeit.

(SHYLOCK, TUBAL and CHUS exit, leaving

SALERIO *and* SOLANIO *sobered.)*

(Slow Fade out.)

Lights up:

GRATIANO *and* JESSICA *together;* GRATIANO *reading* JESSICA's *palm.)*

GRATIANO.   Yes, truly, for look you, the sins of the father are to be laid upon the children—therefore, I promise you, I fear you. For truly I think you are damned. There is but one hope in it that can do you any good, and that is but a kind of bastard hope neither.

JESSICA.   And what hope is that, I pray thee?

GRATIANO.   Marry, you may partly hope that your father got you not, that you are not the Jew's daughter.

(JESSICA suddenly withdraws her hand from GRATIANO and then immediately begins to cover up.)

JESSICA.   That were a kind of bastard hope, indeed! So the sins of my mother should be visited upon me.

GRATIANO.   Truly then I fear you are damned both by father and mother: thus when I shun Scylla, your father, I fall into Charybdis, your mother: well, you are gone both ways. *(Comes closer to JESSICA).*

JESSICA.   I shall be saved by my husband—he hath made me a Christian.

GRATIANO.   Truly, the more to blame he. We were Christians enow before, e'en as many as could well live, one by another. This making of Christians will raise the price of hogs—if we grow all to be pork-eaters, we shall not shortly have a rasher on the coals for money. *(Draws closer still.)*

(LORENZO enters.)

JESSICA.   I'll tell my husband, what you say—here he comes.

LORENZO.   *(Angry)* I shall grow jealous of you shortly, Gratiano if you thus get my wife into corners.

JESSICA. He tells me flatly there's no mercy for me in heaven, because I am a Jew's daughter: and he says you are no good member of the commonwealth, for, in converting Jews to Christians, you raise the price of pork.

LORENZO. I shall answer that better to the commonwealth than you can the getting up of the negro's belly: the Moor is with child by you, Gratiano.

GRATIANO. She is indeed more than I took her for.

LORENZO. How every fool can play upon the word! I think the best grace of wit will shortly turn into silence, and discourse grow commendable in none only but parrots. Come, let us prepare for dinner.

GRATIANO. That is done, sir—we have all stomachs.

LORENZO. Goodly Lord, what a wit-snapper are you!

(GRATIANO *smiles intimately at* JESSICA *and exits.*)

LORENZO. Gratiano speaks an infinite deal of nothing, more than any man in all Venice. His reasons are as two grains of wheat hid in two bushels of chaff: you shall seek all day ere you find them, and when you have them they are not worth the search.
The fool hath planted in his memory
An army of good words, and I do know
A many fools that stand in better place
Garnished like him, that for a tricksy word
Defy the matter.

(*Places crucifix around her neck as a gift.*)

Let us go to dinner.

JESSICA. Nay, let me praise you while I have a stomach.

LORENZO. No, pray thee, let it serve for table-talk—
Then, howsome'er thou speak'est, 'mong other
things
I shall digest it.

JESSICA. Well, I'll set you forth.
Go a little before, and I shall come anon.

(LORENZO exits, JESSICA takes hold of crucifix as if it were red-hot and rips it off.)

(Blackout.)

Lights up:

PORTIA's *house.* BASSANIO, *disguised as* ARRAGON *is discovered with his back to audience examining the three safes.* NERISSA, *sitting uneasily on the divan, suddenly moves to entrance as* PORTIA *arrives.*

NERISSA. Quick, quick, The Prince of Arragon hath ta'en his oath, and comes to his election presently.

PORTIA. Behold, there stand the caskets noble prince.

(PORTIA raises her glasses to examine ARRAGON who is. of course, BASSANIO—*shakes her head, and then proceeds)*

If you choose that wherein I am contained,
Straight shall our nuptial rites be solemnized:
But if you fail, without more speech, my lord,
You must be gone from hence immediately.

BASSANIO. I am enjoined by oath to observe three things—
First, never to unfold to any one
Which casket 'twas I chose; next, if I fail
Of the right casket, never in my life
To woo a maid in way of marriage;
Lastly,
If I do fail in fortune of my choice,
Immediately to leave you and be gone.

PORTIA. To those injunctions every one doth swear,
That comes to hazard for my worthless self.

BASSANIO. And so have I addressed me. Fortune now
To my heart's hope! *(He turns to look upon the caskets)*
Gold, silver, and base lead.
"Who chooseth me must give and hazard all he hath"
You shall look fairer, ere I give or hazard.
What says the golden chest? ha! let me see:
"Who chooseth me shall gain what many men desire."
What many men desire! that "many" may be meant

By the fool multitude, that choose by show,
Not learning more than the fond eye doth teach.
I will not choose what many men desire,
Because I will not jump with common spirits,
And rank me with the barbarous multitudes.
Why, then to thee, thou silver treasure-house!
Tell me once more what title thou dost bear:
"Who chooseth me shall get as much as he deserves."
And well said too; for who shall go about
To cozen fortune and be honourable
Without the stamp of merit. But to my choice.
"Who chooseth me shall get as much as he deserves."
I will assume desert
And instantly unlock my fortunes here.

(He opens the casket, and starts back amazed.)

PORTIA.   Too long a pause for that which you find there.

BASSANIO.   What's here? The portrait of a blinking idiot,
Presenting me a schedule! *(Holds up picture of
Alfred E. Newman of* Mad *magazine)* I will read it.
How much unlike art thou to Portia!
How much unlike my hopes and my deservings!
"Who chooseth me shall have as much as he deserves."
Did I deserve no more than a fool's head?
Is that my prize? are my deserts no better?

PORTIA.   To offend and judge are distinct offices . . .

BASSANIO.   And of opposed natures. *(He unfolds the paper)*
"The fire seven times tried this—
Seven times tried that judgement is,
That did never choose amiss.
Some there be that shadows kiss,
Such have but a shadow's bliss:
There be fools alive, I wis,
Silvered o'er—and so was this,
Take what wife you will to bed,
I will ever be your head:
So be gone, you are sped."
Still more fool I shall appear
By the time I linger here.
With one fool's head I came to woo,
But I go away with two.

> Sweet, adieu! I'll keep my oath,
> Patiently to bear my wroth.

(He departs)

PORTIA. Thus hath the candle singed the moth:
> O, these deliberate fools! when they do choose,
> They have the wisdom by their wit to lose.

(NERISSA enters hurriedly.)

NERISSA. Madam, there is alighted at your gate
> A young Venetian, one that comes before
> To signify th'approach of his lord,
> From whom he bringeth sensible regreets:
> To wit, besides commends and courteous breath,
> Gifts of rich value . . . Yet I have not seen
> So likely an ambassador of love.
> A day in April never came so sweet,
> To show how costly summer was at hand,
> As this fore-spurrer comes before his lord.

PORTIA. No more, I pray thee. I am half afeard,
> Thou wilt say anon he is some kin to thee,
> Thou spend'st such high-day wit in praising him,
> Come, come, Nerissa, for I long to see
> Quick Cupid's post that comes so mannerly.

NERISSA. Bassanio—Lord Love, if thy will it be!

(PORTIA reflects for a moment, then begins to apply make-up.)

PORTIA. *(Irritably)* Come, draw the curtain, Nerissa.

(Fade out.)

Lights up.

SHYLOCK, SOLANIO, ANTONIO *and a* GAOLER

SHYLOCK. Gaoler, look to him—tell not me of mercy—
> This is the fool that lent out money gratis.
> Gaoler, look to him.

ANTONIO. Hear me yet, good Shylock.

SHYLOCK. I'll have my bond, speak not against my bond,
  I have sworn an oath that I will have my bond:
  Thou call'dst me dog before thou hadst a cause,
  But since I am a dog beware my fangs,
  The duke shall grant me justice. I do wonder,
  Thou naughty gaoler, that thou art so fond
  To come abroad with him at his request.

ANTONIO. I pray thee, hear me speak.

SHYLOCK. I'll have my bond—I will not hear thee speak.
  I'll have my bond, and therefore speak no more.
  I'll not be made a soft and dull-eyed fool,
  To shake the head, relent, and sigh, and yield
  To Christian intercessors. Follow not—
  I'll have no speaking, I will have my bond.

SOLANIO. It is the most impenetrable cur,
  That ever kept with men.

ANTONIO. Let him alone,
  I'll follow him no more with bootless prayers.
  He seeks my life—his reason well I know;

SOLANIO. I am sure, the duke
  Will never grant this forfeiture to hold.

ANTONIO. The duke cannot deny the course of law:
  For the commodity that strangers have
  With us in Venice, if it be denied,
  Will much impeach the justice of the state.
  Since that the trade and profit of the city
  Consisteth of all nations. Therefore, go.
  These griefs and losses have so bated me,
  That I shall hardly spare a pound of flesh
  Tomorrow to my bloody creditor.
  Well, gaoler, on. Pray God, Bassanio come
  To see me pay his debt, and then I care not!

  (They go.)

  (Fade out.)

VARIATIONS ON THE MERCHANT OF VENICE

Lights up on

BALTHASAR *sitting in vest and trousers, mixing a drink, listening to the wireless. Beside him on a rack are his judicial robes and wig. During the course of the scene in which the voice on the wireless sounds like a Sunday sermon,* BALTHASAR *slowly dons his Barrister's garb.*

VOICE ON WIRELESS.   The world is still deceived with
            ornament.
In law, what plea so tainted and corrupt,
But, being seasoned with a gracious voice,
Obscures the show of evil? In religion,
What damned error, but some sober brow
Will bless it, and approve it with a text,
Hiding the grossness with fair ornament?
There is no vice so simple, but assumes
Some mark of virtue on his outward parts:
How many cowards, whose hearts are all as false
As stairs of sand, wear yet upon their chins
The beards of Hercules and frowning Mars;
Who, inward searched, have livers white as milk?
And these assume but valor's excrement
To render them redoubted. Look on beauty,
And you shall see 'tis purchased by the weight,
Which therein works a miracle in nature,
Making them lightest that wear most of it:
So are those crisped snaky golden locks
Which made such wanton gambols with the wind,
Upon supposed fairness, often known
To be the dowry of a second head,
The skull that bred them in the sepulchre.
Thus ornament is but the guiled shore
To a dangerous sea; the beauteous scarf
Veiling an Indian beauty; in a word
The seeming truth which cunning times put on
To entrap the wisest.

(A hymn is then sung by a chorus.)

(By the end of the broadcast, BALTHASAR *is entirely costumed and transformed. He checks his watch while*

Lights slowly fade out.)

261

Lights up.

The hall of PORTIA's *house at Belmont; the curtains are drawn back from before the caskets.*

BASSANIO, PORTIA, GRATIANO, NERISSA.

PORTIA.   I pray you tarry, pause a day or two
    Before you hazard, for in choosing wrong
    I lose your company; therefore, forbear awhile.
    There's something tells me (but it is not love)
    I would not lose you, and you know yourself,
    Hate counsels not in such a quality;
    But lest you should not understand me well—
    And yet a maiden hath no tongue but thought—
    I would detain you here some month or two
    Before you venture for me. I could teach you
    How to choose right, but then I am forsworn.
    So will I never be, so may you miss me;
    But if you do, you'll make me wish a sin,
    That I had been forsworn. Beshrew your eyes,
    They have o'er-looked me and divided me,
    One half of me is yours, the other half yours—
    Mine own I would say: but if mine then yours,
    And so all yours.
    I speak too long, but 'tis to pass the time,
    To eke it and draw it out in length,
    To stay you from election.

BASSANIO.   Let me choose,
    For as I am I live upon the rack.

PORTIA.   Upon the rack, Bassanio, then confess
    What treason there is mingled with your love.

*(*BASSANIO *starts for a moment—then recovers.)*

BASSANIO.   None but that ugly treason of mistrust,
    Which makes me fear th'enjoying of my love.
    There may as well be amity and life
    'Tween snow and fire, as treason and my love.

PORTIA.   Ay, but I fear you speak upon the rack
    Where men enforced do speak any thing.

BASSANIO.   Promise me life, and I'll confess the
   truth.

PORTIA. Well then, confess and live.

BASSANIO. "Confess" and "love"
    Had been the very sum of my confession:
    O happy torment, when my torturer
    Doth teach me answers for deliverance.
    But let me to my fortune and the caskets.

PORTIA. Away then! I am locked in one of them—
    If you do love me, you will find me out.

    *(After a moment, BASSANIO rises, goes directly to
    lead safe, opens it, withdraws portrait contained therein,
    and turns to PORTIA.)*

BASSANIO. What find I here?
    Fair Portia's counterfeit! What demi-god
    Hath come so near creation? Move these eyes?
    Or whether, riding on the balls of mine,
    Seem they in motion? Here are severed lips,
    Parted with sugar breath—so sweet a bar
    Should sunder such sweet friends. Here in her hairs
    The painter plays the spider, and hath woven
    A golden mesh t'entrap the hearts of men,
    Faster than gnats in cobwebs—But her eyes!
    How could he see to do them? having made one,
    Methinks it should have power to steal both his,
    And leave itself unfurnished; yet look, how far
    The substance of my praise doth wrong this shadow
    In underprizing it, so far this shadow
    Doth limp behind the substance. Here's the scroll,
    The continent and summary of my fortune.
    "You that choose not by the view
    Chance as fair and choose as true:
    Since this fortune falls to you,
    Be content, and seek no new,
    If you be well pleased with this,
    And hold your fortune for your bliss,
    Turn you where your lady is,
    And claim her with a loving kiss."
    A gentle scroll . . .*(He turns to PORTIA)*
    Fair lady, by your leave,
    I come by note, to give and to receive.
    Like one of two contending in a prize
    That thinks he hath done well in people's eyes,

Hearing applause and universal shout,
Giddy in spirit, still gazing in a doubt
Whether those peals of praise be his or no,
So thrice-fair lady stand I, even so,
As doubtful whether what I see be true,
Until confirmed, signed, ratified by you.

PORTIA.   You see me, Lord Bassanio, where I stand,
Such as I am. Though for myself alone
I would not be ambitious in my wish
To wish myself much better, yet for you
I would be trebled twenty times myself—
A thousand times more fair, ten thousand times
More rich.
That only to stand high in your account,
I might in virtues, beauties, livings, friends,
Exceed account. But the full sum of me
Is some of something which, to term in gross,
Is an unlessoned girl, unschooled,
     unpractised,
Happy in this, she is not yet so old
But she may learn; happier than this,
She is not bred so dull but she can learn;
Happiest of all is that her gentle spirit
Commits itself to yours to be directed,
As from her lord, her governor, her king . . .

(They kiss)

Myself and what is mine to you and yours
Is now converted. But now I was the lord
Of this fair mansion, master of my servants,
Queen o'er myself; and even now, but now,
This house, these servants, and this same myself,
Are yours—my lord's!

BASSANIO.   Madam, you have bereft me of all words,
Only my blood speaks to you in my veins,
And there is such confusion in my powers,
As after some oration fairly spoke
By a beloved prince there doth appear
Among the buzzing pleased multitude,
Where every something, being blent together,
Turns to a wild of nothing, save of joy,
Expressed and not expressed.

(As they kiss, GRATIANO *and* NERISSA *stealthfully enter.)*

NERISSA.   My lord and lady, it is now our time,
That have stood by and seen our wishes prosper,
To cry, good joy; good joy, my lord and lady!

GRATIANO.   My lord Bassanio and my gentle lady,
I wish you all the joy that you can wish
For I am sure you can wish none from me
And when your honours mean to solemnize
The bargain of your faith, I do beseech you,
Even at that time I may be married too.

BASSANIO.   With all my heart, so thou canst get a wife.

GRATIANO.   I thank your lordship, you have got me one.
My eyes, my lord, can look as swift as yours.
You saw the mistress, I beheld the maid.
You loved, I loved, for intermission
No more pertaining for me, my lord, than you.
Your fortune stood upon the caskets there,
And so did mine too, as the matter fall;
For wooing here until I sweat again,
And swearing till my very roof was dry
With oaths of love, at last—if promise last,
I got a promise of this fair one here,
To have her love, provided that your fortune
Achieved her mistress.

PORTIA.   *(Irritated)* Nerissa, is this true?

NERISSA.   Madam, it is, so you stand pleased withal.

BASSANIO.   *(Incredulous)* And do you, Gratiano, mean
good faith?

GRATIANO.   Yes, faith my lord.

BASSANIO.   *(Cynical)* Our feast shall be much honour'd in
your marriage. But who comes here? Lorenzo and his
Jessica and my old Venetian friends Salario . . .

SALANIO.   Salanio.

BASSANIO.   And Salanio.

SALARIO.   Salario.

BASSANIO. Welcome hither,
    If that the youth of my new interest here
    Have power to bid you welcome . . . *(To* PORTIA*)*
    By your leave, I bid my very friends and
    countrymen, Sweet Portia, welcome.

PORTIA. So do I my lord.
    They are entirely welcome.

LORENZO. I thank your honour. For my part, my lord,
    My purpose was not to have seen you here,
    But meeting with Salerio by the way,
    He did entreat me, past all saying nay,
    To come with him along.

SALERIO. I did, my lord.
    And I have reason for it. Signior Antonio
    Commends him to you.

(He gives BASSANIO *a letter.)*

BASSANIO. Ere I ope his letter,
    I pray you, tell me how my good friend doth.

SALERIO. Not sick, my lord, unless it be in mind—
    Nor well, unless in mind: his letter there
    Will show you his estate.

*(*BASSANIO *opens the letter.)*

GRATIANO. Your hand, Salerio. What's the news from
        Venice?
    How doth that royal merchant, good Antonio?
    (Aside) I know he will be glad of our success,
    We are the Jasons, we have won the fleece!

SALERIO. I would you had won the fleece that he hath
    lost.

(They talk apart.)

PORTIA. There are some shrewd contents in yon same paper,
    That steals the colour from Bassanio's cheek—
    Some dear friend dead, else nothing in the world
    Could turn so much the constitution
    Of any constant man. What, worse and worse!
    (She lays her hand upon his arm)
    With leave, Bassanio, I am half yourself,

And I must freely have the half of anything
That this same paper brings you.

BASSANIO. O sweet Portia,
Here are a few of the unpleasant'st words
That ever blotted paper. Gentle lady,
When I did first impart my love to you,
I freely told you all the wealth I had
Ran in my veins—I was a gentleman—
And then I told you true: and yet, dear lady,
Rating myself at nothing, you shall see
How much I was a braggart. When I told you
My state was nothing, I should then have told you
That I was worse than nothing; for indeed,
I have engaged myself to a dear friend,
Engaged my friend to his mere enemy,
To feed my means . . .
But is it true, Salerio?
Have all his ventures failed? What, not one hit?
From Tripolis, from Mexico, and England,
From Lisbon, Barbary, and India?
And not one vessel scape the dreadful touch
Of merchant-marring rocks?

SALERIO. Not one, my lord.
Besides, it should appear, that if he had
The present money to discharge the Jew,
He would not take it: never did I know
A creature that did bear the shape of man
So keen and greedy to confound a man.
He plies the duke at morning and at night,
And doth impeach the freedom of the state,
If they deny him justice. Twenty merchants,
The duke himself, and the magnificoes
Of greatest port, have all persuaded with him,
But none can drive him from the envious plea
Of forfeiture, of justice, and his bond.

PORTIA. Is it your dear friend that is thus in trouble?

BASSANIO. The dearest friend to me, the kindest man,
The best-conditioned and unwearied spirit
In doing courtesies: and one in whom
The ancient Roman honour more appears
Than any that draws breath in Italy.

PORTIA. What sum owes he the Jew?

BASSANIO. For me, three thousand ducats.

PORTIA. What, no more?
>Pay him six thousand, and deface the bond;
>Double six thousand, and then treble that,
>Before a friend of this description
>Shall lose a hair through Bassanio's fault.
>First, go with me to Church, and call me wife,
>And then away to Venice to your friend;
>For never shall you lie by Portia's side
>With an unquiet soul! You shall have gold
>To pay the petty debt twenty times over.
>*(Goes for cheque book)*
>But let me hear the letter of your friend.

BASSANIO. *(Reads)* "Sweet Bassanio, my ships have all
>miscarried, my creditors grow cruel, my estate is
>very low, my bond to the Jew is forfeit, and since, in
>paying it, it is impossible I should live, all debts are
>cleared between you and I, if I might but see you at
>my death: notwithstanding, use your pleasure—if your
>love do not persuade you to come, let not my letter."

PORTIA. O love, dispatch all business and be gone!

(BASSANIO looks grimly at letter—then at GRATIANO—then finally at JESSICA, who quails inwardly but keeps her gaze constant. LORENZO then looks to others, registering their grim look to JESSICA, approaches her, and protectively places arm around her and turns to rest.)

(Lights up on TUBAL and CHUS studying a plan. They make some marks on it. Agree certain details, then fold it up and stash it away. They synchronize their watches, look at one another, embrace slowly but fondly and exit on opposite sides.)

(Fade out.)

Sound bridge: Military drum tattoo in darkness.

Lights up.

*A British court of Justice. A great judge's bend center,
behind it, a magistrate wearing judicial wig, etc.*

*On stage right, the Christians—ANTONIO, SALANIO,
GRATIANO, JESSICA etc.—are in conversation. On stage
left, a bare bench awaits the arrival of TUBAL and
SHYLOCK. In dock area beside Magistrate's bench,
ANTONIO sits.*

DUKE.   What, is Antonio here?

ANTONIO.   Ready, so please your grace.

DUKE.   I am sorry for thee—thou art come to answer
A stony adversary, an inhuman wretch
Uncapable of pity, void and empty
From any dram of mercy.

ANTONIO.   I have heard
Your grace hath ta'en great pains to qualify
His rigorous course; but since he stands obdurate,
And that no lawful means can carry me
Out of his envy's reach, I do oppose
My patience to his fury, and am armed
To suffer with a quietness of spirit
The very tyranny and rage of his.

DUKE.   Go one, and call the Jew into the court.

SOLANIO.   He is ready at the door, he comes, my lord.

DUKE.   Make room, and let him stand before our face.

*(SHYLOCK confronts DUKE. At this point,
BASSANIO and PORTIA arrive. Embraces between
ANTONIO and BASSANIO. General greetings from
all to PORTIA and BASSANIO. DUKE knocks for
order. PORTIA and BASSANIO take their places, nearby
LORENZO, JESSICA and GRATIANO.)*

DUKE.   Shylock, the world thinks, and I think so too,
That thou but leadest this fashion of thy malice
To the last hour of act, and then 'tis thought
Thou'lt show thy mercy and remorse more strange
Than is thy strange apparent cruelty;
And where thou now exacts the penalty,
Which is a pound of this poor merchant's flesh,

Thou wilt not only loose the forfeiture,
But touched with human gentleness and love,
Forgive a moiety of the principal;
Glancing an eye of pity on his losses,
That have of late so huddled on his back;
Enow to press a royal merchant down,
And pluck commiseration of his state
From brassy bosoms and rough hearts of flint,
From stubborn Turks and Tartars, never trained
To offices of tender courtesy.
We all expect a gentle answer, Jew.

SHYLOCK.   I have possessed your grace of what I purpose,
And by our holy Sabbath have I sworn
To have the due and forfeit of my bond.
If you deny it, let the danger light
Upon your charter and your city's freedom!
You'll ask me why I rather choose to have
A weight of carrion flesh than to receive
Three thousand ducats: I'll not answer that!
But say it is my humour, is it answered?
What if my house be troubled with a rat,
And I be pleased to give ten thousand ducats
To have it ban'd? what, are you answered yet?
Some men there are love not a gaping pig.
Some that are mad if they behold a cat.
And others when the bag-pipe sings i'th'nose
Cannot contain their urine: for affection.
Mistress of passion, sways it to the mood
Of what it likes or loathes. Now, for your answer:
As there is no firm reason to be rendered.
Why he cannot abide a gaping pig:
Why he, a harmless necessary cat:
Why he, a woollen bag-pipe: but of force
Must yield to such inevitable shame
As to offend, himself being offended;
So can I give no reason, nor I will not,
More than a lodged hate and a certain loathing
I bear Antonio, that I follow thus
A losing suit against him! Are you answered?

BASSANIO.   This is no answer, thou unfeeling man,
To excuse the current of thy cruelty!

SHYLOCK.   I am not bound to please thee with my answers!

BASSANIO.   Do all men kill the things they do not love?

SHYLOCK.   Hates any man the thing he would not kill?

BASSANIO.   Every offence is not a hate at first!

SHYLOCK.   What, wouldst thou have a serpent sting thee
    twice?

ANTONIO.   I pray you, think you question with the Jew
    You may as well go stand upon the beach
    And bid the main flood bate his usual height;
    You may as well use question with the wolf
    Why he hath made the ewe bleat for the lamb;
    You may as well forbid the mountain pines
    To wag their high tops and to make no noise
    When they are fretted with the gusts of heaven:
    You may as well do anything most hard,
    As seek to soften that—than which what's harder?
    His Jewish heart. Therefore, I do beseech you,
    Make no more offers, use no farther means,
    But with all brief and plain conveniency
    Let me have judgement and the Jew his will!

BASSANIO.   For thy three thousand ducats here is six.

SHYLOCK.   If every ducat in six thousand ducats
    Were in six parts and every part a ducat
    I would not draw them, I would have my bond!

(The BRITISH PARTY *stage right, improvise an angry
reaction.)*

DUKE.   How shalt thou hope for mercy, rendering none?

SHYLOCK.   What judgement shall I dread, doing no wrong?
    You have among you many a purchased slave,
    Which, like your asses and your dogs and mules,
    You use in abject and in slavish parts,
    Because you bought them—shall I say to you,
    "Let them be free, marry them to your heirs?
    Why sweat they under burthens? Let their beds
    Be made as soft as yours, and let their palates
    Be seasoned with such viands?" You will answer
    "The slaves are ours." So do I answer you:

The pound of flesh, which I demand of him
Is dearly bought, 'tis mine, and I will have it:
If you deny me, fie upon your law!
There is no force in the decrees of Venice!
I stand for judgement. Answer—shall I have it?

(The BRITISH PARTY *again react bitterly.)*

DUKE.   Upon my power, I may dismiss this court,
Unless Bellario, a learned doctor,
Whom I have sent for to determine this,
Come here today.

SOLANIO.   My lord, there stays without
A messenger with letters from the doctor,
New come from Padua.

DUKE.   Bring the letters; call the messenger.

BASSANIO.   Good cheer, Antonio! what man, courage yet:
The Jew shall have my flesh, blood, bones, and all,
Ere thou shalt lose for me one drop of blood.

*(*SHYLOCK *takes a knife from his girdle and kneels to
whet it.)*

ANTONIO.   I am a tainted wether of the flock,
Meetest for death. The weakest kind of fruit
Drops earliest to the ground, and so let me;
You cannot better be employed, Bassanio,
Than to live still, and write mine epitaph.

DUKE.   Came you from Padua, from Bellario?

MESSENGER.   *(Bows)* From both, my lord. Bellario greets your
grace. *(He presents a letter: the* DUKE *opens and reads it.)*

BASSANIO.   Why doest thou whet thy knife so earnestly?

SHYLOCK.   To cut the forfeiture from that bankrupt there.

GRATIANO.   Not on thy sole, but on thy soul, harsh Jew,
Thou mak'st thy knife keen: but no metal can,
No, not the hangman's axe, bear half the keenness
Of thy sharp envy: can no prayers pierce thee?

SHYLOCK.   No, none that thou hast wit enough to make.

GRATIANO.   O be thou damned, inexorable dog,

And for thy life justice be accused!
Thou almost mak'st me waver in my faith,
To hold opinion with Pythagoras
That souls of animals infuse themselves
Into the trunks of men: thy currish spirit
Governed a Wolf, who hanged for human slaughter,
Even from the gallows did his fell soul fleet,
And whilst thou layest in thy unhallowed dam.
Infused itself in thee: for thy desires
Are wolvish, bloody, starved, and ravenous.

SHYLOCK.   Till thou canst rail the seal from off my bond,
Thou but offend'st thy lungs to speak so loud:
Repair thy wit, good youth, or it will fall
To cureless ruin. I stand here for law.

(GRATIANO *leaps towards* SHYLOCK *but is
intercepted by* BASSANIO. *General clamour
interrupted by* JUDGE *knocking for order.*)

DUKE.   This letter from Bellario doth commend
A young and learned doctor to our court:
Where is he?

MESSENGER.   He attends here hard by
To know your answer, whether you'll admit him.

DUKE.   With all my heart:
Go give him courteous conduct to this place.
Meantime, the court shall hear Bellario's letter . . .

(Hands letter to CLERK*)*

"Your grace shall understand that at the receipt of
your letter I am very sick, but in the instant that your
messenger came, in loving visitation was with me a young
doctor of Rome, his name is Balthazar. I acquainted him
with the cause in controversy between the Jew and
Antonio the merchant; we turned o'er many books
together; he is furnished with my opinion, which
bettered with his own learning, the greatness whereof I
cannot enough commend, comes with him at my
importunity to fill up your grace's request in my stead.
I beseech you, let his lack of years be no impediment to
let him lack a reverend estimation, for I never knew so
young a body with so old a head. I leave him to your

gracious acceptance, whose trial shall better publish his
commendation."

You hear the learned Bellario, what he writes. And here,
I take it, is the doctor come.

(As BALTHAZAR *enters, the* BRITISH GROUP *is
abuzz with anxious whispered conversation.)*

Come you from old Bellario?

BALTHAZAR.   I did, my Lord. *(Hands him document.)*

DUKE.   You are welcome. Take your place . . .
Are you acquainted with the difference
That holds his present question in the court?

BALTHAZAR.   I am informed throughly of the cause.
Which is the merchant here, and which the Jew?

DUKE.   Antonio and old Shylock, both stand forth.

(They step forward.)

BALTHAZAR.   Is your name Shylock?

SHYLOCK.   Shylock is my name.

BALTHAZAR.   Of a strange nature is the suit you follow,
Yet in such rule that the Venetian law
Cannot impugn you as you do proceed.
You stand within his danger, do you not?

ANTONIO.   Ay, so he says.

BALTHAZAR.   Do you confess the bond?

ANTONIO.   I do.

BALTHAZAR.   Then must the Jew be merciful.

SHYLOCK.   On what compulsion must I? Tell me that.

BALTHAZAR.   The quality of mercy is not strained,
It droppeth as the gentle rain from heaven
Upon the place beneath. It is twice blessed:
It blesseth him that gives, and him that takes,
'Tis mightiest in the mightiest, it becomes
The throned monarch better than his crown:
His sceptre shows the force of temporal power,
The attribute to awe and majesty,

Wherein doth sit the dread and fear of kings:
But mercy is above this sceptred sway,
It is enthroned in the hearts of kings,
It is an attribute to God himself;
And earthly power doth then show likest God's
When mercy seasons justice. Therefore, Jew,
Though justice be thy plea, consider this,
That in the course of justice none of us
Should see salvation: we do pray for mercy,
And that same prayer doth teach us all to render
The deeds of mercy. I have spoke thus much,
To mitigate the justice of thy plea,
Which if thou follow, this strict court of Venice
Must needs give sentence 'gainst the merchant there.

SHYLOCK.   My deeds upon my head! I crave the law,
The penalty and forfeit of my bond.

BALTHAZAR.   Is he not able to discharge the money?

BASSANIO.   Yes, here I tender it for him in the court,
Yea, twice the sum. *(Offering cheque.)* If that will
not suffice,
I will be bound to pay it ten times o'er,
On forfeit of my hands, my head, my heart.
If this will not suffice, it must appear
That malice bears down truth.

And I beseech you,
Wrest once the law to your authority—
To do a great right, do a little wrong,
And curb this cruel devil of his will.

BALTHAZAR.   It must not be, there is no power in Venice
Can alter a decree established:
'Twill be recorded for a precedent,
And many an error by the same example
Will rush into the state. It cannot be.

SHYLOCK.   A Daniel come to judgement: yea, a Daniel!
O wise young judge, how I do honour thee!

BALTHAZAR.   I pray you, let me look upon the bond.

SHYLOCK.   *(Snatching a paper from his bosom)* Here 'tis,
most reverend doctor, here it is.

BALTHAZAR. *(Taking the paper)*
Shylock, there's thrice thy money offered thee.

(With cheque in hand.)

SHYLOCK. An oath, an oath, I have an oath in heaven.
Shall I lay perjury upon my soul?
No, not for Venice.

BALTHAZAR. *(Perusing the paper)* Why, this bond is forfeit,
And lawfully by this the Jew may claim
A pound of flesh, to be by him cut off
Nearest the merchant's heart. Be merciful,
Take thrice thy money, bid me tear the bond.

SHYLOCK. It doth appear you are a worthy judge,
You know the law, your exposition
Hath been most sound: I charge you by the law,
Whereof you are a well-deserving pillar,
Proceed to judgement: by my soul I swear,
There is no power in the tongue of man
To alter me. I stay here on my bond.

(The BRITISH GROUP *smoulder audibly as*
ANTONIO *speaks with passion.)*

ANTONIO. Most heartily I do beseech the court
To give the judgement.

BALTHAZAR. Why then, thus it is.
You must prepare your bosom for his knife.
For the intent and purpose of the law
Hath full relation to the penalty,
Which here appeareth due upon the bond.
Therefore, lay bare your bosom.

SHYLOCK. Ay, his breast,
So says the bond, doth it not, noble judge?
"Nearest his heart", those are the very words.

BALTHAZAR. It is so. Are there balance here, to weigh
The flesh?

TUBAL. I have them ready.

*(He places a black case onto the gallery rail before him.
The* BRITISH GROUP *react in an outraged manner.)*

BALTHAZAR. Have by some surgeon, Shylock, on your charge,
To stop his wounds, lest he do bleed to death.

SHYLOCK. Is it so nominated in the bond?

(He examines bond.)

BALTHAZAR. It is not so expressed, but what of that?
'Twere good you do so much for charity.

SHYLOCK. I cannot find it, 'tis not in the bond.

(He gives it back to BALTHAZAR.*)*

BALTHAZAR. You merchant, have you anything to say?

ANTONIO. But little; I am armed and well prepared.
Give me your hand, Bassanio, fare you well!
Grieve not that I am fall'n to this for you:
For herein Fortune shows herself more kind
Than is her custom; it is still her use,
To let the wretched man outlive his wealth,
To view with hollow eye and wrinkled brow
An age of poverty; from which ling'ring penance
Of such misery doth she cut me off.

(They embrace.)

Repent not you that you shall lose your friend.
And he repents not, that he pays your debt.
For if the Jew do cut but deep enough,
I'll pay it instantly with all my heart.

BASSANIO. Antonio, I am married to a wife
Which is as dear to me as life itself,
But life itself, my wife, and all the world,
Are not with me esteemed above thy life.
I would lose all, ay, sacrifice them all
Here to this devil, to deliver you.

SHYLOCK. We trifle time, I pray thee pursue sentence.

BALTHAZAR. A pound of that same merchant's flesh is
thine,
The court awards it, and the law doth give it.

SHYLOCK. Most rightful judge!

BALTHAZAR. And you must cut this flesh from off his breast,
The law allows it, and the court awards it.

SHYLOCK.   Most learned judge—a sentence—come prepare.

*(ANTONIO removes jacket and comes downstage with
BASSANIO standing behind him to give active support.
SHYLOCK comes downstage as well. He turns to
BALTHAZAR, expecting him to bring ANTONIO
to him, but BALTHAZAR returns his look with a
steely gaze.)*

*(SHYLOCK slowly approaches ANTONIO. When he
arrives, ANTONIO slowly unbuttons his shirt and
presents his breast. BASSANIO takes hold of
ANTONIO's shoulders to help him through the ordeal.
As SHYLOCK raises his knife, the BRITISH GROUP
audibly have an intake of breath and before it can make
its mark, BALTHAZAR speaks:)*

BALTHAZAR.   Tarry a little, there is something else.
This bond doth give thee here no jot of blood—
The words expressly are "a pound of flesh".
But, in the cutting it, if thou dost shed
One drop of Christian blood, thy lands and goods
Are by the laws of Venice confiscate
Unto the state of Venice.

(Pause.)

SHYLOCK.   Is that the law?

BALTHAZAR.   *(Opens book)* Thyself shalt see the act:
For, as thou urgest justice, be assured
Thou shalt have justice more than thou desir'st.

SHYLOCK.   I take this offer then—pay the bond thrice,
And let the Christian go.

BASSANIO.   Here is the money.

BALTHAZAR.   Soft!
The Jew shall have all justice—soft, no haste—
He shall have nothing but the penalty.
Therefore, prepare thee to cut off the flesh.
Shed thou no blood, nor cut thou less nor more
But just a pound of flesh; if thou tak'st more
Or less than a just pound, be it but so much
As makes it light or heavy in the substance,
Or the division of the twentieth part

Of one poor scruple, nay, if the scale do turn
But in the estimation of a hair,
Thou diest and all thy goods are confiscate.

(Pause.)

BALTHAZAR.   Why doth the Jew pause? Take thy forfeiture.

SHYLOCK.   Give me my principal, and let me go.

BASSANIO.   I have it ready for thee, here it is.

BALTHAZAR.   He hath refused it in the open court,
He shall have merely justice and his bond.

SHYLOCK.   Shall I not have barely my principal?

BALTHAZAR.   Thou shalt have nothing but the forfeiture
to be so taken at thy peril, Jew.

SHYLOCK.   Why then the devil give him good of it!
I'll stay no longer question.

(He turns to go.)

BALTHAZAR.   Tarry, Jew.
The law hath yet another hold on you . . . *(He reads
from book.)* It is enacted in the laws of Venice,
If it be proved against an alien,
That by direct or indirect attempts
He seek the life of any citizen,
The party 'gainst the which he doth contrive
Shall seize one half his goods, the other half
Comes to the privy coffer of the state,
And the offender's life lies in the mercy
Of the duke only, 'gainst all other voice.
(He closes the book.)
In which predicament, I say, thou stand'st:
For it appears by manifest proceeding,
That indirectly and directly too
Thou hast contrived against the very life
Of the defendant; and thou hast incurred
The danger formerly by me rehearsed.
Down, therefore, and beg mercy of the duke.

GRATIANO.   Beg that thou mayst have leave to hang
thyself,
And yet thy wealth being forfeit to the state,

Thou hast not left the value of a cord,
Therefore thou must be hanged at the state's charge.

DUKE.   That thou shalt see the difference of our spirit,
I pardon thee thy life before thou ask it:
For half thy wealth, it is Antonio's—
The other half comes to the general state,
Which humbleness may drive unto a fine.

BALTHAZAR.   Ay, for the state, not for Antonio.

DUKE.   What mercy can you render him, Antonio?

GRATIANO.   A halter gratis, nothing else, for God's sake.

ANTONIO.   So please my lord the duke and all the court
To quit the fine for one half of his goods,
I am content; so he will let me have
The other half in use, to render it
Upon his death unto the gentleman
That lately stole his daughter;
Two things provided more, that, for this favour,
He presently become a Christian;
The other, that he do record a gift
Here in the court, of all he dies possessed
Unto his son Lorenzo and his daughter.

DUKE.   He shall do this, or else I do recant
The pardon that I late pronounced here.

SHYLOCK.   Nay, take my life and all, pardon not that.
You take my house, when you do take the prop
That doth sustain my house; you take my life,
When you do take the means whereby I live.

DUKE.   From naught at first thou cam'st to little wealth
From little unto more, from more to most.
If your first curse fall heavy on thy head
And make thee poor and scorn'd of all the world,
'Tis not our fault, but thy inherent sin.

SHYLOCK.   What? Bring you scripture to confirm your
wrongs?
Preach me not out of my possessions.
Some Jews are wicked, as all Christians are.
But say the Tribe that I descended of
Were all in general cast away for sin,

Shall I be tried by their transgression?
The man that dealeth righteously shall live,
And which of you can charge me otherwise.

DUKE.   Sham'st thou not to justify thyself
As if we knew not thy profession?
If thou rely upon thy righteousness,
Be patient and thy riches will increase.
Excessive wealth is cause of covetousness,
And covetousness. O 'tis a monstrous sin.

SHYLOCK.   Ay, but theft is worse.

DUKE.   If yet thou holdeth wealth then let it buy
Some balm to cure the rancour of thy soul

SHYLOCK.   I prithee sir, disdain me not my wealth.
I am a Jew, and therefore I am lost.

DUKE.   'Tis through our sufferance of your hateful lives
Who stand accursed in the sight of heaven,
That fierce afflictions are befallen,
And therefore make no further protestation.
(Pompously) The hand of law and dignity of state
Shall not impeach the edict here proclaimed.

SHYLOCK.   Most reverend, lord. Let none presume
To wear an undeserved dignity.
O, that estates, degrees and offices,
Were not derived corruptly, and that clear honour
Were purchased by the merit of the wearer—
How many then should cover that stand bare!
How many be commanded that command!
How much low peasantry would then be gleaned
From the true seed of honour!

DUKE.   Thine insolence doth now untread our mercy
And stirs that wrath that we were loth to show.

SHYLOCK.   *(Looks about the court, then bursts out
contemptuously)*
Who hateth me but for my happiness?
Or who is honour'd now but for his wealth?
Rather had I a Jew be hated thus
Than pitied in a Christian poverty
For I can see no fruits in all your faith
But malice, falsehood and excessive pride.

VARIATIONS ON THE MERCHANT OF VENICE

(An EXPLOSION is heard outside. It shatters the courtroom and causes the Union Jack to fall. CHUS, TUBAL and OTHERS suddenly reveal weapons.)

(The BRITISH OFFICERS are disarmed.)

(JESSICA leaves LORENZO's side and takes up defensive position with SHYLOCK.)

CHUS. Governor, now partake my policy.
First know, there is an army sent before
Enter'd the garrison and underneath
In several places are field-pieces pitch'd,
Bombards, whole barrels full of gunpowder,
That on the sudden shall dissever it,
And batter all the stones about your ears
Whence none can possibly escape alive.

ANTONIO. O fatal day, to fall into the hands
Of such a traitor and unhallowed Jew.

(SHYLOCK now comes before the court under cover of CHUS, TUBAL, etc.)

SHYLOCK. He hath disgraced me and hindered me half a million, laughed at my losses, mocked at my gains, scorned my nation, thwarted my bargains, cooled my friends, heated mine enemies—and what's his reason? I am a Jew. Hath not a Jew eyes? hath not a Jew hands. organs, dimensions, senses, affections, passions? fed with the same food, hurt with the same weapons, subject to the same diseases, healed by the same means, warmed and cooled by the same winter and summer, as a Christian is? If you prick us do we not bleed? if you tickle us, do we not laugh? if you poison us, do we not die? and if you wrong us, shall we not revenge? if we are not like you in the rest, we will resemble you in that. If a Jew wrong a Christian, what is his humility? Revenge. If a Christian wrong a Jew, what should his sufferance be by Christian example? Why, revenge. The villainy you have taught me I will execute, and it shall go hard but I will better the instruction.

(SHYLOCK turns on his heel and walks out of the courtroom.)
(Several of the guerillas force the BRITISH GROUP

282

into a huddle, then step back to take aim. The weapons are raised and as the first shots are fired and the first bodies begin to fall, the BLACKOUT is immediate.)

Sound of whirring ambulance is heard in the distance and the VOICE OVER resumes the story of the King David Hotel incident with slides illustrating the text.)

VOICE. At midnight, about 200 men of the army and police were working under glare lamps with cranes and bulldozers to reach people still buried under concrete blocks and fallen masonry at the site of the King David Hotel. As the rescue proceeds, all border posts have been shut, all street-corners are blocked with armoured cars and barricades, and a curfew is in force throughout Jerusalem.

Dates of first performances

Hamlet 20th January, 1965, Akademie der Kunst, Berlin
Macbeth May 1969, May Festival, Wiesbaden Staatstheater
The Shrew 18th October 1973, Hot Theatre, The Hague
Measure for Measure June 1975, Open Space Theatre, London
Variations on The Merchant of Venice 17th May 1977, Open Space Theatre,
   London.